The Changing
Spanish Family

# The Changing Spanish Family

*Essays on New Views in Literature, Cinema and Theater*

Edited by TIFFANY TROTMAN

McFarland & Company, Inc., Publishers
*Jefferson, North Carolina, and London*

LIBRARY OF CONGRESS CATALOGUING-IN-PUBLICATION DATA

The changing Spanish family : essays on new views in
  literature, cinema and theater / edited by Tiffany Trotman.
      p.     cm.
    Includes bibliographical references and index.

    ISBN 978-0-7864-6404-3
    softcover : 50# alkaline paper ∞

    1. Spanish literature — 20th century — History and criticism.
  2. Family in literature.   3. Mothers in literature.   4. Family in
  motion pictures.   5. Mothers in motion pictures.   I. Trotman,
  Tiffany Gagliardi.
  PQ6073.F33C43    2011
  860.9'3552 — dc23                                2011021742

BRITISH LIBRARY CATALOGUING DATA ARE AVAILABLE

© 2011 Tiffany Trotman. All rights reserved

*No part of this book may be reproduced or transmitted in any form
or by any means, electronic or mechanical, including photocopying
or recording, or by any information storage and retrieval system,
without permission in writing from the publisher.*

Front cover images © 2011 Shutterstock

Manufactured in the United States of America

*McFarland & Company, Inc., Publishers
  Box 611, Jefferson, North Carolina 28640
     www.mcfarlandpub.com*

# Table of Contents

*Introduction*
    TIFFANY TROTMAN . . . . . . . . . . . . . . . . . . . . . . . . . . . . . . . . . . 1

1 — Why We Are All in the Club: *El club de las malas madres*
    CATHERINE BOURLAND ROSS . . . . . . . . . . . . . . . . . . . . . . . . . . 9

2 — Hypermodern Families in Ángela Vallvey's *Los estados carenciales*
    TIFFANY TROTMAN . . . . . . . . . . . . . . . . . . . . . . . . . . . . . . . . . 24

3 — All Turbulent on the Home Front: Unfulfilled Working Mothers in Almudena Grandes' *Atlas de geografía humana*
    LORRAINE RYAN . . . . . . . . . . . . . . . . . . . . . . . . . . . . . . . . . . . 40

4 — New Conceptions of Family in Contemporary Galician Narrative: Visions of Maternity in the Works of María Xosé Queizán and Teresa Moure
    MARISOL RODRÍGUEZ RODRÍGUEZ . . . . . . . . . . . . . . . . . . . . . . 59

5 — Feminism and Motherhood in the Police Novels of Alicia Giménez Bartlett
    RENÉE CRAIG-ODDERS . . . . . . . . . . . . . . . . . . . . . . . . . . . . . . 75

6 — Charting the New Nuclear Family in Pedro Almodóvar's *Los abrazos rotos*
    SAMUEL AMAGO . . . . . . . . . . . . . . . . . . . . . . . . . . . . . . . . . . 93

7 — Recovering Gender: Motherhood and Female Identity in *El pájaro de la felicidad* and *Gary Cooper que estás en los cielos*
    DIANA M. BARNES . . . . . . . . . . . . . . . . . . . . . . . . . . . . . . . . 109

8 — Picking a Fight with Domestic Violence: New Perspectives on Patriarchy in Contemporary Spanish Cinema
    PAUL BEGIN . . . . . . . . . . . . . . . . . . . . . . . . . . . . . . . . . . . . 126

9 — Meet the Nihilists: The Disintegration of the Contemporary
    Spanish Family in Pedro Aguilera's *La influencia*
        AMY L. TIBBITTS .................................. 141
10 — Parents on Stage in Contemporary Spanish Theater
        CANDYCE LEONARD ................................. 159
11 — Basque Identity on Stage: History, Family Constructs, and
    the Troubled Mother in Maite Agirre's *Bilbao: Lauaxeta,
    tiros y besos* and Teresa Calo Fontán's *El día en que inventé
    tu nombre*
        TRACIE AMEND .................................... 180
12 — Mother-Daughter Relationships in Contemporary Spanish
    Theater
        CRISTINA CASADO PRESA ........................... 198

*About the Contributors* ..................................... 215
*Index* ...................................................... 217

# Introduction

## Tiffany Trotman

Family. It is a word that conjures up many images and sentiments. Photographic images of extended or nuclear families. Feelings of happiness or anger. Perhaps even smells and tastes from family meals. As individuals, we are fairly certain of what "family" means to us. But if we are to step backward from our own families and reexamine the notion of this critical institution within the wider society, it is clear that there is no longer a single cultural definition of family.

The concept of "family" is not stagnant. It has changed, as have most things, over the course of time. We are living in a time that has redefined family in many variant ways and has seen a phenomenal change in what defines this social institution. In the late twentieth century and early twenty-first century, economic and cultural changes have forged new definitions of family in much of the Western world.

Spain, a nation whose history has been strongly influenced by centuries of Catholic conservatism, is among the many Western countries that have embraced, in recent times, non-traditional families. This change is the result of a multitude of factors including the end of Franco's dictatorship, the liberalization of society, economic reforms, Spanish feminism, and more recently Socialist constitutional reforms recognizing the rights of same-sex partners. This book is a study in the cultural manifestations that have resulted from the redefining of family within Spanish society. That is to say, each chapter examines how authors, filmmakers or playwrights are engaging with the changing fabric of Spanish culture and more specifically with the question of what it means to be a part of a "Spanish family."

Sociologist Inés Alberdi has explored the changes within Spanish family life in her book *La nueva familia española* (1999) and has drawn several conclusions. Her analysis examines new family values that center on diversity, equality, cohesion and solidarity. Diversity in Spanish families has resulted from a modification of societal norms and consequently legitimacy has arisen around non-traditional relationships. For example, marriages without children or children outside of marriage are now considered acceptable, albeit alternative options. Additionally, same-sex partnerships have been legally granted the same civil rights as heterosexual partnerships and according to a survey by the CIS (Centro de Investigaciones Sociológicas), a majority of the population supported this change.

Alberdi argues that the Spanish family is no longer defined by a patriarch but rather a balance between partners. This new equality between partners has extended itself to their children; sons are no longer privileged above daughters. Children are no longer seen as a "gift from God" but are instead planned, fewer, and better cared for than in the past. While many things have changed in the definition of the Spanish family, Alberdi argues that solidarity and cohesion have continued to be fundamental. The web of familial relations has not been broken as family homes, vacations, and get-togethers continue to be important within Spanish culture.

In Spain today, individuals make choices about what their family will look like, rather than society. Perhaps most importantly, there are choices, rather than a single route to familial bliss, and these choices are constantly changing. According to Alberdi, based on CIS surveys, one can predict continued shrinkage in family size, an increase in the number of women in the workforce, an increase in sexual liberation, education levels and greater tolerance towards divorce and abortion.

Perhaps one of the most notable changes to the family structure in Spain since the 1960s has been the move away from the extended family model to the nuclear family.[1] While the extended family model was the ideal espoused during the Franco years and may still be the predominant model in Northern Spain, it has slowly eroded in part due to the changing economic role of women. In her study *Women in Contemporary Spain,* Anny Brooksbank Jones attributes some of this change to the increased availability of contraception as well as the liberalization of abortion laws (87). She cites the tendency among urban and middle-class groups to defer marriage and childrearing and underscores a transition made clear by Inés Alberdi between a predominantly traditional model to a "legal rational" family unit which has resulted in a greater diversity in family models and values (Alberdi 1996). The composition of the home has changed radically. Today 27 percent of Spanish homes are either solo parent or couples without children (del Campo 110), a figure that would have astounded the population had it been predicted in the 1960s.

As in the rest of the Western world, Spain has experienced ever-increasing divorce and separation rates. Typically, solo parents are women, as divorced women are less likely to remarry than their male counterpart. Between 1938 and 1981 divorce was effectively banned as marriage was the domain of canonical law. With reforms in 1978, however, civil marriages were recognized and subsequently in 1981 divorce was legalized. The result was an onslaught of legal separations and divorces. According to Brooksbanks Jones separation is typically sought by the woman, a fact that underscores women's "affective and economic dependency on men over the last 20 years" (91).

To a certain extent, the radical changes in the definition of family can be attributed to legislative changes that occurred during the Spanish Transition. The Spanish Constitution does not define family, however, it does require the state to support the institution of family. To that end, Spanish Civil Code has seen several modifications to ensure that the rights of different families are protected. Changes to the Civil Code in May and July 1981 effectively gave men and women equal rights as well as equality to children conceived within or outside of the institution of marriage. These changes also required fidelity of both husband and wife rather than just on the part of the woman. Additionally, paternal responsibilities were recognized and the right to pursue paternity through the judicial system was granted. Additionally, de facto couples were recognized in 1981.

The passage of the legislative bill 13/2005 in June 2005 further contributed to the redefining of family. Through 13/2005 the Spanish government legalized gay marriage and provided same-sex married couples with access to the rights of adoption. Spain has become one of the most progressive countries in Europe and perhaps the world through its elimination of all legal distinctions between same-sex and heterosexual unions. Consequently, gay and lesbian parents are further redefining parenthood in contemporary Spain.

The aim of this book is to begin a conversation about how these radical changes in the composition of Spanish families is translating into Spanish culture. In other words, are "new" families making their way into the cultural products of society in the form of novels, films, television and theater. Certainly within North American popular culture today, there are a multitude of examples of television programs and films that depict non-heternormative families. Is this change in culture also occurring in Spain? This was the question that was posed to colleagues as they embarked on their research of contemporary Spanish culture.

The first five chapters focus on new representations of family in Spanish narrative. In the first of these, Catherine Bourland Ross identifies the increase of parenting literature published in Spain and examines, in detail, Lucía Etxebarria's *El club de las malas madres*, a practical and realistic guide to surviving parenthood. The essay considers Etxebarria's approach to motherhood and its attempts to destroy myths of the "ideal mother" that are perpetuated through both traditional Spanish society and contemporary media. In addition, Bourland Ross's essay provides critical details about the unequal social structures within Spanish society as well as the lack of support to provide for the well-being of working mothers and their children.

Chapter 2, "Hypermodern Families in Ángela Vallvey's *Los estados carenciales*," investigates the multitude of alternative family models that compose contemporary Madrid society. Tiffany Trotman identifies the wide variety of family structures included in Vallvey's novel, including custodial fathers, same-sex parents, and polyandrous unions within the context of what Gilles Lipovetsky calls "hypermodern times."

In Chapter 3, "All Turbulent on the Home Front: Unfulfilled Working Mothers in Almudena Grandes' *Atlas de la geografía humana*," Lorraine Ryan explores the maternal experiences and quest for self-realization of two female colleagues, Ana and Rosa. Having both embraced domesticity at a young age, their experiences of motherhood have been overshadowed by the level of self-abnegation exacted by the intensive mothering model. Underlying their jaundiced views of motherhood are the seismic socio-cultural shifts of the Transition, which have resulted in a radically different, and altogether more discerning, attitude towards motherhood among Spanish women. As well as examining how democratization has occasioned a more critical attitude to motherhood, Ryan also highlights Grandes' sexualization of the Transitional mother. She concludes that the tribulations of the mothers in *Atlas* belie the notion of maternity as the ultimate source of fulfillment for Spanish women.

In Chapter 4, "New Conceptions of Family in Contemporary Galician Narrative: Visions of Maternity in the Works of María Xosé Queizán and Teresa Moure," Marisol Rodríguez Rodríguez explores the ways in which two Galician women writers deal with new conceptions of family in their narrative. Queizán's writings, including her novel *Ten o seu punto a fresca rosa* (2000) and her essay *A escrita da certeza* (1991), incorporate controversial themes, such as motherhood, pedophilia and alternative sexualities. Moure's novel, *A xeira das arbores* (2004), focuses on the experiences of a single mother who combines family life and a professional career. The novel, a long monologue, reflects on the protagonist's life and battle against the stereotypes that affect women, such as maternity as an obstacle to achieve success in one's career and prejudicial views about women's sexuality.

Renée Craig-Odders' essay, "Feminism and Motherhood in the Police Novels of Alicia Giménez Bartlett," examines the personal rejection of motherhood by Petra Delicado, the detective-protagonist of this popular series of crime novels. Through the identification of a post-feminist perspective in Giménez Bartlett's work, Craig-Odders outlines the evolution of Petra's views towards motherhood in various novels and concludes that the female detective's stance is ultimately conservative. While unique in her position as female detective, Petra's position/derision of motherhood and her devotion to her professional career indicate a support for a more traditional, patriarchal society. Later novels in the series introduce the topic of work/life balance and blended families through Petra's marriage and consequent acquiring of four stepchildren.

Chapters 6 through 9 explore depictions of family in contemporary Spanish cinema. Samuel Amago's essay "Charting the New Nuclear Family in Pedro Almodóvar's *Los abrazos rotos*" identifies a new configuration of family within the films of Spain's most famous director. Unlike the authors discussed in the previous chapters, Almodóvar's work marks a move away from non-traditional families to his first traditional family unit. After thirty years and seventeen films, Almodóvar has created his first film that features a nuclear family in a traditional configuration including a positive, caring father figure. This essay explores the significance of Almodóvar's first heteronormative family and evolution of the paternal figure within his works while also considering important motifs within *Los abrazos rotos*, including the use of cartographic imagery, an emphasis on technologies of representation and the importance of reflexive historical inquiry.

In Chapter 7, "Recovering Gender: Motherhood and Female Identity in *El pájaro de la felicidad* and *Gary Cooper que estás en los cielos*," Diana M. Barnes analyzes two female protagonists from Pilar Miró's films and their processes of re-self definition through inner exile. The female women's actions are seen as testaments to the rupturing of cultural paradigms of motherhood established during the Franco regime. Barnes' study builds on a growing area of investigation that highlights the gap in expectations and ideals between Franco's mothers and their post–Franco daughters. She notes the novelty and importance of the incorporation of females as subject figures in cinema during the Transition period.

In Chapter 8, "Picking a Fight with Domestic Violence: New Perspectives on Patriarchy in Contemporary Spanish Cinema," Paul Begin considers three contemporary films, *Te doy mis ojos* (Icíar Bollaín, 2003), *El Bola* (Achero Mañas, 2000), and *La buena estrella* (Ricardo Franco, 1997), all of which offer alternative forms of patriarchy that share certain contemporary notions of shared labor, interracial marriage, and adoption. In these three films patriarchy is systematically dissected and reformulated to match more progressive views of masculinity and family. Each film accomplishes this by contrasting a "traditional" father and a modern father, one who defies on several levels the conventions of masculinity. Begin pays particular attention to the films' cinematic codes, their adherence to realism, and the potential for social intervention with regards to fostering egalitarian relationships and domestic violence.

Amy L. Tibbitts' essay, "Meet the Nihilists: The Disintegration of the Contemporary Spanish Family in Pedro Aguilera's *La influencia*," considers the contemporary Spanish family as a post-modern wasteland. Tibbitts interprets the film's framework as a negative re-visioning of the mother/child relationship and the institution of the family in general. The disjointedness and extreme isolation of the subjects suggests that there is no future for the family as a stabilizing social force in the contemporary Spanish social landscape. The film's rapt attention to hopelessness redraws the notion of social cohesion and, instead, pushes the spectator to question (and perhaps acknowledge) that such cohesion ever existed.

The final three chapters explore contemporary families within the context of Spanish theater. In Chapter 10, "Parents on Stage in Contemporary Spanish Theater" Candyce Leonard profiles the trajectory of contemporary Spanish theater within the twenty-first century taking into consideration characters in the role of a parent. Her discussion concludes that the topic of alternative families is occurring at the margins of theater culture and that mainstream theater continues to be less "politically challenging and more crowd pleasing." Leonard identifies a slow increase in the publication and production of plays with new characterizations of parents and indicates that this may be a signpost of an increasingly open environment. The essay provides a useful examination of plays that approach the topic written or published between 1995 and 2010.

In Chapter 11, "Basque Identity on Stage: History, Family Constructs, and the Troubled Mother in Maite Agirre's *Bilbao: Lauaxeta, tiros y besos* and Teresa Calo Fontán's *El día en que inventé tu nombre*," Tracie Amend links two plays to the tendency of twenty-first Spanish dramatists to engage in a re-examination of recent history in order to address shifting identities. In the case of the two plays, the female protagonists explore two roles: unconventional motherhood, and their place within Basque (and Spanish) national history. In both plays, the female characters' positions as mothers and Basque citizens become two intertwining (and often conflicting) forces in their lives, particularly when the women are forced to confront the past. In these two Basque plays the dramatists explore the topic of dual culture/nationality through the prism of the family construct and defines this essential unit as a cornerstone in the process of nation-building.

Finally, Cristina Casado Presa's essay "Mother-Daughter Relationships in Contemporary Spanish Theater" embarks on an investigation of this critical relationship beginning with the patriarchal paradigm established through Federico García Lorca's *La casa de Bernarda Alba* (1939). Building upon this conservative tradition, she undertakes an analysis of mother-daughter relationships in three plays written by the contemporary female playwrights Concha Romero, Lidia Falcón and Pilar Pombo. Her approach underscores the importance of the female voice of the playwrights as they address the topic of this most volatile and important familial relationship. Ultimately, Casado Presa draws interesting conclusions regarding the long shadow of Bernarda Alba.

Together these essays evidence that Spanish culture is beginning to reflect, through novels, cinema and theater, the dramatic changes to the structure of families in contemporary society. Through these creative works, the process of normalization and acceptance of non-traditional families is advancing. While family affection and conflict will ever be a part of our social relations, the constitution of the family is changing. Families today come in many different variations but the one constant through all these changes is that Spaniards value their families above all else.

## NOTES

1. For more information about statistics related to changes in Spanish families see Salustriano Del Campo and María del Mar Rodríguez-Brioso, "La gran transformación de la familia española durante la segunda mitad del siglo XX." *REIS: Revista de Investigaciones Sociológicas* (October–December 2002): 103–165.

## WORKS CITED

Alberdi, Inés. *La nueva familia española*. Madrid: Ediciones Taurus, 1999.
Alberdi, Inés. "Nuevos roles femeninos y cambio familiar." *Sociología de las mujeres españolas*, ed. María Antonia Garcia de León. Madrid: Editorial Complutense, 1996, pp. 41–68.
Brooksbank Jones, Anny. *Women in Contemporary Spain*. Manchester, UK: Manchester University Press, 1997.
Del Campo, Salustriano, and María del Mar Rodríguez-Brioso. "La gran transformación de la familia española durante la segunda mitad del siglo XX." *REIS: Revista de Investigaciones Sociológicas*. (October–December 2002): 103–165.

# 1

# Why We Are All in the Club
## *El club de las malas madres*

CATHERINE BOURLAND ROSS

In 2009, Lucía Etxebarria co-wrote a book with Goyo Bustos entitled *El club de las malas madres* [The Bad Mothers' Club][1] a first-person narrative recounting the lives of today's Spanish mothers—their problems and their perks. Similar to the authors other books of the same genre, including *Supermami: mil maneras de ser una mamá feliz* [Supermommy: One Thousand Ways to be a Happy Mom] (2009) by Care Santos and *Diario de una madre imperfecta* [Diary of an Imperfect Mother] (2010) by Isabel García-Zarza, Etxebarria, is a woman with a career and a child, and through her writing strives to transform society by proving that one must break taboos in order to survive motherhood. These authors are not alone. In fact, the abundance of Spanish books published in the past ten years dealing with issues surrounding motherhood identify a market niche of mother-readers searching for literature about and for them.[2] As Susan Maushart suggests in the title to her book on mothering, motherhood changes everything, even if we pretend it does not (Maushart). These author/mothers recognize the need for literature about their experiences and want to share it with their readers.[3]

In this chapter, I will examine *El club* as an exemplar of contemporary Spanish motherhood literature, a genre that I define as having three general characteristics. First, these books are authored or co-authored by mothers who draw on their own experiences to craft their discussion. Second, the authors exhibit some degree of skepticism or antipathy toward traditional social norms of motherhood. And third, these books emphasize women's obligatory emotional involvement in mothering as a key source of tension in contemporary ideals of motherhood. As examples of the genre, I illustrate these three characteristics in each of the mentioned books on motherhood and compare it to the perspective of *El club*.

First, in the prologue of her book *Supermami*, Care Santos explains that she is not an expert in child psychology, nor is she trained in medicine or education; she is a mother and, "[é]sta es la única autoridad que me avala a la hora de escribir estas líneas" [that is the only authority I have to write these lines] (13). Etxebarria and Bustos also underline the fact that they are not specialists, stating: "Este libro no viene avalado por pediatra, psicólogo o especialista infantil alguno. Lo hemos escrito un profesor y una madre. Tampoco es un libro de *parenting*, ni pretende serlo. Es el testimonio de lo que hemos vivido y, a veces, hablamos también de lo que hemos leído" [This book does not come endorsed by a pediatrician, psychologist or infant specialist. A mother and a teacher have written it. Neither is it a parenting book, nor does it want to be. It is the testimony of what we have lived and, sometimes, we also talk about what we have read] (22).

As an example of speaking against traditional norms, Isabel García-Zarza starts her book with an explanation of motherhood not being what we imagine. She tells us that we grow up with myths about motherhood, feeling that there is one specific way to be a mother (10–11). She explains that we are sold the idea that motherhood is the direct route to happiness, but that many times we feel like we have lost the way, since we do not always experience motherhood as happiness (10). Santos emphasizes these same ideas when she recounts the emotions that are part of motherhood — guilt, disappointment, frustration, anger — all based on "la cantidad de falsedades que te vendieron como ciertas cuando te hablaban de la supuestamente idílica maternidad" [the quantity of lies they sold you as truths when they talked about the supposedly idyllic motherhood] (22). Etxebarria views this same perspective from the fact that no one fits into to the ideal version of a mother, which is why she talks about her club for bad mothers. These illustrations demonstrate that pressure to feel certain positive emotions about mothering create a key source of tension for mothers.

*El club* is an important representative of this strain of motherhood literature, and it also has unique characteristics that make it particularly worthy of analysis. Through a close examination of *El club*, I will show how one particular mothering book challenges and reinforces motherhood ideas. I also hope to illuminate the power of the genre as a whole. I will also attempt to explain why the myth of the good mother continues to exist, how consumer society influences parenting roles, what this says about women's roles in the private sphere, and what effect this ideal has on the emotional wellbeing of women.

Etxebarria, a well-known Spanish author and winner of the prestigious Premio Nadal in 1998 for her novel *Beatriz y los cuerpos celestes*, has written eight novels, a book of poetry, three books of essays (nonfiction), two biographies and two collections of short stories, all of which deal with women's issues, with the possible exception of her most recent novel (*Lo verdadero es un momento de lo falso*) [*The Truth Is but a Moment of Falseness*]. *El club* is her most recent work of nonfiction, co-written with Goyo Bustos, a man with no children himself, but who writes about his experiences as a teacher.

The structure of the work is themed chapters, such as "Ser madre" [Being a Mother] or "La infancia" [Infancy], in which both authors offer anecdotal evidence in support of their opinions on the subject, distinguishing themselves through a change of font and paragraph, as well as in tone and point of view. While Etxebarria writes in her characteristically ironic, confrontational tone, Bustos employs a much more didactic style, full of examples from his experience as a classroom teacher. Although the book is not classified as a self-help manual, it does attempt to address what it takes to raise a child and how to improve the experience. As a guide to surviving parenthood, *El club* works to reevaluate the roles of parents, the role of government, and what it means to raise a child. Through its literary strategies, the book exposes the deceptiveness of the "ideal woman" who can participate equally in public and private contexts. By illuminating how public and private roles continue to be mutually exclusive, the authors show how the structures in place within Spanish society, though much changed over the past four decades, continue to foster the dangerous ideology of an "ideal woman" that ultimately contributes to women's oppression.

Dr. Jane Swigart, in her 1991 book entitled *The Myth of the Bad Mother: The Emotional Realities of Mothering*, states that before she had children she, "vaguely believed that women were either good mothers who made their children happy or bad mothers who made them miserable" (5). After giving birth to her children, Swigart "realized how much we use these myths—of good and bad mothers—to obscure the chaotic, sometimes overwhelming experiences that child-rearing inevitably stirs up in us" (5–6). As expressed in her writing, Swigart came to believe that all mothers eventually realize that there is no perfect mother (7).

In contrast to Swigart, Etxebarria, in the introduction to *El club*, claims that most women are bad mothers, asking, "¿a veces se enfada, a veces está harta, a veces llora y a veces, muchas veces, no está en condiciones de dar lo mejor de sí misma? Estupendo. Bienvenida al Club de las Malas Madres. Recuerde: no somos las mejores pero somos la mayoría" [Do you sometimes get mad, fed up, cry? And sometimes, perhaps many times, are you unable to give the best of yourself? Stupendous. Welcome to the Bad Mother's Club. Remember: We're not the best but we're the majority] (21). Although somewhat ironic and self-denigrating in tone, this introduction to the book allows its readers, especially mothers, to feel part of something—to feel like they are not alone. By inaugurating a club for bad mothers, Etxebarria insists that women shed the guilt that accompanies mothering and instead accept that as much as "se esfuerza por ser la Mejor Madre Posible" [she tries to be the Best Possible Mother] all mothers end up "más perdida que un bebé en un bosque" [more lost than a babe in the woods] (21). In her description of her life as a mother, Etxebarria details her days and her nights, giving a description of a dedicated caretaker who still does not fit into the category of a good mother:

> No soy una buena madre pero pago las facturas de mi hija (el colegio, la comida, los canguros, la ropa, los juguetes, el pediatra, y muy a mi pesar, las Barbies), apenas duermo para poder llevarla al colegio todos los días, dedico la mayor parte de mi tiempo libre a su cuidado y todo mi espacio mental para pensar en ella. No soy una buena madre, como no lo somos ninguna.
>
> [I am not a good mother but I pay my daughter's bills (school, food, babysitters, clothes, toys, pediatrician, and much to my dismay, Barbies), I hardly sleep in order to be able to take her to school every day, I dedicate the better part of my free time to her care and all of my mental space is for thinking about her. I am not a good mother, none of us is] [20].

Etxebarria explains the demands of mothering, working, surviving — all aspects of the balancing act that is being a parent. As Etxebarria illustrates, she, like most women, does all that she can to be the best mother possible, but yet, most women feel that they fall short of what is demanded of them. By defining the pressures that overwhelm many mothers, Etxebarria not only explains why she does not consider herself a good mother, but she also gives a definition of what a good mother must be, referencing an outdated and impossible ideal. In addition to all the aspects of parenting listed by Etxebarria — paying bills, giving up personal freedom, depriving oneself of sleep, worrying about the child, being available for transport to and from school — a mother must also enjoy every aspect of mothering. It is not enough to do all that is required; it must be enjoyable as well. Much of the guilt surrounding motherhood comes from the fact that women do not enjoy the work of mothering as they expected to, an expectation based upon incomplete information or some times outright lies.

Why do women still feel the pressure to succumb to the externally defined, impossibly achieved version of motherhood? Part of the problem is that the concept of the ideal or good mother has existed for a long time, in both mythology and history. According to Spanish feminist critic Carmen Sáez Buenaventura, the specific concept of the good mother that exists today in Spanish culture dates back to the nineteenth century. She writes that in nineteenth century Spain, the ideal mother figure was the Virgin Mary and any mother received, "las más grandes recompensas celestiales, cuanto mayor fuera su dedicación y sacrificio hacia la infancia" [the greatest heavenly reward, the bigger her dedication and sacrifice to the children] (9). She goes on to explain that many mothers see themselves as products of "madres imperfectas, inadecuadas" [imperfect, inadequate mothers] and the hope is to become this idea of the ideal mother that their own mothers were unable to achieve (11–12).

The original mythology surrounding the ideal mother dates back even further than the nineteenth century, explains María Asunción González de Chávez in her work *Familia, maternidad y paternidad*, showing that historically, "La mujer, tal como se representa en la imagen de Eva, de Pandora o de todas las figuras femeninas maléficas de la mitología, es considerada LA CULPABLE y el chivo expiatorio de todos los males" [Woman, as she is represented in the image of Eve, of Pandora or of all the other evil female figures in mythology, is considered THE GUILTY ONE and the scapegoat of all evil] (49). Women fall into the category of the bad mother, such as Eve and the other mythological figures above, when they do not dedicate themselves fully to their children or otherwise do not fit into the virtuous definition of the good mother. To be a good mother: "es necesaria la supresión de todo rasgo de egoísmo, de erotismo y de hostilidad. Las madres, además, no deben dejar transparentar sus ansiedades, necesidades, conflictos, y deben cancelar todos los sentimientos negativos y los síntomas de sufrimiento; tienen la obligación de ser autosuficientes, serenas, felices y perfectas (omnipotentes)" [it is necessary to suppress every trace of selfishness, of eroticism and of hostility. Mothers, furthermore, should not let their anxieties, necessities, conflicts be seen, and they should negate all negative feelings and symptoms of suffering; they have the obligation to be self-sufficient, serene, happy and perfect (omnipotent)] (46). When things do not coincide with this idealized image of a mother, González de Chávez claims that women feel inadequate (47). That the suppression of all negative emotions is a necessary aspect of being a good mother leads to fears that, if one does not enjoy her position of mother, that means she is a bad mother. However, these suggestions that define an ideal mother have no place in reality, as they are uncontrollable and impossible. Sáez Buenaventura calls for a reframing of the definition of a "good mother" by removing goodness and replacing it with the idea that individuals do the best they can, given their individual circumstances.

Not only does this historical image of the perfect, self-sacrificing mother cause guilt in today's mothers, as González de Chávez suggests, but along with the historical, traditional views of the perfect mother come today's portrayal of an ideal mother. Etxebarria explains that media, especially magazine advertisements, always choose to portray mothers as happy, busy women who have time to clean their house, fix dinner, and happily take care of their children. However, she argues that "la madre real no tiene tiempo de hacerse la manicura ni de retocarse las raíces, ha ganado diez kilos con el embarazo y su casa se parece más a un campo de batalla que a la mansión de la actriz de moda" [a real mother does not have time to get a manicure or touch up her roots, she has gained ten kilos with her pregnancy and her house looks more like a battle ground than like a fashionable actress's mansion] (42). She claims that Spanish society advertises aspects of identity that are opposed: "Nuestra sociedad es perfeccionista y quiere individuos perfectos.... Nuestra sociedad ha convertido el goce en un modelo, y el goce inmediato en el valor supremo. Y un niño no es goce ni inmediatez. Un hijo implica renuncia y perspectiva. Y, sobre todo, implica aceptar que la perfección no existe" [Our society is perfectionist and wants perfect individuals.... Our society has converted pleasure into a model, and immediate pleasure into a supreme merit. And a child is not pleasure nor immediate. A child implies renunciation and perspective. And, above all, it implies accepting that perfection does not exist] (20–21). A child does not fit into the valued characteristics of today's individual, where looks, perfectionism, and enjoyment are key qualities of a good lifestyle. Upon closer examination, Etxebarria insists that society preaches individualism and narcissism, while being a parent requires responsibility and altruism (42). She claims that society sets up certain expectations about how life should be lived; personal freedom, youthfulness and beauty are all valued more than collaboration, cooperation and partnership (42). However, having a child changes how we value both the superficial and collaborative aspects of society and reinforces the fact the perfectionism is unattainable.

The realization of the impossibility of achieving perfection also affects relationships, adding a consumer quality to them that encourages consumers to return or dispose of what does not work. Susan Maushart suggests that many relationships are based on the possible eventuality of an end, be it divorce or separation (62–63). If the relationship does not meet the guidelines of a satisfactory interaction, the relationship can be easily ended, just like an unsatisfactory purchase can be returned. Etxebarria states that "las parejas se fundan en uniones provisionales que, aunque en muchos casos terminen siendo duraderas, mantienen la ilusión de ser fácilmente disolubles" [couples are founded on provisional unions that, even if in many cases are long-lasting, maintain the illusion of being easily dissolved], stating that the whole concept of marriage is in a crisis (53). However, children are constant and forever; once one becomes a parent, there is no going back. According to Etxebarria, a child implies a lifelong commitment with no cancellation clause (54). Loss of liberty and autonomy also accompany the birth of a child. Modern consumerist philosophy focuses on individualism, narcissism and instant gratification; parenting is its antithesis. Having a child means a "high-risk" investment without guarantees, and for this reason maternity is losing a great part of its symbolic prestige (54). Consumerist society affects not only our choices of purchases but also of partners and of how many children we have — the basic components of social interactions.

In addition to society's effect on both childrearing and even birth rates, media portrayals also cause anxiety for both parents and children, due to the psychological and social pressure they exert. Etxebarria tells us that, "Si nos fiamos en las portadas de *¡Hola!* o de programas del corazón, la madre vive en un limbo de algodón de azúcar en el que todo es ternura, paz y calma, drogada ella por una corriente de amor de ida y vuelta que va y viene de y hacia su hijo y que la transforma en un ser beatífico de eterna sonrisa" [If we trust the covers of *¡Hola!* or certain television programs, mothers live in a limbo of cotton candy in which everything is tenderness, peace, and calm, drugged by a current of love that comes and goes to and from her child and transforms her into a beatified being with an eternal smile] (55). Women not only strive to be the perfect mother, but they must enjoy doing it, exuding calm love and unconditional acceptance all the while. Women have to deal with the historical, religious implications of motherhood, and above and beyond those traditional models of mothers, today's examples of motherhood — after having been retouched from the photo shoots — make women more prone to be self-critical, as they do not experience their children as the media portrays how this experience should be and appear.

Not only do these patterns of false portrayals exist for adult women who mother; children also suffer from early interaction with media. Etxebarria mentions the enormous amount of ads broadcast during child-friendly television time, claiming that, "por cada cinco minutos de dibujitos hay otros cinco minutos de anuncios, y muchos de estos anuncios también tienen dibujitos, con lo cual los niños no diferencian entre lo que es entretenimiento y lo que es publicidad" [For every five minutes of cartoons, there are another five minutes of commercials, and many of these commercials are also cartoons, meaning that children cannot differentiate between what is entertainment and what is advertising] (242), although the European Union only allows ten minutes of commercials for every thirty-minute program. This amount of consumerist messaging poses a problem for children. Perhaps an even bigger problem, however, are the messages that these commercials convey to their viewers, both young and old. According to a study from the Consejo Audiovisual de Andalucía (CAA) cited by Etxebarria, "La mayoría de los anuncios de televisión destinados a niños son <<sexistas, socialmente conservadores y consumistas>>" [The majority of television ads destined for children are <<sexist, socially conservative and consumerist>>] and "la publicidad infantil transmite valores inadecuados, realiza presentaciones equívocas, promociona alimentos poco saludables, y anima a la violencia y la agresividad" [child advertising transmits inadequate values, makes misleading presentations, promotes unhealthy foods, and encourages violence and aggression] (243). If children are watching two hours of television each day, it is equivalent to forty minutes of advertising during the viewing segment. These commercials reinforce antiquated roles for girls and boys and cause consumerist notions at an early age. Etxebarria suggests that "los avispados publicistas han caído en la cuenta del chollo y han ido como lobos tras los niños, intentando imponer desde la más tierna infancia modelos de consumo propios de adultos" [clever publicists have discovered the gift and have gone like wolves after children, trying to impose, from a young age, adult-like consumer models] (240). Since many parents spend their days apart from their children, with the children in daycare and the parent(s) at work, "[m]uchas, de forma consciente o inconsciente, tienden o tendemos a intentar compensar nuestra falta de tiempo por la vía material. Y les compramos todo lo que piden" [many of us, consciously or unconsciously, tend to compensate for our lack of time through material ways. And we buy them whatever they ask for] (240). Parents have the responsibility to provide for their children — clothing, care, medicine, food — these are all part of what it means to be a parent. However, parental guilt is also a major part of parenting. Historically, men have been charged with being the material providers for children; now, however, men and women both provide financially for the child(ren) in many cases. Even if the affective part of childrearing falls on the mother, both parties must deal with the basic needs of the child. That parents both have or choose to work while someone else tends to their child enables them to provide material possessions for the child, many times based on the guilt that they are not present as much as they would like. Guilt does work — and it sells, too.

Parenting manuals work much in the same way — playing on parental guilt while reinforcing traditional, non-helpful models of parenting. While one manual deems co-sleeping to be the best way to raise a child, another claims that co-sleeping is harmful to children (21). Etxebarria exclaims that, with such contradictory opinions, it is easy to be confused and frustrated (21). Most of the books refer to mothers, and not parents, by which they imply that women are assumed to be the primary caregivers of children. Etxebarria and Bustos discuss the body of literature on parenting present in Spain, stating that many books come from the United States of America, are translated from English, and do not account for Spanish customs, such as meal times and working hours (22). But in Spanish-authored books on parenting:

> nos sorprendió el tratamiento ultraconservador que se les daba a ciertos temas. Si uno lee a según qué autores se diría que al niño hay que domarlo antes de quererlo y, sobre todo, hay que desconfiar de la criatura por principio. También resultaban excesivamente culpabilizadores para la madre, sobre la que cargaban, cómo no, toda la responsabilidad — por no decir culpa — de los problemas o fracasos de los

hijos. En casi ninguno se hablaba de madres solas, de familias monoparentales o de las familias con dos padres o madres del mismo sexo. Y el lenguaje resultaba francamente poco asequible.

[the ultraconservative treatment of certain things surprised us. If you read some authors, you would say that you first have to tame a child before loving them, and that you should always distrust the child. They were also excessively blaming the mother, on whom they placed all of the responsibility — and the guilt — of the problems and failures of their children. In almost none did they talk about single mothers, one-parent families or families with two fathers or two mothers of the same sex. And the language was frankly inaccessible] [22].

The perspective of these books on childrearing shows how Spanish society still holds onto traditional norms of parenting, considering a two-parent, heterosexual family as the only family unit possible. In her book, Etxebarria tries to redress some of these wrongs by using the term "progenitores" [parents] instead of "padre" [father] or "madre" [mother], while understanding that "eso no quiere decir que el núcleo familiar tenga que estar formado por dos adultos necesariamente" [this does not mean that the nuclear family has to be formed by two adults necessarily] (29). The authors also claim that, although this is a book for anyone interested in children — teachers, parents, grandparents, etc — they have still found, particularly in the case of Bustos in his position as a school teacher, that "la sociedad sigue siendo sexista y tiende a cargar sobre la mujer la responsabilidad del cuidado de los hijos" [society continues to be sexist and tends to load the responsibility of the care of children on women] (29). The invisible, private, unremunerated work that women do in their home continues to be overlooked by authors, government, and social practices.

Women still exercise more responsibility in the private sphere than men. As Bustos points out, women are the ones who, in the majority, tend to handle issues relating to childcare and any other sort of dependency care. According to Bustos, with the incorporation of women into the workforce this social and work model (workdays from nine in the morning to seven in the evening) has not changed: women have simply been added to the system that men followed, but with the additional load of everything related to children being still on women's shoulders (103). He contends that the sharing of responsibilities for child raising in Spain is a utopia, stating that:

en la puerta de los colegios, en la tutorías, renunciando a parte de su sueldo o cogiéndose el día libre para ir al médico con el niño, lo que hay, en la inmensa mayoría de los casos es madres, no padres. Y madres muy agobiadas o culpables por no llegar a ser la *superwoman* imposible que la sociedad exige: trabajadora modelo, madre modelo y, además, monísima y arreglada.

[at school doors, at tutoring, giving up part of their salary or taking a day off to go to the doctor with their child, what there is, in the immense majority of the cases is mothers, not fathers. And overwhelmed, guilty mothers for not being the impossible superwomen that society requires: model worker, model mother, and, furthermore, cute and put together] [103].

The family model remains the same, even with women forming a major part of the Spanish workforce — only now with women as part of it. Above and beyond the fact that women now have double responsibilities — inside and outside of the home — they are still influenced by external pressures to be cute, well-dressed and organized. Spanish society has changed, and these changes affect such integral parts of Spanish society, such as eating lunch together as a family at home, which for many families is an impossibility (105). A 2010 article in *El País* by Silvia Blanco states that until women have children, they experience equality in work, social and romantic circumstances. However, upon becoming pregnant, "el discurso igualitario ... se estampe contra una realidad aún sexista" [the egalitarian discourse crashes into a reality that is still sexista] (Blanco). Quoted in the article, professor of labor relations and gender studies Fefa Vila Núñez states that the person who postpones or sacrifices her career continues to be the woman, and not having a job implies the loss of economic independence, reinforcing traditional gender roles between men as material providers and women as emotional caretakers (Blanco).

In a 1997 study of the Spanish family, David Reher discovered that the "adjustment to the new role of women [as wage earners] has been hindered by the resistance to change of society as a whole, and especially of men, who have insisted that women continue to fulfill their traditional roles of mothers and homemakers" (277). This, he explains, makes life much more complicated for women, as there are not enough hours in the day to continue to play the same roles that they did as homemakers (277). Spanish society still has not adjusted to allow for equal burden sharing between men and women in childrearing. A more recent study by the Centro de Investigaciones Sociológicas (CIS) [Center for Sociological Research] from March 2010 shows that popular opinion believes that women hold fewer positions of power due to their familial obligations (question 16) and that it is the responsibility of the government to adopt measures so that companies can facilitate family life with work life (question 18). People surveyed also agreed that the ideal situation was one in which both adult members of the family worked outside the home and shared responsibilities for the care of the home and the children equally (question 20), although when asked who actually did the household chores, only 25 percent responded that they were divided equally (question 33). The difference between the ideal of equally sharing responsibilities and the reality of the situation of the Spanish family underlines the fact that women still work more inside the home than men.

Work in dependency care has historically been devalued, as it is equated with women's work.[4] Iris Young, a political philosopher and author of the article "Autonomy, Welfare Reform, and Meaningful Work," explains, "Contemporary societal devaluation of care work can be partly attributed to getting only part of the feminist message about women's equality. Feminists criticized a social division of labor that defined women's proper place as performing unpaid work at home for men and children," excluding women from other opportunities outside of the home since they were "needed" at home (51). She continues to explain that "social policies render domestic work increasingly invisible and devalued, all over the world social policy implicitly relies on the assumption that time and energy available for unpaid domestic work are expandable" (52). Women are not compensated for their domestic work, yet they continue to spend time on these chores, taking time away from other important parts of their lives, such as paid work and time with one's partner. Spanish sociologist Elena Vásquez explains that, "Las madres se sienten presionadas en el sentido de que si trabajan, abandonan a sus hijos y si no trabajan fuera del hogar y lo hacen como ama de casa, la sociedad les responde con una desvalorización de su trabajo" [Mothers feel pressured in the sense that if they work, they abandon their children and if they don't work outside the home and work as a housewife, society responds by devaluing their work] (92). Even if women do work outside the home, they tend to earn an average of 24 percent less than men, according to a statistic from IE Business School (Blanco). Dependency work is devalued — if a women works in the industry as a care worker or if she stays at home to take care of her children, she has little value in society in large part because value is equated with income.

Etxebarria discusses the lack of support for women in Spain in the home. She cites statistics about domestic and dependency work in Spain from a recent study by the Ecobarómetro which say that seven out of every ten Spanish men (69.2 percent) do no household chores, while 56 percent think that women should quit their jobs to dedicate themselves to housework (42–43). According to statistics from Eurostat, in all of the European union, "Not only are many more women than men involved in looking after children in all countries, but they also spend much more time doing so" (57). In eight of the countries mentioned, "women in the 20 to 49 age group looking after children spent 45 hours or more a week on this activity" (57). Looking at the time women spend on unremunerated chores, it is not surprising that so many women feel like bad mothers and feel as though they are doing something wrong when presented with the idealized version of mothers presented by the media.

Spanish women struggle to be the idealized women portrayed through the media and traditional views of women. Etxebarria remembers a picture of Christina Aguilera on the cover of ¡Hola! magazine which was so changed through Photoshop that she looked like a Botticelli painting, suggesting that motherhood is a sublime, almost religious experience (56). However, the reality is different, and the problem is finding a solution. Etxebarria hopes that motherhood will eventually be another facet, not the only function, of a woman (50). She suggests that childcare centers need to be aware of the different hours that people work, and that the nationalized care system needs to offer alternatives for care over the summer when children are not in school (99). She complains that mothers are forced to be imaginative in order to fulfill their double responsibilities in workforce as well as caring for their children (99). She also see a problem within the governmental structure in that, "España se sitúa entre los últimos países de la Unión Europea en lo que se refiere al gasto social a favor de las familias, y sin embargo estamos entre los países con la carga impositiva más alta de Europa. En cristiano: pagamos muchos impuestos y recibimos muy pocas ayudas sociales" [Spain is situated among the last of the countries of the European Union in what is called social spending for families, and yet we are among the highest in tax burdens in Europe. Clearly speaking: we pay a lot of taxes and we get very little help] (99). She calls for a restructuring of social policies that support families and allow for "igualdad de oportunidades y cohesión social" [equality of opportunities and social cohesion], as well as the wellbeing of children and mothers (101).

The role of the government is one of the few issues upon which Bustos and Etxebarria do not agree. Bustos argues that it is up to a family to provide "ese entorno estable, feliz y rico en estímulos necesario para su desarrollo, un modelo positivo de conducta, unos principios morales, mucho cariño y mucha seguridad" [a stable, happy, rich environment with the necessary stimuli for development, a positive model of conduct, moral principles, and a lot of love and security] (84); that is not the responsibility of the government or of schools. He calls this his "verdad incómoda," using Al Gore's terminology ("an inconvenient truth"), about the need for familial and labor conciliation (102). Instead of more care outside of the home, Bustos calls for "permisos — y dineros — para poder pasar más tiempo con los hijos, hacer que las jornadas laborales de ambas partes coincidan en lo posible" [permission — and money — to spend more time with children, making workdays that coincide when possible] (102–103). How possible a solution this is, or how much help that would provide to overburdened parents is debatable at best. The current system causes anxiety and guilt; it does not work.

Even though women are firmly ensconced in the workplace, and "a nadie le sorprende ir al juzgado y encontrarse con una mujer presidiendo una sala, o ir al hospital y que le opere una mujer, o entrar en un aula universitaria y escuchar a una mujer sentando cátedra" [no one is surprised to go to a courtroom and see a woman presiding over it, or go to the hospital and have a women operate on them, or enter into a university classroom and hear a women giving a class], it is still unusual to see men as the caretakers of children (51). For many decades, women have been working to reconcile their public space with their private responsibilities. Reher believes that "women will demand, and eventually get, this type of [domestic] burden-sharing" (277), but it has not happened yet. And much is at stake. Etxebarria explains that for this reason — the overburdening of responsibilities — many women choose to have only one child (51). She points to the fact that "ser madre no es un deseo universal e irrefrenable compartido por todas las mujeres, ya que, si así fuera, no seríamos individuos autónomos sino pura reducción fisiológica, mero determinismo biológico" [being a mother is not a universal, overwhelming desire shared by all women, since, if it were, we would not be autonomous individuals but only a physiological reduction, mere determinism] (51–52). Being a woman does not necessarily mean being a mother; however, mothering does affect a large percentage of women.

Women who have careers, or women who must work outside the home for financial reasons, have various obstacles placed in front of them. First, they have to resolve the feelings of guilt that they have from not being superwoman, fearing that they are bad mothers; that they are raising their children poorly; that they don't spend enough time with their children; that they are not performing well at work due to pressures at home; that they are not thin enough, pretty enough, well-dressed enough, etc. Somehow the idea of the ideal mother, the good mother continues to affect women, through media portrayals of perfect women and through self-help and parenting books suggesting paths to happiness and guilt-free parenting. In addition to confronting these media ideals and discarding them as impossible, Spanish women struggle with unequal division of labor at home. As Etxebarria says, "por mucho que se nos hable de la incorporación de los padres al trabajo del cuidado de los hijos, lo cierto es que en casi todos los casos el hombre delega en la mujer todo lo concerniente al hogar y a la prole" [as much as they talk about the incorporation of fathers in the care of children, what is certain is that in almost all cases men delegate everything concerning the home and the children to women] (42). These aspects of mothering suggest that women still work under the illusion that having it all is possible, that one can balance — not just juggle — a career and a family. Women believe that they can be the manicured, groomed, well-dressed, skinny media image of what a mother should be and still be able to do the dishes, clean the house, and bathe the children. In *El club de las malas madres*, however, Goyo Bustos and Lucía Etxebarria write to expose the dangerous models these beliefs represent — and the impossibility of perfection, especially when it comes to parenting.

The perspective of the authors of *El club* allows the readers to view the current situation of mothers in Spain, to analyze the difficulties and drawbacks of being a mother, but also to recognize the importance of motherhood. Etxebarria's sometimes ironic tone and her recounting of her own experiences with her daughter, as well as Busto's interactions with children and mothers through his work at school, illustrate how to accept the role of motherhood, how to fight for new ways of viewing it, and why we need to discard the idea of the good mother. The book also delves into governmental and corporate biases that keep current unequal burdens on women, leading to the delayed age of the first child (30.83 years of age according to the article in *El País*) and the low Spanish birthrate. The book also demonstrates the need for more literature on mothering in Spain, a need that has already been seen in the recent barrage of books published on the subject.

Consumerism, the relegation of women to the home, and the pressure on women to enjoy motherhood all combine to explain why women experience motherhood in ways that are unexpected. *El club de las malas madres* calls into question the myth of the good mother, the influence of consumerism on parenting, the emotional well-being of women, the unequal structures in place within Spanish society, showing how, even though the idea of equality exists — and is the ideal for most citizens — women continue to suffer from inequality in both the private and the public spheres.

## Notes

1. All translations from English to Spanish in this essay are mine. Page numbers for subsequent quotations from sources are given parenthetically.
2. Many other books fit into this category of contemporary Spanish motherhood. Please see *El precio de un hijo* by Josune Aguinaga, *Todo por un hijo* by Olga Ruiz, and *Madres e hijas* edited by Laura Freixas for other examples.
3. Another popular source of information for and about mothers is blogs. García-Zarza's own book is based on her popular blog, and Santos lists other mothering blogs in her book (Santos 183).
4. Dependency care is defined as the care, especially unpaid, of the young or the elderly. For more information on dependency care, please see *The Subject of Care: Feminist Perspectives on Dependency*, eds. Eva Feder Kittay and Ellen K. Feder (New York: Rowman and Littlefield, 2002).

## Works Cited

Blanco, Silvia. "Me veo como mi madre en los setenta." *El País*. 9 October 2010 <http://www.elpais.com/articulo/espana/veo/madre/setenta/elpepiesp/20101009elpepinac_16/Tes>. Accessed 9 October 2010.

Centro de Investigaciones Sociológicas. Barómetro Marzo 2010. Estudio 2831. <http://www.cis.es/cis/opencms/-Archivos/Marginales/2820_2839/2831/e283100.html>. Accessed 9 October 2010.

Etxebarria, Lucía, and Goyo Bustos. *El club de las malas madres*. Madrid: mr ediciones, 2009.
Eurostat. *The Life of Men and Women in Europe: A Statistical Portrait*. Luxembourg: Office for Official Publications of the European Communities, 2002. <http://epp.eurostat.ec.europa.eu/cache/ITY_OFFPUB/KS-43-02-680/EN/KS-43-02-680-EN.PDF>. Accessed 7 Oct. 2010.
García-Zarza, Isabel. *Diario de una madre imperfecta*. Barcelona: Viceversa Editorial, 2010.
González de Chávez, María Asunción. *Familia, maternidad y paternidad*. Alcalá de Henares: Ayuntamiento de Alcalá de Henares, 1995.
Maushart, Susan. *The Mask of Motherhood: How Becoming a Mother Changes Everything and Why We Pretend It Doesn't*. New York: New, 1999.
Reher, David S. *Perspectives on the Family in Spain, Past and Present*. Oxford: Clarendon Press, 1997.
Sáez Buenaventura, Carmen. "El hecho maternal: la mística, el mito y la realidad." *Subjetividad y ciclos vitales de las mujeres*. Ed. María Asunción González de Chávez. Madrid: Siglo Veintiuno Editores, 1999.
Santos, Care. *Super mami: mil maneras de ser una mamá feliz*. Barcelona: Grijalbo, 2010.
Swigart, Jane. *The Myth of the Bad Mother: The Emotional Realities of Mothering*. New York: Doubleday, 1991.
Vásquez, Elena. "Demografía y cambios culturales." *Las representaciones de la maternidad: debates teóricos y repercusiones sociales*. Eds. C. Fernández-Montraveta, et al. Madrid: Instituto Universitario de Estudios de la Mujer, UAM, 2000.
Young, Iris M. "Autonomy, Welfare Reform, and Meaningful Work." *The Subject of Care: Feminist Perspectives on Dependency,* eds. Eva Feder Kittay and Ellen K. Feder (New York: Rowman and Littlefield, 2002).

# 2

# Hypermodern Families in Ángela Vallvey's *Los estados carenciales*

TIFFANY TROTMAN

At the end of the nineteenth century, the realist novel in Spain clearly defined the image of the "angel del hogar" [angel of the home] and established a stereotype that heavily influenced representations of motherhood/parenthood in Spanish culture through the mid–late twentieth century. These representations continued throughout the twentieth century however significant changes to the role of women in the 1960s began to slowly alter the expected roles of women and consequently the dynamics of Spanish households. In the 1960s labor shortages resulted in a liberalization of Spanish economic policies consequently encouraging women to enter the workforce. These changes initiated a new period of women's rights and a renegotiation of the roles of both mother and father within the Spanish home. Fathers began to assume greater responsibility for the raising of children and professional women began to balance work and parenting. While family continues to be the central focus of Spanish life, the definition of the Spanish family has been radically transformed in recent years. This transformation has occurred in the private realm however popular culture, in the form of narrative, cinema and theater, is reflecting these changes in the public sphere through works that contemplate "new families." This essay will explore the contemporary writer, Ángela Vallvey's depictions of new family in her novel *Los estados carenciales* [Happy Creatures] (2004).[1]

Ángela Vallvey is both a journalist and prize-winning writer, having received prestigious awards for her children's literature, poetry and narrative. She is among a new generation of female novelists in Spain that have enjoyed tremendous success due to the mass marketing of their books which primarily focus on women and contemporary issues. In 2002, she published her novel *Los estados carenciales*, and was subsequently awarded in that same year with the prestigious *Premio Nadal* for the work. Critics have lauded the novel for its contemporary relevance as a satire of self-help manuals. While this interpretation of the work is both interesting and accurate, the focus of this study relates to a separate aspect of the novel, that is, the author's exploration of new manifestations of family within contemporary Spanish culture.

In her book *La nueva familia española*, sociologist Inés Alberdi discusses several changes within the fabric of the Spanish family. Two aspects of particular relevance to the study of Vallvey's novel are the importance of individualism and the existence of new choices. Individualism, the importance of one's private life, the sense of life's quick passing have all resulted in urgency for immediate gratification. Rather than considering another's interests or even society's interest over one's own, people are choosing themselves first. Additionally, Spanish society now allows an individual to consider different choices in relation to their family structure, not just heterosexual marriage and children. Spaniards are now able to choose among various possibilities including the traditional family, a non-traditional family and also the "family-optional" model. There no longer exists a single path to establishing a family but rather a multitude of possible paths.

Before embarking on an exploration of parenthood or family as developed in Vallvey's novel it is important to examine briefly the central theme of the novel, which is the age-old question "What is happiness?" and how this relates to the subtheme of modern families. Through a myriad of characters with varying circumstances, Vallvey attempts to gather perspectives on this question. It is this aspect of the novel that has drawn critics and reviewers to label the work as a satire of self-help manuals. The question of what constitutes happiness leads to a secondary and more practical issue. How does one attain happiness? Vallvey has commented on these two universal questions in various interviews. When asked if "happiness" refers to an unachievable utopia or an attainable reality in an interview conducted by *Fusión*, Vallvey responded that it is possible to be happy and satisfied with life but that unfortunately we tend to sabotage this possibility through a "tendencia extrañamente masoquista hacia la tortura y la autoflagelación" [a strange masochistic tendency towards torture and self-abuse].[2] She further explained that the goals that we set for ourselves are so elevated that the consequence is that "vivimos en un estado de constante ansiedad y frustración" [we live in a constant state of anxiety frustration].

In *Los estados carenciales*, Vallvey adopts a philosophy developed by Arthur Schopenhauer in *The World as Will and Representation* to engage with the topic of happiness. Like Schopenhauer, she stresses the importance of first knowing who we are and what we actually have in order to be happy.

Schopenhauer's influence is highlighted through the division of the novel in three parts that refer explicitly to the distinctions that one must make to avert a constant state of disappointment. The three sections of the novel, "Lo que representamos" [What we represent], "Lo que tenemos" [What we have] and "Lo que somos" [What we are], stress the importance of not living based on our desires or our will, but rather the reality of who we truly are and what we can realistically achieve.[3] Interestingly, this philosophy lends itself well to the development of new representations of family, as the characters in the novel are not encumbered by traditional expectations of their roles as men or women but rather engage with life based on their own personal desires. They create their own families based on who they are and what they actually have rather than what they might wish to be and what others might expect of them. In a subtheme related to the universal question of how one achieves happiness, Vallvey explores the composition of family in contemporary Spain.

At its core *Los estados carenciales* is the story of a broken marriage between successful fashion designer Penélope and her artist husband, Ulises. After several years of tolerating Ulises' adulterous escapades with several gallery owners and nude models, Pénelope walks out, leaving her husband to care for their three-month-old son, Telémaco. Their family story thus becomes that of a solo-father and a non-custodial mother. In addition to these characters, whose story binds the novel's three parts, there are a myriad of others whose circumstances provide perspective on the theme of happiness. Some of the characters create families that transcend the boundaries of traditional families while others, who have followed a more conservative route, struggle to maintain their relationships within contemporary society.

Vallvey's characters are all drawn together through a weekly evening meeting at an institution called the *Academia*. The meeting, established by Penélope's father, Vili, is a space apart from the bustling, construction-plagued city of Madrid. At the *Academia*, individuals from various walks of life meet to discuss philosophical issues under Vili's tutelage. While Penélope displays her latest couture designs in the top European and American fashion shows, Ulises befriends the members of the *Academia* he attends each week. The details of the *Academia* attendees' lives are revealed through an open dialogue facilitated by Vili, a retired philosopher.

Vallvey's characters, above any other feature of the novel, illustrate the hypermodern atmosphere of contemporary Madrid while also demonstrating an increasing variation in the definition of family in Spanish culture. In order to better understand the environment in which these variations in family have developed it is helpful to consider the ideas of the contemporary French philosopher Gilles Lipovetsky. His theory of hypermodernity is particularly relevant to the cultural atmosphere and the characters developed in the novel.

## Lipovetsky and Hypermodernity

In his two books *The Empire of Fashion: Dressing Modern Democracy* (1994) and *Hypermodern Times* (2005), Gilles Lipovetsky describes and analyses various aspects of contemporary culture. In particular he focuses on "the unprecedented reign of fashion, the metamorphoses of ethics ... the new relations between the sexes, the explosion of luxury and the change in consumer society" (Tavoillot viii). According to Lipovetsky significant changes in our cultural fabric have yielded a new society that he refers to as "hypermodern."

How does Lipovetsky define *hypermodernity*? Hypermodernity is the result of the postmodern exertion of an individual's subjective autonomy. Through this exertion, individuals are freed from restrictive social guidelines, and consequently personal differences multiply (Charles 6). Lipovetsky suggests that the result of this increased autonomy is a two-sided phenomenon or impact that affects everyone, to varying degrees. This impact is reflected in a positive, strengthening force and counterbalancing negative, destroying force. In *Hypermodern Times* he writes, "Two opposite trends can be discerned. On the one hand, more than ever, individuals are taking care of their bodies, are obsessed by health and hygiene, and obey medical guide-lines. On the other hand, individual pathologies are proliferating, together with the consumption characteristic of *anomie*, and anarchic behavior" (33). Thus people living in a hypermodern society seek out and benefit from a multitude of products and services to enhance their personal health. In counterbalance however anxiety and depression abounds.

In addition to this troubling dichotomy, hypermodernity implies an overwhelming exertion of independence:

> Hypercapitalism is accompanied by its double: a detached hyperindividualism, legislating for itself but sometimes prudent and calculating, sometimes unrestrained, unbalanced and chaotic. In the functional universe of technology, dysfunctional behavior is on the increase. Hyperindividualism does not coincide merely with the interiorization of the model of *homo oeconomicus*, pursuing the maximization of his own interests in most spheres of life (education, sexuality, procreation, religion, politics, trades union activities), but also with the destructuring of the old social forms by which behavior was regulated, with a rising tide of pathological problems, psychological disturbances and excessive behavior. Through its operations of technocratic normalization and the loosening of social bonds, the hypermodern age simultaneously manufactures order and disorder, subjective independence and dependence, moderation and excess [33].

While the hyperindividualism of this age allows one to make more non-traditional choices, in this case with respect to family composition, it turns it back on the social support networks that ensure stability within society.

Thus, the new *hypermodern* society reflects both the benefits and the consequences of postmodernity. While man is free to be whatever type of individual he or she desires, there are psychological implications of this freedom. Gone are the "triumphalist visions of the future" as they are replaced by an emotional tone of insecurity. Lipovetsky describes the negative impact of this new society writing:

> Instead of being lightened, our burden has become heavier.... On the one hand, the society of fashion endlessly incites us to enjoy the increasingly numerous pleasures of consumption, leisure and wellbeing. On the other, life is becoming less light-hearted, more stressful, more anxious. The increasing insecurity of people's lives has supplanted the carefree "postmodern" attitude. [Hypermodernity] appears as a paradoxical combination of frivolity and anxiety, euphoria and vulnerability, playfulness and dread. Within this context, the label "postmodern" which announced a new birth has become, in its turn, a vestige of the past, a "realm of memory" [40].

As Sébastian Charles explains in his article "Paradoxical Individualism: An Introduction to the Thought of Gilles Lipovetsky," "every increase in autonomy occurs at the expense of a new dependency" (8). So while individuals are more able to define a new path in life, there are consequences of forging this road.

Lipovetsky's hypermodern society is twenty-first century urban Madrid society. As will be demonstrated, the characters' life circumstances and their relationships illustrate the liberation and pathologies described in *Hypermodern Times*. *Los estados carenciales* reflects many aspects of the delicate hypermodern balance through a focus on the affect of hypermodernity on family life. The characters in the novel importantly demonstrate a multitude of variants on the contemporary family including: fathers as primary-care-givers, non-custodial mothers, same-sex parents, middle-aged new mothers and even a polyandrous family. Through careful development of these figures, the reader gains insight into the changing face of family in what was forty years ago, a highly restrictive, Catholic society. Interestingly, the novel also examines the functioning of traditional models of family within the hypermodern milieu. With this background established, it is time to turn to the novel and look in greater depth at the families that Vallvey profiles.

## *Hypermodern Families*

### Single Parents: Consumption, Pathologies, Individualism and the Euphoric Present

The principal "alternative family" in *Los estados carenciales* is that of Penélope and Ulises. While the role of solo parents is not new to Spanish culture (mothers have been raising their children alone in Spain for many years, particularly during and in the wake of the Spanish Civil War), Vallvey's novel explores the role of solo parents from the perspective of custodial fathers. Ulises represents a new breed of father within the whole of Western culture. They are intimately, involved and indeed, completely responsible for the daily care of their children. In Spain, primary care giving fathers are a new, variant on the modern family. These new fathers have forged their way through the battles of parenthood successfully despite, in most cases, not having had fathers who demonstrated paternal childrearing. For example, in the novel, Ulises describes feeling desperate when his own father was widowed and left to raise two young sons. He describes his as a father that "ni siquiera sabía abrir la nevera" [didn't even know how to open the fridge] (75). A further example can be found in a traumatic childhood experience he relates. Shortly after his mother's death, Ulises' drawing pens were stolen while at school. Seeking comfort from his father, he is told "Búscate la vida, yo no quiero saber nada" [Sort it out yourself, I don't want anything to do with it] (76). Ulises' relationship with his father represents an old standard for the paternal role.

It is in contrast to this generational precedent that young Spanish men like Ulises are successfully assuming the role of caregiver. In leaving her husband with their three-month-old son Penélope expects Ulises to fail miserably at the task of parenting and to beg her to return. Her expectations, and that of other women, in the novel, are crushed when he proves extremely competent. It is not just Penélope who doubts his abilities. Luz, a middle-aged member of the *Academia*, imagines Ulises and Telémaco struggling to survive in a cramped, run-down apartment:

> Se imaginaba a Ulises trajinando en una cocina antigua, alentando la leche del niño en un erolo agrietado y frotándose las manos para combatir el frío que entraría por las rendijas de la oscura ventana en invierno.... Un hombre joven, probablemente poco diestro en las tareas del hogar, viviendo solo junto a un bebé llorón y hambriento, constantemente agarrado a sus piernas con desesperación.
>
> [She imagined Ulysses slaving away in an old kitchen, heating the little boy's milk in a cracked saucepan and, in winter, rubbing his hands together to combat the cold air wafting in through the cracks in the dark window.... A young man, probably little skilled in household tasks, living alone with a crying, hungry child always hanging about his legs in desperation] [49].

Luz's preconceptions are dashed when she is invited by Ulises to return to their apartment one evening. The narrator describes her reaction: "Por eso le sorprendió más, cuando Ulises abrió la puerta de su casa, encontrarse con un cálido hogar decorado con tonos teja y avellana, de ventanas cubiertas con estores de médula y suelo de parquet de roble americano" [So she was amazed when Ulises opened the front door and she found herself in a cozy home painted in tones of straw and hazelnut, with woven wood blinds and parquet flooring made of American oak] (49). Vallvey's description of the comfortable apartment that Ulises maintains further underscores the destruction of the stereotype that men are unable to nurture children or sustain a warm environment devoid of a woman's influence in the home.

In addition to maintaining a good home for his son, Ulises follows routines and carefully considers his responsibility as Telémaco's father. He avoids taking Telémaco out too late, or in bad weather. In one incident he chastises Penélope for requesting to see Ulises after his bedtime and during a torrential downpour. Furthermore, the care with which Ulises packs Telémaco's diaper bag clearly illustrates his focused parenting:

> El padre abrochó la chaquetilla del pequeño mientras lo sostenía junto a su pecho, cogió el paraguas y se echó al hombro un bolso de bebé donde había metido, además del biberón con el agua para Telémaco, un chándal firmado por Ágata Ruis de la Prada (le gustaba llevar uno siempre, por si surgía un imprevisto y el niño se manchaba, o se mojaba y había que cambiarlo rápidamente), toallitas higiénicas y dos chupetes de recambio, entre otras cosas.
>
> [Ulysses held the little boy against his chest whilst he buttoned his jacket, then picked up the umbrella and slung the baby bag over his shoulder. It contained: a bottle of water, an extra set of clothes — in this case a track suit designed by Ágata Ruiz de la Prada (he always took extra clothes in case something happened and the boy got himself dirty or wet himself) — some wipes, two spare dummies and a few other things] [74].

Ulises plans carefully for his outings with Telémaco. Vallvey's description is indicative of a new type of father who is willing and able to take his young children on excursions in the absence of their mothers.

Despite the dissolution of his marriage to Penélope, Ulises also demonstrates his thoughtful parenting by maintaining weekly contact with Telémaco's grandparents. He ensures that Telémaco visits his maternal grandfather, Vili, as well as his maternal great-grandmother, Araceli, in her rest home. In a further extension of his role as caregiver, Ulises eventually asks Araceli to move into his apartment and it is there that she spends the final days of her life. Unlike most of the characters in the novel, Ulises is stable and maintains a healthy balance in his life. While there is no doubt that Ulises is a seducer of women, he does not let this interfere with his parental responsibilities.

Ulises illustrates the positive side of Lipovetsky's theory benefiting from the independence achieved in hypermodernity without suffering from the pathologies. The key to Ulises' happiness lies in his ability to live in the present. Lipovetsky describes domination by the present as a principal factor of hypermodernity. In *Hypermodern Times* he discusses the reorganization of society along the logic of fashion that is temporal by its very nature. He describe a hedonistic culture which:

incites everyone to satisfy their needs immediately, it stimulates their clamor for pleasure, idolizes self-fulfillment, and sets the earthly paradise of well-being, comfort and leisure on a pedestal. Consume without delay, travel, enjoy yourself, renounce nothing: the politics of a radiant future have been replaced by consumption as the promise of a euphoric present [37].

At times, this life approach comes at a high price to those around Ulises. In particular, Penélope has suffered the emotional consequences of his infidelity. However her ex-partner appears energized by the freedom that he enjoys.

In addition, Ulises lives with a spirit of hyper-renewal. His life is intensely focused on the "euphoric present" rather than the past or the future. In the final section of the novel, entitled "Lo que somos" [What we are], Ulises contemplates his approach to life in contrast to his wife's approach: "A diferencia de Penélope, tú nunca miras atrás. Sabes que no puedes cambiar el pasado. Cada día, al despertar, sientes la llamada de la aventura, adviertes que la vida es un estado de ánimo, y el ánimo una forma de vida. Eres un hombre nuevo cada nuevo día que amanece" [Unlike Penelope, you never look back. You know that you cannot change the past. Every day, when you wake up, you feel the call of adventure, you sense that life is a state of mind and that mindset is a form of life. You are new man each new day] (293). It is because of his focus on the present that Ulises is less burdened then most of the characters in the novel.

Penélope, in contrast, displays both sides of the dichotomy associated with Lipovetsky's hypermodern individual. Her hyper-individualism has come at the price of psychological wellbeing. In the second part of the novel, Penélope reflects on the dissolution of her marriage. Through this reflection, one sees that she is innately hyper-individualistic. This is most acutely evidenced through her rejection of motherhood and quick, post-natal insertion into professional life. During an interview for a position as a designer with a top Spanish design house she is asked:

> *¿Está usted casada?*
> Sí, pero acabo de dejar a mi marido y a mi hijo, y sólo espero de la vida que no ponga en mi camino más maridos ni más hijos de aquí en adelante. No tengo obligaciones familiares, si es eso lo que le preocupa — mintió un poco. Pero no del todo.
>
> ["Are you married?"
> "Yes, but I have just left my husband and son, and all I require of life is that it doesn't place any more husbands or children in my path ever again. I have no family obligations, if that is what you are worried about." She lied a little, but not completely] [86].

This rejection of children and marriage illustrates the dismantling of old institutions that began in postmodernity and continues into hypermodernity.

Penélope views marriage as a failed institution because it comes with no guarantees that one will feel the same way about the person one marries in a few years time. This opinion rings clearly of an individual driven by an impulse to buy-in according to consumerist policies, regardless of whether it is a product, an institution or a marriage (250).

As a non-custodial mother, she throws herself into her work becoming the "nueva *wonder girl* de la moda española" [the new wunderkind of Spanish fashion] (158). Because of her extreme independence, Penelope feels her professional ambitions cannot be achieved while also parenting. She explains "su capacidad nacía de algún rincón más complejo y recóndito, dentro de sí misma. Y un marido — incluso un hijo, carne de su carne — no podría evitar que la sacase a la luz y disfrutara de ella" [her abilities were born in some complex, hidden place inside herself. And no husband — nor even a son, her own flesh and blood — would prevent her from dragging them out into the light and taking full advantage of them] (87). The tone of Penelope's interior monologue rings of resentment towards family members that could potentially curtail her success. Thus her contact with Ulises and Telémaco is limited to at most a single visit once every three months. She financially supports her husband and child through monthly payments while sending regular gifts of clothing from the latest catwalk shows depicting children's fashions.

Unfortunately Penélope suffers the emotional consequences of her hyperindependence through an anxiety-plagued existence. Sébastian Charles describes this suffering as a state in which "Narcissus is gnawed by anxiety; fear has imposed itself on his pleasures, and anguish on his liberation" (13). Lipovetsky writes:

> Abandoned to himself ... the individual finds himself deprived of the social structures that endowed him with an inner strength that enabled him to face up to life's trials and tribulations.... The more socially mobile the individual is, the more we witness signs of exhaustion and subjective "breakdowns"; the more freely and intensely people wish to live, the more we hear them saying how difficult life can be [56].

The chapter titles in the second part of the novel clearly refer to Penélope's fragility. They include *La culpa, La obligación, La angustia, La postergación, La dependencia, El temor, La preocupación, El miedo a lo desconocido* [Guilt, Duty, Anxiety, Procrastination, Dependence, Dread, Worry, Fear of the Unknown]. Penélope states that she believes life is a fight to the death against all of these things. In describing her insidious battle against worry she ruminates, "La preocupación es un mal cultural epidémico.... Es una bestia carnicera, muy libidinosa. Nos seduce y nos devora, y a veces ni siquiera lo hace por ese orden" [worry is a cultural malaise of epidemic proportions.... It is a lustful, carnivorous beast. It seduces and devours us, and sometimes not even in that order] (262). Penélope fights a personal battle against insecurity that is so prevalent in society she believes it tangible to the senses. She explains, "la preocupación y la culpa desprenden cierto olor mohoso, y hacen que la gente se escabulla corriendo del lado de quienes sueltan esa pestilencia. Bastante tienen con la propia" [Worry and guilt have a particular musty odor that sends people scurrying away from anyone who gives off the stench. Everyone has quite enough worry and guilt of their own] (265).

Prior to shifting the lens away from these two key characters in the novel towards other figures that clearly represent new manifestations of parenthood, it is important to acknowledge the link between Ulises and Penélope to the principal characters of Homer's *Odyssey*. The naming of these characters draws a clear link between the two works. In Vallvey's work however an inversion of roles is clear with Penélope departing home and leaving Ulises behind to care for their child. She is a hostile, counterpart to the Homer's Penélope. Unlike the faithful characters described by Homer, Vallvey's protagonists are disloyal and unfaithful to anyone other than themselves.[4]

While Ulises' role as solo father and Penélope's complete rejection of motherhood are one example of the changing definition of family, many others appear in the novel. Interestingly they are all introduced through the forum of the *Academia*. The existence of the *Academia* indicates an unspoken desire for institutions that provide meaning within a hypermodern world. The individuals that attend the meeting grapple with the emptiness, anxiety, and unrest that Lipovetsky describes in his writing. The omniscient narrator describes the group as "seres ansiosos y aturdidos buscando lucidez e indicios, aunque fuesen temporales, de que viver no era una tarea absurda" [they were all bewildered, anxious souls in search of clarity and some indication, however provisional, that living was not an absurd act] (28). In the next section I will explore the new family constructs of several other attendees to the *Academia*.

## Polyandry: The Clamor for Pleasure

Among the variants on family in *Los estados carenciales,* Vallvey also includes a polyandrous union. Mireia Amorós, a 43-year-old bank director, is a strong independent woman. One evening while at the *Academia* Mireia becomes engaged in a debate regarding whether there is sufficient space for more than one lover/mate in a woman's life at any one time. Through this conversation, we learn that Mireia has been married twice. In recent years, her first husband (Luis) fell on difficult times and Mireia, with the consent of her second husband (Pedro), invited him to move back in to their marital home. In order to contribute to the household, Luis began to take care of the housekeeping and cooking for his ex-wife and her new husband. The result was a blissful existence for all three individuals involved. Shortly thereafter, Mireia began sleeping with Luis again and Pedro accepted the arrangement with a simple, "La carne no es nada más que carne, cariño" [Flesh is nothing more than flesh, my darling] (141). As two husbands and one wife, they live happily under the same roof.

Mireia is considering becoming pregnant and raising a child within this new family. The narrator relates, "Mireia estaba convencida de que atravesaba una etapa de vida excelente para tener un hijo, daba igual que fuera de uno o de otro de sus maridos. Luis podría ocuparse del niño mientras ella y Pedro trabajaban. Lo de menos eran los apellidos o los genes de crío" [Mireia was convinced that this would be an excellent time to have a child. It really didn't matter which of her two husbands was the father. Luis could look after the child while she and Pedro worked. Surnames and genetics were the least of it] (141). Thus we see here not just a break from a traditional family in the sense of two partners but also a reaffirmation of the role of men as primary care givers. Mireia is a strong woman determined to create the family she desires. She believes ultimately that she has "todo el derecho del mundo de vivir con su marido y con su ex marido bajo el mismo techo" [She had all the right in the world to live with her husband and her ex-husband under the same roof] (139). Several members of the *Academia* reject Mirieia's assertions that a woman can capably love more than one man at a time however this only strengthens her resolve. She is a hypermodern character exercising her extreme independence and her strong resolve ensures that she cannot be convinced that there is anything wrong with the arrangement that has brought her and her two husbands a great deal of happiness.

## SAME-SEX PARENTS: HYPER-RECOGNITION

Vallvey's contemplation of the various definitions of family extends beyond what she intends with Ulises and Penélope and Mireia. David Molina is another character that regularly attends the *Academia*. He and his partner Óscar have fathered a child through surrogacy. David complains that his family experiences the same trials and tribulations as any other however without any of the advantages of a normal family. His mother, in particular, criticizes his "familia extraña, anormal, sin sentido y *contra natura*" [odd, abnormal, meaningless and unnatural family] (68). Daniel and Óscar, as a de facto couple, have abandoned the institutions available and accepted within his mother's Catholic idealization of Spanish culture and forged their own path. He relates, "Para mi madre, saber que tenemos hijo, concebido por inseminación artificial con una madre de alquiler, un hijo que es sólo mío y no de Óscar, demuestra que somos degenerados que nos acolamos a los grandes planes que su Dios católico tenía revistos para el universo" [For my mother, knowing that we have a son conceived by artificial insemination using a surrogate mother, a child that is mine alone and not Óscar's, just proves that we are a pair of degenerates who don't fit in with the grand plan that her Catholic God had for the universe] (68). Within the realm of hypermodernity, Daniel has chosen a path open to the hyperindividual. As a consequence, however he suffers the pathologies mentioned before. His situation has left him feeling like "un soldado cojo en medio de una batalla" [a lame soldier caught up in a battle] (66).

David's family circumstances provide an ideal theme for Vili's philosophical teachings at the *Academia*. In an attempt to provide some perspective on the situation, he asks the groups to define "normal family" by giving examples. Several possibilities are offered including the Spanish Royal Family and the family from *Little House on the Prairie*. Ultimately, David suggests, "La Sagrada Familia... La Virgen María, san José y el niño Jesús. Un patrón clásico, un prototipo que lleva funcionando más de dos mil años sin que haya encontrado competencia que pueda destronarlo. La familia ideal universal" [The Holy Family... The Virgin Mary, St. Joseph and the baby Jesus; a classic model, a prototype that has remained unrivalled for more than two thousand years. It is the universal perfect family] (67). Vili accepts this paradigm of the normal family and undertakes a comparison between the Holy Family and David's same-sex family. Ultimately he concludes that there is little difference between the two. Vili likens David's use of a surrogate to the Virgin Mary's pregnancy by asking the group:

> –¿Y cómo fue engendrado Jesucristo?
> La chica de los pendientes de aro volvió a intervenir.
> –¡Fue engendrado por la gracia de Dios! ¡A través del Espíritu Santo en forma de paloma!— dijo como se ese incidente bíblico le llenara de un particular regocijo.
> –¿De verdad?— Vili sonrió—. Así que una paloma, ¿eh? Bien, bien.... Que me aspen, pero a mí eso me suena a inseminación artificial, que es lo mismo que hicisteis tú y Óscar junto con la madre de vuestro hijo.
>
> *["And how was Jesus conceived?"*
> The girl with the hoop earrings joined in again.
> "He was conceived by the grace of God! Through the Holy Spirit in the form of a dove!" she said, as if that particular Biblical episode filled her with a special glee.
> "Really?" Vili smiled... "A dove, eh? Well, well... You know, that sounds awfully like artificial insemination, which is exactly what you and Óscar did with the mother of your child"] [69].

Vili successfully reformulates David's notion of "normality" by relating his circumstances to what David considers to be the ideal normal family. In so doing, he reconnects this hypermodern character to an institution (Catholicism) that provides him with a sense of legitimacy. Vili concludes, "En fin.... No sé de qué te quejas, la verdad. ¡Si incluso Dios fundó una Sagrada Familia de lo más disfuncional, *quod erat demostrandum*! Lo que es bueno para Dios debe ser bueno para ti. Y sobre todo para tu madre, si es tan religiosa. Díselo así en cuanto tengas la oportunidad, David" [So.... I don't really know what you are complaining about. If God himself created a highly dysfunctional Holy Family, *quad erat demonstrandum*! If it was good enough for God it should be good enough for you, and more specifically, for your mother, if she's so religious. Tell her so, as soon as you get the chance, David] (70). Vili's well-argued demonstration of the validity and perhaps sanctity of the relationship David's family underscores the importance of recognizing multiple variations in family construct. Like Pénelope, David has fallen victim to anxiety and suffering due to the non-traditional nature of his relationship however within the realm of the *Academia* he can experience some positive affirmation of his individuality.

While the *Academia* does host several characters that assert their hyperindividualism through non-traditional choices, there are also members who have lived very traditional lives. These characters' family relationships are not as solid as they would have once been however. Hypermodernity has taken its toll. In the next section, I will briefly explore two conformist families and demonstrate how Vallvey reveals the tenuous nature of these relationships.

## *Traditional Families in a Hypermodern World*

### CATHOLIC FAITHFULNESS?

One of the women that opines on Ulises' abilities to raise Telémaco on his own is Luz Sanahuja, a 44-year-old Catholic woman whose traditional wedding and marriage are described in detail in the chapter entitled *Matrimonio de Luz* [Luz's Wedding]. At the time of her wedding she was completely content and devoid of anxiety. However, after 22 years of a satisfactory marriage and several children, Luz "descubrió que sus sueños se habían marchitado y que su cielo, antaño indestructible y redondo, empezaba a requebrajarse sobre su cambeza" [discovered that her dreams had withered and that her indestructible, round sky was beginning to show cracks above her head] (37). Luz's life is lonely now that her children have grown up, her husband has retreated into silence and she has no hopes for her future. She feels that she has lost her life to such an extent that she will never recover it (38). This state of desperation results in an addiction to tranquilizers that temporarily pacify her anxiety. After a rendezvous with Ulises in which she engages in an evening of adulterous sex, she is inspired to quit her addiction and re-engages with life. It is as if the contact with Ulises, who lives with the spirit of hyper-renewal has been contagious for Luz. She reflects, "hacía mucho tiempo que no notaba de manera tan clara y rotunda cómo la vida vibraba en torno a ella" [it had been a long time since she had noticed with such clarity and depth how life vibrated around her] (53).

Unlike Penelope who pursues her career without consideration of her family, Luz abandoned her language studies shortly after marriage to dedicate her life to creating a "perfecto orden doméstico" [perfect domestic order] (37). Despite her greatest intentions, this effort does not bring unending happiness to Luz. Her model Catholic family no longer provides the key to happiness that it was intended in part due to the changing expectations of hypermodernity. Luz is not content to feign happiness for the sake of her husband and children; she must actually feel it. Through an uncharacteristic assertion of her individuality and independence (a one-night stand with Ulises) she begins to feel alive again. This character challenges the relevance of traditional, religious marriage within the hypermodern world.

## Togetherness

Another failed model of family that springs from the traditional realm of marriage is the coupling of Francisco de Gey and his wife Laura Yanes. Francisco is one of the sadder participants in the *Academia*. When they married, Laura was a vulnerable, dependent woman who undertook the household chores with routine precision. He looked after her and she looked after him in a simpatico undertaking of "togetherness." The couple's marriage consisted of "almas confundidas la una con la otra, sin individuación.... Amor pleno y entregado a la más absoluta esclavitud del uno al otro [two entwined souls without individualization.... Total love devoted to mutual and absolute enslavement] (90). Whilst Francisco progressively moved up the professional ladder, the relationship flourished however when he lost his job and eventually became long-term unemployed, Laura was forced to become the breadwinner. Francisco decides, with his wife's support to write the book he always dreamed about, however after several unsuccessful attempts, Laura tires of her husband and for the first time in their partnership, she asserts her independence.

Laura and Francisco's marriage follows a "Togetherness" philosophy of families established in the 1950s: "*Togetherness*, así se llamaba al, <<espíritu comunitario>> del que gozaban algunos matrimonios, en teoría afortunados, modélicos. Parejas que comulgaban unidas en todos los frentes de la vida, que lo compartían todo, incluidos los sentimientos más terribles" ["togetherness" was the name given to the "community spirit" enjoyed by a few, in theory fortunate, marriages. Couples that presented a united front in all aspects of life and who shared everything, even the most terrible of feelings] (89).

This couple represents the opposite of the relationship between Penelope and Ulises in which both partners seek independence and freedom at any cost. For Francisco and Laura this sort of independence inspired fear: "tuvieron miedo de existir cada uno por su cuenta. Un pavor atávico y de naturaleza desconocida, a esa bola espesa y negra, pesada como la carga de un condenado, que es la libertad" [they were afraid to exist alone on their own account. The idea inspired a strange atavistic fear of freedom, as if it were a dense black ball that weighed heavier than a death sentence] (90). The conflict between their relationship and Laura's hypermodern desire for independence and freedom results in the dissolution of their marriage.

## Conclusion

In this essay, I hope I have captured a snapshot of the various alternative or new families that Vallvey portrays in *Los estados carenciales* and also reflected on these characters through the theoretical lens established by Lipovetsky in his depiction of hypermodern times. In addition, I have briefly examined the status of traditional marriages within this milieu as they are depicted in the novel. There are many other aspects of this novel that are ripe for critical analysis including the intertextual references to Homer's epic *The Odyssey* so clearly established through the central figures' names. In addition, I have just briefly touched on the theme of the novel, "What is happiness?" which also merits further exploration.[5]

Perhaps the most salient conclusion of the reader and the author can be found in the final pages of the novel. Within the Notes of the Author at the conclusion of the work, Vallvey again links her novel to the ideas established by Schopenhauer. In answer to the question, "What is happiness?" she offers the following advice, "Contra lo que pudiera parecer, la felicidad no es el arte de saber conformarse, si bien es posible que sí lo sea el de aprender a disfrutar de lo que somos, y secundariamente de lo que tenemos, sin preocuparnos demasiado por aquello que es evidente que jamás podremos ser o por lo que tendremos" [Contrary to appearances, happiness is not the art of knowing how to conform, although it might well be learning how to enjoy what we are, and secondly what we have without worrying too much about what we will never be or never have] (365). Within the context of the modern family, this serves as an incentive to create the family one desires and to seek happiness within that construct rather than worrying about finding happiness within conformity.

## Notes

1. This is the title given to the translation of *Los estados carenciales* into English by Margaret Jull Costa (London: Penguin, 2004).
2. Page numbers for subsequent quotations from this source are given parenthetically. All translations are mine.
3. Page numbers for subsequent quotations from this source are given parenthetically. All translations are mine.
4. This particular aspect of the novel warrants further investigation.
5. This theme invites the insertion of a multitude of philosophers' ruminations on the topic throughout the text.

## Works Cited

Alberdi, Inés. *La nueva familia española*. Madrid: Ediciones Taurus, 1999.
Charles, Sébastien. "Paradoxical Individualism: An Introduction to the Thoughts of Gilles Lipovetsky." Trans. Andrew Brown. In *Hypermodern Times*, ed. Gilles Lipovetsky. Cambridge, UK: Polity, 2005.
Lipovetsky, Gilles. *The Empire of Fashion*. Trans. Catherine Porter. Princeton, NJ: Princeton University Press, 2002.
\_\_\_\_\_. *Hypermodern Times*. Trans. Andrew Brown. Cambridge, UK: Polity, 2005.
Schopenhauer, Arthur. *Schopenhauer: The World as Will and Representation*. Trans. Judith Norman, Alistair Welchman and Christopher Janaway. Cambridge, UK: Cambridge University Press, 2010.
Tavoillot, Pierre-Henre. Foreword. In *Hypermodern Times*, ed. Gillies Lipovetsky. Cambridge, UK: Polity, 2005.
Vallvey, Ángela. *Happy Creatures*. Trans. Margaret Jull Costa. London: Penguin, 2004.
\_\_\_\_\_. *Los estados carenciales*. Barcelona: Ediciones Destino, S.A., 2008.

# 3

# All Turbulent on the Home Front
## *Unfulfilled Working Mothers in Almudena Grandes'* Atlas de geografía humana

### LORRAINE RYAN

This essay, which explores Almudena Grandes' portrayal of unfulfilled mothers in *Atlas de geografía humana* (2005), takes as its point of departure the distinction between the younger and older generations of Spanish women writers made by Catherine Davies in her study, *Spanish Women's Writing, 1849–1996*. Davies classifies women writers such as Clara Janés and Ana Rossetti as the older generation, born in the 1940s and 1950s. She further defines the younger generation, including Grandes, as those born in the late 1950s and 1960s as "the younger generation, experiencing the Transition when they were children or adolescents, [who] would note the change of the 1960s less and would tend to take civil and political rights for granted. On the other hand, they would have to face new levels of unemployment, drug cultures and AIDS" (193). Catherine Davies notes that gender has become a salient concern in Spanish society, superseding both class and regional identity as the most significant forms of categorization (194). For Almudena Grandes, gender has been, until the publication of *El corazón helado* (2006) that marked a thematic shift to historical memory, among the foremost of her concerns. From the beginning of her literary career, she has demonstrated a deep desire to demonstrate the effect of seismic social changes on Spanish women, and, in so doing, to approximate a more nuanced definition of Spanish womanhood, which has tended to be reduced to a binary dichotomy of the liberal, Transitional woman and the conservative Francoist "ángel del hogar." Her first novel, *Las edades de Lulú* (1989) caused uproar as it explicitly chartered the sexual odyssey of a teenager, and contained masochistic scenes. Refusing to be typecast as the high priestess of Spanish eroticism, Grandes next embarked on the rationalization of gender roles and performance, which can be understood as the socially prescribed models of gender and a consequent assimilation of the dominant gender model. Gender roles are part of a conundrum inextricably linked with radical social change in Spain. This issue underlies and indeed moulds Grandes' narrative reconceptualization of maternity in novels such as *Malena es un nombre de tango* (1994), *Modelos de mujer* and the short story *La buena hija* which features in Laura Freixas' acclaimed 1996 collection *Madres e hijas*.[1] In these texts, differing, and oft, incompatible gender ideologies collide and produce dissension between mother and daughter, but rather than recur to simplistic binary oppositions, Grandes creates characters who are a composite of conservatism and liberalism.

Prior to embarking on a detailed analysis of the author's shattering of deeply seated maternal myths in *Atlas*, it is first important to define the sociological concept of generation as this is critical to understanding her perspective. A generation is a social unit that matures at the same time, and, in adulthood, shapes the social order (Mannheim 152). Generations usually transmit the edicts of the dominant order to the upcoming generation. Of special pertinence to this analysis is Julio Aróstegui's definition of la *generación activa* [the active generation]. It consists of those between the ages of 25 to 45 who control the dominant political, social and cultural terrains (125). Grandes' coming of age, that is, her accession to the *generación activa* status precipitated a questioning of the imbrication between generational status and gender autonomy. Institutionally, the image of a putative convergence between the two is promoted. Grandes' generation, which came to adulthood during the Transition, should have obtained all the rights to which women are entitled within an egalitarian society.

However, it is the divergence between generational status and gender autonomy that underlines Grandes problematization of gender in her novels. Instead of a symbiosis between these two elements, Grandes' generation has been confronted with remnants of traditional thinking regarding appropriate feminine behavior and the disappointing divergence between political rhetoric and the realities of an unequal and at times discriminatory workplace. This generation, which reached adulthood during the Transition, believed that they would be liberated from the shackles that previously impeded women's development in Spain. Grandes comments, "nosotras, [...] fuimos adolescentes en un país adolescente, pertenecemos a una generación que se iba a comer el mundo, todo estaba a nuestro favor" [we were teenagers in a teenager country, we belonged to a generation who was going to eat up the world, everything was in our favor] (Llorente 2).[2] Grandes' contention is corroborated by statistics, which evidence that the acceleration of social change in Spain often causes it to be overestimated. The rate of employment for women in Spain is lower than in other European countries (Tezanos 107). Variables such as social class and education are also highly important factors in women's experience of equality. The range of possibilities open to women within a liberal democracy has been impeded by extant gender inequalities. The pleasure of apparent triumphs has also been marred by the absence of any help and the pressure of having to cope with both the demands of the private and public sphere: "Para muchas mujeres ha significado trabajar el doble, esforzarse el doble" [For many women this has meant working and striving twice as hard] (La Argentinidad).

The treatment of pregnant women within the workplace also belies institutional claims that egalitarianism has been achieved. Unbeknown to their female employees, some companies perform pregnancy tests on them. Ángel Panero, Vice President of CEOE (Confederación Española de Organizaciones Empresariales [Spanish Confederation of Business Organizations], has termed pregnancy, an "enfermedad muy contagiosa" [a very contagious disease] (qtd. in Falcón 42). An overview of the high court cases in Spain over the last 10 years demonstrates that pregnancy in the business world is fraught with difficulty. The volatility of the mother's health in the months ensuing the delivery of the child is often used to vindicate the employer's covert desire to dismiss her (Fernández Rodríguez 15).

The realities of female employment contrasts sharply with the egalitarian institutional discourse that promotes women's rights. For Grandes, this disparity only serves to reinforce her conviction that the current struggle for equality lacks vigor: "Cada vez que celebramos el Día de la Mujer, el 8 de marzo, pienso: en un país que no cumple el principio básico de igual trabajo, igual salario, ¿de qué hablan los políticos? Esa idea que teníamos de que el progreso es una línea recta, que no hay vuelta atrás, estaba equivocada" [Every time we celebrate Women's Day on the 8th of March, I think, "In a country which does not fulfill the basic principles of equal working conditions and salary, what are the politicians talking about. That idea we had that progress would be straightforward, that there is no turning back, was wrong"] (Grandes qtd. in Pérez Oliva, 2007).In a similar manner to other women writers, Grandes herself has experienced dismissal and the belittlement of her success due to her gender.

Many attribute the prominence of women writers to their eminent marketability and the desire of the literary world to enhance their liberal credentials by promoting women (Henseler 25). This has engendered some reluctance on the part of women writers to be associated with what is perceived as "women's literature." Grandes' experience of this cultural elitism, which contains decidedly sexist overtones, has strengthened her conviction that gender equality is yet to be fully achieved in Spain. Female writers' gender is considered an intrinsic part of their writing in a way that would be inconceivable for a man. She writes: "en el mundo literario prevalece un principio de discriminación sexual que obliga a las escritoras a pronunciarse a cada paso acerca del género" [In the literary world a principle of sexual discrimination prevails which forces women writers to give their opinions on gender at every step] (Rodríguez Villouta). Grandes' personal experience buttresses her conviction that the institution of gender, which has not advanced as much as is proclaimed in public fora, still restricts the gamut of a woman's potentialities and the recognition accorded to her achievements.

Grandes' *generación activa* status also implies that she is concerned with the transmission of a liberal conception of gender to the next generation. This has proved itself to be a difficult process as the newer generation is more conservative. Grandes feels that they have observed the toll that "el doble jornada" [the double day] taken on their mothers and, therefore, understandably, rejected this model. Their conservatism has been undoubtedly fomented by the sterile and mercenary atmosphere of current day Spain, which she finds repugnant. Grandes is appalled by what has replaced the hypocrisy of Francoism, namely vulgar ostentation and unbridled selfishness (Grandes and Llamazares, 2008: 53). She questions the steadfastness of her generation's values and their commitment to the forging of a progressive and enlightened Spain. The values they fought for seem irrelevant to the generation that will soon replace them. This means that her generation's values will not be perpetuated and might eventually cease to influence society. An even more alarming prospect for Grandes is that the reactionary conservatism of her childhood might replace the liberalism for which her generation fought so hard. In an interview with *El País* she explained, "se puede retroceder y se pueden perder conquistas sociales que han costado mucho. Educamos a nuestras hijas pensando en que los cambios eran irreversibles, pero ahora ya no soy tan optimista" [it can regress and social advances which have been very difficult to achieve can be lost. We brought up our children thinking that the changes were irreversible, but now, I am not so optimistic] (Grandes qtd. in Pérez Oliva). Grandes' novels do not offer any facile solutions to the problem of gender inequality but rather seek to elucidate how her generation negotiates the complexities of gender.

Much of Almudena Grandes' writing can be construed as a contestation of the maternal instinct: replete with angry and frustrated mothers for whom motherhood has been a complete parenthesis of unfulfillment. Her novels give motherhood a distinctly negative valence. Furthermore, the strictures of motherhood implied by these characters' attitudes make the idea of a biological need to mother a child somewhat apocryphal. This can be interpreted as an iconoclastic deconstruction of the tenets that upheld Francoist gender ideology, such as ascriptive motherhood. Nash notes that the Regime promoted "la concepción global de la mujer como el ángel del hogar, cuyo destino biológico y social era la maternidad" [the global conceptualization of the woman as the "angel of the house" whose biological and social destiny was motherhood] (280).

The convergence of Church and State assured that the traditional, conservative ethos, which was characteristic of both institutions and manifested itself most strongly in the terrain of personal morality and sexual mores, permeated every facet of life. This discriminatory discourse was complemented by the work of the *Sección Femenina de Falange* [the Falange's Women Section]. The following text demonstrates how State policy was enmeshed in the official doctrine: "El verdadero deber de las mujeres para con la Patria consiste en formar familias con una base exacta de austeridad y alegría" [Women's real duty for the Homeland consists in forming families on an exact base of austerity and happiness] (Primo de Rivera 12–14).

Ascriptive motherhood implicitly assumes the existence of a maternal instinct, which presupposes a womanly propensity for childrearing and nurturing. It is inherently discriminatory, a fact which Sherry Ortner elucidates succinctly:

> There is something genetically inherent in the male of the species that makes them the naturally dominant sex; that "something" is lacking in females, and as a result women are not only naturally subordinate but in general quite satisfied with their position, since it affords them protection and the opportunity to maximize maternal pleasures, which to them are the most satisfying experiences of life [71].

Scientific research has invalidated the notion of an innate maternal instinct. Klineberg has divided the maternal instinct into two separate stages. The mother, before conceiving, experiences prematernal desire, which is the urge to have a child. Ensuing the delivery of the child, the mother experiences post maternal desire (qtd. in Ferro 59). It is imperative that we now focus on the definition of instinct provided by Laplanche and Pontalis, which is an inherited biological instinct with little variation between individuals (1983 qtd. in Ferro 57). This does not correspond, in any sense, to desire, which always implies subjectivity, and certainly not any biological necessity. Furthermore, Ferro maintains that desire vacillates with social tendencies (63). Crawford and Unger have also substantiated the social constructiveness of the maternal instinct. They convincingly argue that the worryingly high rates of abortion and infanticide throughout history belie its naturalness (349). Furthermore, they argue that men are highly capable, and indeed adept, at "mothering" when the situation arises. They observe that single fathers who perform this nurturing role identify themselves as caring, understanding and nurturing: research which gives credence to the view that the role itself is instrumental in developing and consolidating supposedly feminine or masculine characteristics (Crawford and Unger 349).

Therefore, the maternal instinct is not a biological given but a socially constructed myth which can prove detrimental to women's well being, especially in a society such as Spain which effects a radical rupture with traditional values in a relatively short period of time. This is the case in the story of two dissatisfied working mothers, Ana and Rosa, in Almudena Grandes' *Atlas de geografía humana*. The narrative voice in each these stories stresses the loss of control that motherhood signifies, impacting as it does on a woman's economic, personal and professional destiny, and gives further validation to the theory that the discourse of motherhood venerates the mother, but not the woman as an entity distinct from her mothering person. Grandes' depiction is remarkably innovative, as these women defy the status quo by discarding the intensive mothering model that dictates that a mother must sacrifice her own needs in order to perfectly fulfill her designated maternal duties (Hayes 1996: 85), and instead seek fulfillment in their personal lives. Ana lets her affair with a married man take precedence over her daughter Amanda's welcome. Rosa, the quintessential "good girl," initiates an affair with the photographer Nacho only to be later rebuffed by unanswered telephone calls. Their primacy of personal relationships pinpoints to a transformation of maternal value systems, which now prioritize the mother's needs and have rejected the self sacrificing Francoist maternal model.

Firstly, I will analyze the maternal trajectory of Ana, who works in a publishing company and became a mother at a young age. Her experience is worthy of analysis as it reflects how the transitional mother alternatively cedes, negotiates and rejects the intensive mother model: in so doing, it repeats Grandes' earlier portrayals of gender freedom as a constantly contested liberty, and lends credence to the view that Spanish gender ideology is composed of an amalgam of liberal and conservative attitudes. As a schoolgirl, Ana had a relationship with her art teacher Félix. Propelled by his desire to become a father, she gets pregnant at nineteen years of age. Their relationship founders, and Ana is eventually forced to confront the seemingly insurmountable challenges of single motherhood: "Tenía veinticuatro años, una hija de cuatro, una familia que había dejado de lamentar mi pérdida, y ningún título, ninguna experiencia, ninguna idea, siquiera aproximada, de cómo iba a lograr ganarme la vida" [I was twenty-four years of age, I had a four year old daughter, a family who had ceased to mourn my loss, no qualifications, no experiences, no idea, not even remote, of how I would earn my living] (86). Her situation is further exacerbated by Félix's refusal to pay child maintenance: a refusal that is grounded in his vehement opposition to the bourgeois nature of education. Only the munificence of Ana's parents allows them to enjoy a reasonable standard of living. Her daughter Amanda has recently gone to live with her father in Paris of her own volition: an event that causes Ana to experience a deluge of emotions, including loneliness, guilt and sadness.

Ana epitomizes the mother of the Transition, in the sense that she is non-traditional and also displays a more questioning, non-conformist attitude towards motherhood. Her evaluation of Amanda's childhood in terms of expenditure could hardly be more antithetical to the self-sacrificing model of motherhood propagated by the Francoist Regime "La niña se chupaba más de la mitad de mi primer sueldo" [The child sucked more than half of my first salary] (87). It is only when Amanda reaches puberty that Ana succeeds in eradicating her self-image as a "rehén perpetua de mi propia hija" [a perpetual hostage of my own daughter] (86). Endeavoring to console herself in the wake of Amanda's departure, she even laments the fact that Félix did not seek to get custody of her eleven years ago when Amanda's maintenance required self-sacrifice on Ana's part.

The fact that Ana's decision to be a mother was a non-subjective one has significant ramifications for the mother-daughter relationship. Her love for her daughter is tempered by regret, as she feels that although she loves her dearly, she has also been "una de mis mayores errores" [one of my biggest mistakes] (83). Following her arrival from Paris, Amanda proceeds to admonish her mother for her foolhardy behavior. Ana counters this by accusing Amanda of being overly conservative. As the argument continues, Ana's ambiguity concerning the mothering role is patent. Rebutting her own mother's belief that her cousin Antonio's childfree state is deplorable, she asserts that Antonio is perfectly content with his life, and furthermore, "tener hijos no es garantía de nada" [having children is not a guarantee of anything] (421). Even more conclusive is the fact that she justifies his lifestyle by saying that she would have also liked to live a similar type of life (421). With this statement, Ana reveals that she was really compelled to engage in motherhood by Félix's desires, not her own. Ana's decision to have a child always is also expounded in terms of Félix's life with no reference to her own hopes and dreams.

Even more significantly, Ana staunchly defends her right to personal happiness. She reminds Amanda that she never disputed her right to live with her father and that she has endured the loneliness that Amanda's absence caused her. She issues her with an ultimatum: either she can accept Ana's domestic arrangements or she can go to live with her father (422). She responds to Amanda's claim that she has become very selfish by unabashedly asserting that her age makes selfishness her prerogative. This assertion marks her not only as a person with healthy self-esteem, but, more definitively, as a woman of the Transition. María Jesus Miranda asserts that women under 45 are characterized by increasing autonomy and that their sense of personal fulfillment is derived from the exterior: the public sphere (80–81). Hence, their lives do not revolve around gaining the approval of their family.

The nascent social mores of the Transition, which promoted women's entry into the public sphere, to a certain extent, illuminate Ana's attitude. Between 1975 and 1995, two million women entered the labor force in Spain (Iglesias de Ussel 28). Ana could be just one of this cohort of women who experienced the conflict of personal ambition and domestic obligations: a conflict that is generated by conflicting value-systems. Women are inculcated in the private sphere with the values of caring, dependence and security: all prerequisites for the ideal mother. These values exist in polarity to those admired in the private sphere, such as initiative, independence, competitiveness and ambition. Ambition, in particular, is generally held to be adversarial to good motherhood. Hence, women often find themselves at an impasse that opposes two options: forsake their personal fulfillment or embrace motherhood and the sacrifices it entails wholeheartedly. Ana's list of grievances demonstrates that many women still continue searching for that all-elusive fulfillment and merely endure, but not condone, the self-sacrifice motherhood entails.

Also comprising the political and social permutations of the Transition were women's growing awareness of their own rights. Further facilitated by greater access to work and contraception, women began increasingly to choose to have fewer children. For many women the effects of the economic crisis in the late 1970s and increased access to university acted as deterrents from motherhood. Consequently, Spain witnessed a sharp decrease in its birth rates. In fact, its birth rate is now one of the lowest in the EU, standing at 1.24 births per woman (Cousins 60). Attendant upon this shift in demographic trends was an iconoclastic depiction of the family. Iglesias de Ussel postulates that negative portrayals of the family now proliferate in the media and that the promotion of legislative and social changes by the feminist movement has had a vital role in transforming women's attitudes towards work and motherhood (31). These measures have culminated in the genesis of a radically different mentality among Spanish women, who "[parece que hayan] rechazado a la familia y al matrimonio como orientación vital" [who seem to have rejected family and marriage as essential orientations] (29) Ana embodies the spirit of this new attitude, not only in her unromantic view of motherhood, but in her regret at having embraced domesticity at too early an age, and having forsaken the opportunity to study abroad and develop her career. Her negative valuation of her domestic life stands in clear opposition to the Francoist idealization of motherhood as the ultimate source of fulfillment for women. Far from being a uniquely satisfying experience, motherhood for these Transition mothers seems to act as an obstacle to what is regarded as a fulfilling life. Certainly, Ana's reminiscences would insinuate that engagement with the public sphere is infinitely more rewarding than enclosure in the private one. Hence, if we reflect on Ana's views in conjunction with the historical permutations of the Transition, the conclusions vindicate the idea that attitudes to motherhood are not fixed signifiers, but are instead dictated by the dominant ideology.

Ana's ambivalence concerning her daughter is not only symptomatic of the particular socio-historical circumstances of the Transition but can also be assessed in relation to the experience of lone motherhood. In Spain, single parent families are becoming increasingly common: the percentage of lone parent families has increased from 6 percent in 1981 to 8.2 percent in 1995 (Alberdi 98). Sociologists concur that this phenomenon is rooted not only in the availability of divorce in Spain but on a more profound level, in the eradication of hypocritical attitudes in Spanish society. Spouses are no longer willing to endure the hardships of an unhappy marriage in order to conform to anachronistic dictates such as "marriage is for life" (Instituto de la Mujer 9). Ana incarnates this new outlook on marriage, as she regards Félix's selfishness and infidelities as intolerable and does not baulk at revealing the extent of her suffering during the marriage. Yet, lone parenthood has significant consequences for the mother-daughter relationship. The absence of one spouse's income has as its obverse increased reliance on the earnings of the mother; as a result, money can often preoccupy the lone mother to an almost obsessive degree (Shaw 144). In Ana's case, we witness her frantic efforts to pay the accumulating bills, which gives rise to her acute awareness of the cost of raising a child. Shaw also adduces loneliness as one of the pitfalls of lone parenthood (145).[3] Certainly, Ana's history of failed relationships testifies to the fact that lone parenthood can adversely affect the mother's relationships: "no les excitaba la idea de irse de vacaciones con una niña de otro" [the idea of going of holidays with another person's child did not excite them] (Grandes 172). Ana also spend the formative years of Amanda's life foregoing her own most basic needs, such as adult company. Thus, it can be argued that the level of self-sacrifice that lone parenthood requires far exceeds that of traditional motherhood. If we recall Ana's declaration that Amanda was one of her biggest mistakes, we can conclude that this level of self-abnegation taints the mother's love with bitterness.

Therefore, it would seem that women's growing involvement within the public sphere corrodes the reverence habitually accorded to the tenets of the private sphere and formulates a more modern version of mothering that promotes the well being of the mother as fundamental. Motherhood never sufficiently fulfilled Ana and now that her new romance has given her that feeling of completion, she relegates her performance as a mother to a second priority. When her daughter confides in Ana that being the daughter of separated parents caused her emotional damage, it does not precipitate a panicky reassessment of her capacities as a mother, as it might have. Instead, Ana joyfully acknowledges her selfishness (453); this prioritization of herself, after all, has caused her life as a woman, not as a mother, to experience intense change as well as a happiness which was previously denied to her by the restrictions of lone motherhood. Her "selfishness" prefigures the emergence of the mother as a sentient being whose life as a person is not subordinated to the interests of family. Although she is the antitype of the patriarchal definition of the "good" mother, she has performed her maternal function admirably well despite the formidable obstacles with which she was confronted. Moreover, she refuses to allow her mothering role to strain her, which in the view of Debold, Malavé and Wilson is vital in order to preserve the mother's uniqueness (88).

Ana has transcended cultural myths that mandate mothering as paramount by honestly and consistently assessing her situation and feelings. Her story augurs the beginning of a hopeful new era for the mother-daughter relationship in Spain, as it surmounts the intangible, but nevertheless formidable, obstacle of cultural expectation. Primacy is accorded to what constitutes the essence of the relationship: the feelings of the mother and daughter as individuals. Ana and Amanda discuss their feelings honestly and struggle for self-definition within the parameters of their relationship. Although this approach is often contentious, it has an expurgative effect on the relationship, ridding it of misunderstandings and ultimately fortifying it.

Ana's colleague, Rosa's solution to her disillusionment with motherhood and bourgeois conformity is altogether more drastic, as she consciously rejects motherhood in order to achieve what she perceives to be self-realization. In short, while Ana privately complains about motherhood and is very much aware of its disappointing realities, Rosa categorically rejects it. Her unambiguous stance is made all the more surprising by the fact that she epitomizes "the good girl." Her life story is devoid of traumatic incidences and instead has all the trappings of respectability. Her education in a convent school passes uneventfully as she is a diligent, docile student in marked contrast to her rebellious sister Angélica (338). In the convent school she is inculcated with certain docility, as the outward manifestations of compliance such as study and good grades ensure that she doesn't suffer the wrath of the nuns (338). Yet, an inexplicable sadness overwhelms her at school.

As a teenager, Rosa had a curfew of 9 o'clock at night. After beseeching her mother to let her stay out longer, the curfew is extended to 9:30 P.M. (340). Significantly, Rosa states that she would never have dared insist on a more lenient curfew, as she does not wish to jeopardize the peaceful relationship she enjoys with her parents (340). Having witnessed her siblings' rebellious behavior, Rosa firmly entrenches herself in the polar opposite position (343). She renounces her own desires in order to comply to the social image of a good girl, which is docile and meek. Analogizing happiness to an addictive drug, she notes that both destroy the will: "Quizás la costumbre de la felicidad es como una de esas drogas dañinas que se asimilan al organismo hasta el punto de llegar a resultar ineficaces e imprescindibles a la vez, destruyendo la voluntad para siempre" [Maybe the habit of happiness is like one of those damaging drugs which are assimilated into the organism to such a degree that they are rendered inefficient and absolutely necessary at the same time, destroying the will forever] (343). The inevitable conclusion to that parallel is that a forfeiture of one's own volition inheres in the attainment of happiness. One particular Saturday, Rosa stays out until two o'clock in the morning. Her transgression merits her a harsh punishment: she is not allowed to go out for a long time. Rosa accepts this with her customary equanimity, yet her conception of happiness is changed forever (343). Further on in the narrative, her reflections on the innocence with which children assume happiness as an entitlement illuminate the conclusion Rosa arrived at following her punishment: namely that compliance assures happiness. After all, children "se niegan a aceptar las reglas de otra vida, no pueden asumir un final diferente" [refuse to accept the rules of another life, they cannot accept another ending] (344). This statement seems to imply that unless one is prepared to assume the risks of an unconventional life, one has to obey the rules of society.

However, an older Rosa re-assesses her conception of happiness. Her reactions to the tribulations of life have always been formulaic and compliant, "esquivando los problemas y las grandes decisiones" [avoiding problems and big decisions] (350). However, the promised happiness has failed to materialize, and blind hope has been superseded by anxiety concerning her age (350). Rosa, like Ana, does not even pretend that domestic life has brought her fulfillment. Rosa was an outstanding student, but never felt that university was the means by which she would realize her potential (16). Consequently, she hinged all her hopes on the life awaiting her after secondary school, when she would travel to exotic countries (16). These plans were thwarted by her involvement with a pop group, where she met her future husband, Ignacio. He convinced her that exams were unnecessary for such a brilliant girl, and, consequently, Rosa decided not to sit her exams. Although Rosa was fully cognizant of the renunciation of her own cherished dreams, it did not unduly disturb her, as married life was, in its incipient stages, exciting and wonderful.

Yet, at this mid-life juncture, with her daily life proceeding at a soporific pace, Rosa is greatly troubled by both the quiescence of her life and the insidious passing of time. The last decade of her life was simply a non-event: so insipid in fact that it does not even constitute a vague recollection: "pero lo cierto es que no los recuerdo, no soy consciente de haberlos vivido" [but what is certain is that I do not remember them, I am not conscious of having lived through them] (18). Her lack of control over her own life is a causal factor in this profound dissatisfaction with her life. After her thirtieth birthday, Rosa ponders on her life, and it certainly seems that the array of her accomplishments is not sufficient to stop her ruminating on what purpose her life has served; neither does it alleviate the feeling of emptiness that gnaws at her internally. It is certainly plausible that Rosa's achievements don't satisfy her because they don't reflect her subjective desires; rather, they indicate the achievements that are deemed appropriate for a mother, such as children, a husband and a talent for cooking. Therefore, in order to satiate her lack of fulfillment, Rosa exhausts herself every day, which allows her no time for reflection on the duplicity of the contract that promised happiness as the corollary of compliance: a contract which her puerile innocence held to be sacrosanct.

Rosa's existential crisis precipitates a re-ordering of her priorities. Far from being her sole reason for existence, Rosa refers to her children only a few times throughout the book (352). The ageing process and her relationship with Nacho are of infinitely more concern to her. At one point, she acknowledges that her affair with Nacho eclipsed her emotional involvement in the children's lives: "no llegaba a vivir de verdad en aquel tiempo" [I did not manage to really live during that time] (352–353). Furthermore, she relishes the chance to travel to Switzerland in order to disconnect totally from the monotony of her daily life. Underlying this new attitude to motherhood, as in Ana's case, is the new spirit of liberalism ushered in by the political changes of the Transition. Cibreiro contends that those Spaniards born during the last two decades of Francoism display a liberal intellectual tendency fashioned from their dual experience of the repression of the dictatorship and the permissiveness of the Transition (133). Rosa personifies their spirit, in the sense that her desire for self-gratification overrides her allegiance to social mandates: a typical characteristic of this generation. Motherhood, in the case of Rosa, is deprived of its habitual reverence, and the shallowness of contemporary society is instead elevated to an issue of supreme importance. Grandes, by this asymmetrical allocation of priority to the aforementioned issues, is subverting the infallibility of the institutions that upheld the Francoist Regime, such as marriage. No longer is marriage regarded as the apogee of a woman's life. Her disillusionment with her life, which is anchored in the incompatibility of her sensuous nature with the monotony of daily domestic life, is tangible: "Esa insoportable sensación de ajenidad, como una sucia y permanente sospecha de vivir atrapada en el cuerpo de otro, la casa de otro, la vida de otro" [This unbearable feeling of distance like a dirty and permanent suspicion of living trapped in another's body, another's house and another's life] (355). Evidently, her sense of self has been distorted by her compliance throughout her life with prior expectations and has thus created an internal tumult between her authentic and her artificial self. Her artificial self is the cheerful person she appears to her family and friends; on the other hand, her authentic self is the person who continually asks what has become of the life from which she expected so much.

Moreover, both Rosa and her husband commit adultery, which was an exclusively male preserve in Franco's era. Women, it was generally held, would be incapable of being unfaithful to the man they loved; according to González Duro, a woman's promiscuity or adultery was invariably attributed to a psychiatric disorder (45).[4] Also, in portraying Rosa as a sexual person, Grandes is attacking the canonical depiction of the mother. The totem of the Francoist Regime, "el ángel del hogar" [the angel of the house] was asexual and docile (Graham 184). Indeed, during that epoch, the whole complex issue of women's sexuality was reduced to the maternal function. Gregorio Marañón contended that women only valued sex for its reproductive ends (González Duro 48).[5] Notwithstanding the changing paradigms of motherhood, the dominant image of mothers as asexual still persists in Western society (Walters 232). Representations of sexual, career-orientated mothers are practically non-existent in Western culture (Kaplan 183). Any portrayals of such mothers, only ever produced during the 1970s in the apex of the feminist movement, invariably satirized them, thus forestalling any serious treatment of the theme (Walters 228). This concept is reversed completely by Grandes as Rosa's sexuality is primordial to her sense of identity: an identity that is menaced by the onset of middle age.

It is now essential to analyze whether the fulfilled mother is an oxymoron. In order to answer that question fully, it must be reiterated that the edicts that previously regulated Spanish society have changed dramatically, but vestiges of a traditional mentality still govern many issues, especially those pertaining to women. Consequently, the generation to which Rosa belongs is defined by its ambivalence. It is precisely this ambivalence concerning social dictates that never leads them to rebel openly and unequivocally (Cibreiro 134). They then find themselves faced with the quagmire of reconciling their outward compliance with a socially prescribed path with their inward desires for self-gratification. Consequently, people like Rosa desperately search for a solution to the gaping void in their lives with only the confused social mores of what Raymond Carr has termed "the schizophrenic society" to guide them

(Carr 199). The mindset of "the schizophrenic society" is exemplified by Rosa's attitude towards her husband. Although she feels utter indifference to him, she still continues to play the part of a dutiful and loving wife, a pretence that only compounds her disquiet.

The private sphere, it would seem, is regulated by immutable laws, which, in Rosa's case, preclude self-fulfillment. Rosa readily admits "por no perder los años, había estado a punto de perderme la infancia de mis hijos" [in order not to miss out on those years, I had been about to miss out on my children's childhood] (353). In the heady excitement of her affair, Rosa felt she was shedding the years, those years that have failed to satiate her hunger for self-fulfillment. Yet this sentiment would seem to be at odds with Rosa's earlier claim that the responsibilities of both working and looking after her children do not bother her. In order to understand these contradictory sentiments, it is vital to recognize the discourse of motherhood itself is now couched in psychological rhetoric (Walter 10). This, in turn, causes mothers to analyze the experience of mothering in terms of self-realization; the fact that working mothers generally have a diminished quality of life only serves to further divest motherhood of its allure (Greer 198). Badinter summarizes the implications of this shift in mothering ideology as follows: "Formerly, a woman's interest was centered on her children; today, it is centered on herself: her emotional and professional life. She no longer builds her existence around her children, but obliges them to adapt to her plans for a personal life" (186). In addition to this, society proffers an array of much more tantalizing options for self-fulfillment and establishes unforgiving criteria for the attainment of the all-elusive happiness, such as beauty, youth and money. Naomi Wolf postulates that the consumerism of Western society instigates a cult of beauty (129). This cult of beauty is primarily based on a process of deferral, which lures women into starvation and other forms of self-deprivation with the promise of eventual happiness, and also subjects women to a rigorous form of accountability. If women do not measure up to the prevailing standards of beauty, a poverty-stricken old age, loneliness and loveliness are their punishments (130). Therefore, women in contemporary Western society are encouraged to seek constant validation through their attractiveness. As they age and their attractiveness diminishes, their sense of self-worth is threatened, as is the case with Rosa. Rosa clearly aspires to this type of fulfillment, as the transience of her youth upsets her greatly.

The shift in Rosa's priorities mirrors this social obsession with conserving a youthful appearance. The onset of maturity often gives rise to a blind panic, whose antidote is found in the affective domain of romance. Rosa chooses an affair to alleviate this anxiety and becomes obsessed with her lover. His attentions salvage her waning self-esteem, as he makes her feel special (183).

Notwithstanding the fact that he doesn't reciprocate her interest, she continues to pursue him, convinced that he can reinvigorate her arid life. Yet there are even more profound undercurrents lurking in the obsessive nature of Rosa's love for Nacho. Alberoni contends that falling in love is simply a nostrum to offset the terror at the empty life that looms ominously before women (69–70). Its superlative qualities as a conduit of self-fulfillment are indisputable. Ethel Person goes as far as to say that romantic love is "perhaps the most important of our cultivated freedoms, [...] perhaps in our time the primary vehicle for self-realization transformation and transcendence" (353–354). Certainly the affair or, more specifically, the feeling that she was still attractive, empowered Rosa. The following analogy demonstrates the magnitude of the change in her life. Significantly, Rosa uses the trope of "[un] sueño de poder ilimitado" [a dream of unlimited power] to describe the hiatus in her life caused by her affair with Nacho (355). The affair restored her feeling of control over the vicissitudes of life, thus countering the impotence that inheres in the ageing process and the failure of a marriage. She is now less sensitive to the rigors of time, as the excitement of her affair accelerates it and, paradoxically, makes it more bearable. Time is no longer relevant as her thoughts now centre exclusively on Nacho; by having an affair, Rosa is asserting her own selfhood and simultaneously freeing herself from the shackles of orthodox views on appropriate womanly behavior.

This path to self-fulfillment, however, is at antipodes to the fulfillment promised by "good" motherhood, which is centered on self-sacrifice and the care of others. Rosa refers to her affair as "un período prolongado de amnesia" [a prolonged period of amnesia] (Grandes 352). It does correspond to amnesia in the sense that Rosa had to cast aside her former self-molded from a socialization process that would have advocated the self-sacrificing model of behavior. González de Chávez postulates that there is an incompatibility between "los deseos como madre y los deseos como mujer" [mothers' desires and women's desires] an antagonism that effectively means that if the mother subscribes to the alternative self-gratifying form of fulfillment, it will adversely affect her performance as a mother (68). Hence, the fulfilled mother is a monolithic category; the mother must derive fulfillment primarily from the function itself and has to retain her non-threatening, desexualized persona in order to conform to social imperatives concerning the so-called good mother. Insofar as her children were concerned, during the affair, Rosa "nunca llegaba a vivir de verdad" [never really lived] (352); she had to relinquish her connection with them in order to explore her own possibilities for self-realization. It is when Rosa ends her affair with Nacho that motherhood reverts to its prior position of relative importance; in order to mark this turnaround and to restore her relationship with her children to its previous level of closeness,

Rosa decides to take the children to Rome on holidays (444). Obviously there is a tension between fulfillment as a woman and fulfillment as a mother, as they are radically opposed in terms of the prioritization of one's self. Fulfillment as a mother demands an almost saint-like altruism, while fulfillment as a woman involves placing one's individual needs first and foremost.

Having decided not to continue her relationship with Nacho, Rosa acquires a serenity born out of taking a more constructive approach to improving her life. She tells her husband that she wants to separate from him. It is noteworthy that both the men in Rosa's life share the same name. In my opinion, this is a strategy to underscore the fact that Rosa has mistakenly associated romance with self-realization. As previously stated, her personal hopes were subsumed by domesticity when she married Ignacio. Upon realizing this, she again embarked on a romance, although of the illicit, adulterous type. Not surprisingly, she rationalized this type of love, so different from the one which was the pivot of her discontentment, would act as the prelude to a more fulfilling chapter in her life. The romance proves to be a painful failure, and it is only when Rosa abandons the two Ignacios that the process of self-acceptance commences. Her experience would indicate that the key to self-fulfillment lies within the self and that a self-esteem that is contingent upon somebody else is only a caricature of the authentic version. Emerging from the nadirs of her existential crisis, Rosa feels that she has regained control over her life. Rosa's dilemma illustrates that motherhood is not necessarily a fulfilling role. It also indicates that mothers now subject the experience to more stringent criteria and are less willing to let their lives be governed by aphorisms.

The focus on the socio-historical context of both Ana and Rosa's dissatisfaction debunks the calcified model of motherhood propagated by the Francoist Regime, as their appraisals of their mothering experiences not only stress their own individuality, but also assimilate the impact of modernization. Rosa also grapples with polarized visions of fulfillment to no avail. The competing discourses of self-sacrifice and self-gratification demand nothing less than complete allegiance to their tenets, thus constraining women by inflexible categorization. Refusing to cede to the insularity imposed by the function of motherhood, Ana combines her motherly duties with a career and a partner, and she also has no qualms about propounding her own jaundiced view of motherhood. Rosa, however, does not reach a definitive end in her quest for self-realization; the euphoria of her affair with Nacho fails to displace the emptiness she feels. Rosa then immerses herself into her children's lives and returns to the familiar routine of never giving herself enough time to think about her life. Her crisis is apparently resolved with this brisk resumption of normal life, but the factors underlying it remain. Complete happiness, it would seem, is illusory in Western societies which alternately promote it as achievable through defiance of social imperatives or compliance; neither of which are particularly enticing options when pitted against the attractions of the other.

Thus, in both cases, the experience of motherhood resists reductionist categorization as the ultimate source of fulfillment. Kristeva's question has of yet remained unanswered: "What is it about this representation [of the patriarchal or Christian Maternal] that fails to take account of what a woman might want or say of the Maternal?" (163). The tribulations of the mothers in this text underline the necessity of reconfiguring motherhood in terms of the mother's own happiness, as both their experiences of motherhood occlude the passage to an infinitely more interesting life. This would also facilitate the evolution of the mother-daughter relationship from a source of conflict to a symbiosis in which self-realization and closeness are not mutually exclusive. Perhaps, this approach would, in the words of Irigaray, "devolverle la vida a esta madre y darle el derecho al placer, al goce, a la pasión" [give the mother back her life and give her the right to pleasure, enjoyment and passion] (14).

## NOTES

1. See Lorraine Ryan, "Nada más que un espejismo: la inquieta realidad de la modernidad española a través de los relatos *La buena hija* de Almudena Grandes y *La hija predilecta* de Soledad Puertólas," in Cinta Ramblado, ed., *Construcciones culturales de la maternidad en España: la madre y la relación madre-hija en la literatura y el cine contemporaneous* (Alicante: Editorial Universidad de Alicante, 2006), pp. 52–68.
2. All translations in this and subsequent translations from English to Spanish are my own.
3. Shaw, in her admirably balanced article on lone motherhood, cites relief at being alone, lack of constraints and increased financial control as benefits accruing from being a single parent (147–149).
4. Sexuality as a cornerstone of women's identity is a characteristic feature of much of Grandes' writing. In *Malena es un nombre de tango*, Malena and Magda both resisted efforts to subdue their sexuality, and hence, sexuality, in that novel, can be viewed as an emancipatory tool. Sara's affair with Vicente in Los aires difíciles also reflects a liberated approach to sexuality. Sexuality also plays a major role in the identities of the characters in *Atlas de geografía humana*.
5. This belief is based, for the most part, on conjecture. In a survey carried out by Serrano Vicens, it was found that 31.2 percent of Spanish women had had extramarital affairs (qtd. in González Duro 45).

## WORKS CITED

Alberdi, Inés. *La nueva familia española*. Madrid: Taurus, 1999.
Alberoni, Frances. *Falling in Love*. Trans.L. Venciti. New York: Random House, 1983.
"La Argentinidad." Entrevista a Almudena Grandes: Uno de los delitos del fue hacer un corte en la memoria, 2007. <http://www.luchadores.wordpress.com/2007/02/04/rntrevista-a-almudena-grandes>. Accessed February 2, 2009.

Aróstegui, Julio. *La historia vivida: Sobre la historia del presente*. Madrid: Alianza Editorial, 2008.
Badinter, Elisabeth. *Man/Woman: The One Is the Other*. London: Collins Harvill, 1989.
Bautista Parejo, Esperanza. "Mujer y democracia en España: Evolución jurídica y realidad social." *Revista de Estudios Sociales y de Sociología Aplicada* 105 (October–December 1996): 49–73.
Carr, Raymond. *Modern Spain, 1875–1980*. Oxford: Oxford University Press, 1980.
Cibreiro, Estrella. "Entre la crisis generacional y el éxtasis sexual: El dilema femenino en *Atlas de geografía humana* de Almudena Grandes." *Romance Studies* 20 (December 2002): 130–141.
Conde, Rosa. *Familia y cambio social en España*. Madrid: Centro de Investigaciones Sociológicas, 1982.
Cousins, Christine. "The Development of a Gendered Social Policy Regime." In *Gendering Spanish Democracy*, eds. Christine Cousins, Monica Threlfall and Celia Valiente. London and New York: Routledge, 2005.
Crawford, Mary, and Rhonda Unger. *Women and Gender: A Feminist Psychology*, 3d ed. New York: McGraw-Hill, 2000.
Davies, Catherine. *Spanish Women's Writing, 1894–1976*. New York: Continuum, 1998.
Debold, Elizabeth, Idelisse Malave and Marie C. Wilson. *Mother-Daughter Revolution: From Good Girls to Great Women*. New York: Bantam, 1994.
Falcón, Lidia. "Violent Democracy." *Journal of Spanish Cultural Studies* 3:1 (2002): 15–28.
Fernández Rodríguez, Vicente. "Familia y trabajo." *Revista de Fomento Social* 57 (2002): 11–24.
Ferro, Norma. *El instinto maternal o la necesidad de un mito*. Madrid: Siglo Veintiuno de España Editores, 1991.
González de Chávez, María Asunción. *Familia, maternidad, paternidad*. Alcalá de Henares: Centro Asesor Mujer, 1995.
González Duro, Enrique. *Represión sexual, dominación social*. Madrid: Akal Editores, 1976.
Graham, Helen. "Gender and the State: Women in the 1940s." In *Spanish Cultural Studies: An Introduction*, eds. Helen Graham and Jo. Labanyi. Oxford: Oxford University Press, 1995, pp. 182–195.
Grandes, Almudena. *Atlas de geografía humana*. Barcelona: Tusquets Editores, 1998.
\_\_\_\_\_. "La buena hija." In *Madres e hijas*, ed. Laura Freixas. Barcelona: Anagrama, 1996, pp. 185–211.
\_\_\_\_\_. *Las edades de Lulú*. Barcelona: Tusquets Editores, 1989.
\_\_\_\_\_. *Malena es un nombre de tango*. Barcelona: Tusquets Editores, 1994.
\_\_\_\_\_, and Gaspar Llamazares. *Al rojo vivo: un diálogo sobre la izquierda de hoy*. Madrid: Antonio Machado Editorial, 2008.
Greer, Germaine. *The Whole Woman*. London: Anchor, 2000.
Hayes, Sheila. *The Cultural Contradictions of Motherhood*. New Haven: Yale University Press, 1996.
Henseler, Christine. *Contemporary Spanish Women's Narrative and the Publishing Industry*. Urbana: University of Illinois Press, 1996.
Iglesias de Ussel, Julio. "Crisis y vitalidad de la familia." *Revista de Occidente* 11: 99 (1997): 21–35.
Instituto de la Mujer. "Informe del Ministerio de Asuntos Sociales sobre la familia española: Una realidad plural y dinámica en constante *evolución*." *Mujeres* 15 (1999): 4–13.
Irigaray, Luce. *Ese sexo que no es uno*. Madrid: Saltés Editorial, 1982.
Kaplan, E. Ann. *Motherhood and Representation: The Mother in Popular Culture and Melodrama*. London and New York: Routledge, 1992.
Kristeva, Julia. "Stabat Mater." *The Kristeva Reader*, ed. Toril Moi. Oxford: Basil Blackwell, 1986 [1977], pp. 160–186.
Llorente, Manuel. "Almudena Grandes dibuja las pasiones humanas a és de cuatro mujeres." *El Mundo*, October 8, 1998. <http://w3.elmundo.es/1998/10/08/cultura/08NO111.html>. Accessed September 9, 2002.

Mannheim, Karl. "The Problem of Generations." *The Sociology of Knowledge*, ed. Karl Mannheim. London: Routledge, 1952, pp. 276–320.
Miranda, María Jésus. *Crónica del desconcierto (actitudes básicas y demandas políticas de las españolas)*. Madrid: Instituto de la Mujer, 1982.
Nash, Mary. "Pronatalismo y maternidad en la España franquista." *Maternidad y políticas de género: La mujer en los estados de bienestar europeos, 1880–1950*, eds. Gisela Bock and Pat Thane. Valencia: Universidad de Valencia, Ediciones Cátedra, 2000, pp. 279–307.
Ortner, Sherry. "Is Female to Male as Nature Is to Culture?" In *Women, Culture and Society*, eds. Michelle Rosaldo and Louise Lamphere. Stanford, CA: Stanford University Press, 1990, pp. 67–88.
Pérez Oliva, Milagros. "La memoria emocionada: El País, February 4, 2007. <http://www.elpais.com/articulo/portada/memoria/emocionada/elpepusoceps/20070204elpepspor_1/Tes>.
Person, Ethel. *Love and Fateful Encounters: The Power of Romantic Passion*. London: Bloomsbury, 1990.
Rodríguez, Villouta, Mili. "Almudena dejó la Grande." June 3, 2007. <http://www.lanacion.cl/prontus_noticias/site/artic/20070602/pags/20070602230232.htm>.
Shaw, Sandra, 1991. "The Conflicting Experiences of Lone Parenthood." In *Lone Parenthood: Coping with Constraints and Making Opportunities*. Graham Crow and Michael Hardy, eds., Hertfordshire: Harvester Wheatsheaf, 1991, pp. 143–156.
Tezanos, José F.. "Notas para una interpretación sociológica del franquismo." *Sistema* 23 10: 2 (1982) 47–101.
Walters, Suzanna-Danuta. *Lives Together/Worlds Apart: Mothers and Daughters in Popular Culture*. Berkeley and Los Angeles: University of California Press, 1992.
Wolf, Naomi. *The Beauty Myth*. London: Vintage, 1991.

# 4

# New Conceptions of Family in Contemporary Galician Narrative

*Visions of Maternity in the Works of María Xosé Queizán and Teresa Moure*[1]

Marisol Rodríguez Rodríguez

Generally speaking, women are a scant presence in the historical canon of Galician literature, a lack that is even more evident in the field of narrative, particularly when compared with developments in poetry and literature for children.[2] However, in the years since 1975, with the Transition to democracy and the designation of Galicia as a *Comunidad Histórica* (Historic Community), together with the gradual assimilation of theories of gender and feminist literary criticism emerging from the Anglo-Saxon world, Galician literature of feminine authorship has experienced progressive growth; this is particularly noticeable in the greater number of women writing narrative.

With the definitive development of the Galician feminist movement,[3] which began to take off in 1976, the mission of women writers has been to conform to the idea of "a room of one's own," that is to say, consciously to empower women with the language to create a transgressive literature that recuperates both the feminine voice and gender diversity, in addition to effecting a re-examination of women's inheritance. In the last twenty years a subdued and gradual development has given way to one that shows more encouraging signs of growth, especially since 2004 when there was an efflorescence of the narrative genre. It is for this reason that literary production is now witnessing a panorama of Galician women narrators who write with the militant and normalizing goal of using Galician language in the narrative genre.

This context frames the narrative works of two Galician writers pertinent to the theme that will be developed in this essay, that of new conceptions of the family, a theme directly linked to the concept of maternity. The chosen authors are from two different generations.[4] The first is María Xosé Queizán (Vigo, 1939– ), who belongs to a generation considered to be fundamental to the revindication of feminist gender consciousness. The second is Teresa Moure (Monforte de Lemos, 1969– ), who belongs to a generation of writers born at the end of the '60s and the beginning of the '70s.

Female-authored narrative in Galicia today has been marked by the committed feminist project of these two writers, who achieve their own place in Galician literature via their corpus of work, in spite of the disparity of opinion as regards their production. Queizán's criticism of the androcentric Galician nationalist model that, in her opinion, has completely ignored feminine history and its precocity in the treatment of polemical themes has resulted in the silencing of her work. For her part, Moure's work is characterized by a favorable reception, as much on the part of the public as the critics and other writers, which has elevated her to be the most representative of Galician women narrative writers of today.

The great difference that separates these writers can also be appreciated in the feminist postures they demonstrate. Queizán defines herself as a follower of a nationalist feminism, the roots of which derive from the feminism that arose in the Enlightenment; she is further strongly influenced by the Marxist feminism evident in her first essays. In a similar manner to Simone de Beauvoir, for whom she feels a profound admiration, Queizán opposes a feminism of difference (personal interview, np).[5] For her part, Moure, as she herself declares in her essay *A palabra das fillas de Eva* [The Word of the Daughters of Eve] subscribes to current, essentialist ecofeminism, taking as her reference the Indian ecofeminist, Vandana Shiva, for whom modern science, as part of the patriarchal domain, devalues the knowledge emanating from other sources, therefore debasing nature and women (*A palabra* 31–32). Moure's philosophy also has affinities with what Mary Mellor has defined as "spiritual ecofeminism," which combines the celebration of the values centered in woman, such as maternity and nourishment, with the celebration of the female body (*Feminismo* 77).

In spite of this divergence of opinion — one that revindicates the "nature" of woman (Moure), the other that openly rejects such a characteristic (Queizán) — it is possible to appreciate numerous similarities in their treatment of the theme of maternity, which brings with it a transformation of the concept of family. This is because among Queizán's numerous preoccupations about women is an emphasis on the themes of social and biological maternity and, therefore, on the diverse models of family, themes that she explores as much in her essays as in her narrative. *Ten o seu punto a fresca rosa* [The Fresh Rose

# 4

# New Conceptions of Family in Contemporary Galician Narrative

*Visions of Maternity in the Works of María Xosé Queizán and Teresa Moure*[1]

MARISOL RODRÍGUEZ RODRÍGUEZ

Generally speaking, women are a scant presence in the historical canon of Galician literature, a lack that is even more evident in the field of narrative, particularly when compared with developments in poetry and literature for children.[2] However, in the years since 1975, with the Transition to democracy and the designation of Galicia as a *Comunidad Histórica* (Historic Community), together with the gradual assimilation of theories of gender and feminist literary criticism emerging from the Anglo-Saxon world, Galician literature of feminine authorship has experienced progressive growth; this is particularly noticeable in the greater number of women writing narrative.

With the definitive development of the Galician feminist movement,[3] which began to take off in 1976, the mission of women writers has been to conform to the idea of "a room of one's own," that is to say, consciously to empower women with the language to create a transgressive literature that recuperates both the feminine voice and gender diversity, in addition to effecting a re-examination of women's inheritance. In the last twenty years a subdued and gradual development has given way to one that shows more encouraging signs of growth, especially since 2004 when there was an efflorescence of the narrative genre. It is for this reason that literary production is now witnessing a panorama of Galician women narrators who write with the militant and normalizing goal of using Galician language in the narrative genre.

This context frames the narrative works of two Galician writers pertinent to the theme that will be developed in this essay, that of new conceptions of the family, a theme directly linked to the concept of maternity. The chosen authors are from two different generations.[4] The first is María Xosé Queizán (Vigo, 1939– ), who belongs to a generation considered to be fundamental to the revindication of feminist gender consciousness. The second is Teresa Moure (Monforte de Lemos, 1969– ), who belongs to a generation of writers born at the end of the '60s and the beginning of the '70s.

Female-authored narrative in Galicia today has been marked by the committed feminist project of these two writers, who achieve their own place in Galician literature via their corpus of work, in spite of the disparity of opinion as regards their production. Queizán's criticism of the androcentric Galician nationalist model that, in her opinion, has completely ignored feminine history and its precocity in the treatment of polemical themes has resulted in the silencing of her work. For her part, Moure's work is characterized by a favorable reception, as much on the part of the public as the critics and other writers, which has elevated her to be the most representative of Galician women narrative writers of today.

The great difference that separates these writers can also be appreciated in the feminist postures they demonstrate. Queizán defines herself as a follower of a nationalist feminism, the roots of which derive from the feminism that arose in the Enlightenment; she is further strongly influenced by the Marxist feminism evident in her first essays. In a similar manner to Simone de Beauvoir, for whom she feels a profound admiration, Queizán opposes a feminism of difference (personal interview, np).[5] For her part, Moure, as she herself declares in her essay *A palabra das fillas de Eva* [The Word of the Daughters of Eve] subscribes to current, essentialist ecofeminism, taking as her reference the Indian ecofeminist, Vandana Shiva, for whom modern science, as part of the patriarchal domain, devalues the knowledge emanating from other sources, therefore debasing nature and women (*A palabra* 31–32). Moure's philosophy also has affinities with what Mary Mellor has defined as "spiritual ecofeminism," which combines the celebration of the values centered in woman, such as maternity and nourishment, with the celebration of the female body (*Feminismo* 77).

In spite of this divergence of opinion — one that revindicates the "nature" of woman (Moure), the other that openly rejects such a characteristic (Queizán) — it is possible to appreciate numerous similarities in their treatment of the theme of maternity, which brings with it a transformation of the concept of family. This is because among Queizán's numerous preoccupations about women is an emphasis on the themes of social and biological maternity and, therefore, on the diverse models of family, themes that she explores as much in her essays as in her narrative. *Ten o seu punto a fresca rosa* [The Fresh Rose

Has Its Spot], a novel published in 2000, presents, in my opinion, the full breadth of her revindications of this theme.

The topic of maternity has been central in feminist theory from Beauvoir to Kristeva, via Rich and Queizán herself. In *Le Deuxième Sexe* [The Second Sex] (1949), Beauvoir had already emphasized that the oppression of women, rooted in biological difference, came out of maternity, suggesting a consequent search for liberty through its rejection. In the seventies Rich's work *Of Woman Born: Motherhood as Experience and Institution* (1976), proposed an alternative focus, maintaining that one should not reject maternity but rather should revindicate it. Rich alludes to the singular nature of such a gift and tries to demonstrate how maternity has been the product of manipulation by the patriarchy, converting it into an oppressive institution. In this manner, Rich bases her contribution to the theme of maternity by breaking down the term into two parts, "experience" and "institution": "I try to distinguish between two meanings of motherhood, one superimposed on the other: the *potential relationship* of any woman to her powers of reproduction and to children; and the *institution*, which aims at ensuring that that potential — and all women — shall remain under male control" (xv). The first word, "experience," refers to the personal experiences that the woman-mother can achieve, distancing and liberating herself from patriarchal society; with the second, "institution," she explores the way in which such a system has exercised its power over the woman-mother.

Consequently, Rich criticizes the role of victim proposed by Shulamith Firestone, in *Dialectic of Sex: The Case for Feminist Revolution*, a text Firestone dedicates to Beauvoir, in which she analyses the concepts of pregnancy, childbirth and education of a child from a patriarchal perspective. For Firestone, the responsibility of childbearing is the cause of woman's oppression, in addition to being a painful process that puts her life at risk: "*Pregnancy is barbaric*" and "Childbirth *hurts*" (188–89). Therefore, Firestone proposes artificial reproduction as a solution to the tyranny of nature; that is to say a total rupture between woman and maternity favoring above all the possibility of extra uterine gestation: "Artificial reproduction is not inherently dehumanizing" (189). According to Firestone, women's liberation comes about through the destruction of the structures of power established by nature and reinforced by men. Women should control the means of reproduction by means of genetic technology (191). In contrast, Rich's posture is that of choice: women should have the right to choose between such a possibility and natural childbirth, in the same way that they choose to become mothers in the first instance. Nevertheless, Rich does not discard artificial reproduction in the future as a solution for women. In a manner analogous to that of Firestone, Rich considers maternity as representing woman's loss of liberty, for which she proposes the term "matrophobia": that is to say the attitude on the part of the woman to eliminating the bonds of motherhood, in order to be able to liberate herself, given that the mother represents the woman who is not free, the martyr: "Matrophobia can be seen as a womanly splitting of the self, in the desire to become purged once and for all of our mothers' bondage, to become individuated and free ... we perform radical surgery" (Rich 238).

Therefore, international feminist criticism has had the objective, from the end of the seventies to the present day, to return primacy to the mother in her individual development as woman, as well as the positive reestablishment of the relationship between mother and daughter. Contemporary discourse on maternity seen through a psycho-analytic lens falls into two schools of thought: those of the United States and those of France. In the first, the focus centers on the mother-child relationship and the effects of maternity on relationships based on gender. Particularly notable are the figures of Nancy Chodorow and Susan Contratto, who, in "The Fantasy of the Perfect Mother" offer a distinct point of view when approaching representations of the mother. The repressive vision of maternity gives way to a new posture, through which priority is given to witnessing and representing motherhood in a positive way, questioning the two prevalent poles of patriarchal cultural ideology: those of guilt and idealization (Chodorow and Contratto 55–59).

In contrast, the French school departs from the connection between maternity and sexuality which, as Hirsch has indicated, had been a taboo theme in feminist criticism (166). French feminists, among whom Kristeva and Irigaray stand out, depart from surmounting the problematics associated with maternity and sexuality to construct a new and liberating discourse of the body. Showing the influence of *Le Deuxième Sexe* [The Second Sex] (1949) of Beauvoir, they present maternity as something alien to women. For Beauvoir, pregnancy becomes alarming when described in the following manner: "[It is] rather horrible that a parasitic body should proliferate within her body; the very idea of this monstrous swelling frightens her" (326). However, Kristeva and Irigaray do not propose maternity as the horrifying act presented in *Le Deuxième Sexe*.[6] In Kristeva's theoretical discourse, the maternal ambit occupies a crucial position. In her essay "Motherhood according to Giovanni Bellini," included in *Desire in Language*, Kristeva begins thus: "Within the body, growing as a graft, indomitable, there is an other. And no one is present, within that simultaneously dual and alien space, to signify what is going on. 'It happens, but I am not there'" (237). As Elizabeth Grosz points out, Kristeva also underscores that maternity obliterates feminine subjectivity, given that the woman-mother can find no autonomy through maternity. The mother becomes the partial object of the being, since only through her can the neonatal necessities be satisfied (Grosz, *Sexual* 79–80).

For her part, Irigaray expounds the necessity of woman being represented beyond her maternal role. Consequently, her project promotes an autonomous position that permits the reestablishment of women's genealogical base. In contrast to de Beauvoir and Firestone, Irigaray advocates the assumption of the maternal function as a means to favor women's development. Thus, the concept of maternity should be reformulated and the relationship of the woman and the mother should not be that of separation and rivalry. Irigaray emphasizes the fact that a woman lacks her own symbolic order, which obstructs access to an independent representation of her maternal function (*Why different?* 18–19).

Queizán's contribution to the theme is developed principally in "Parir o pensamento," [Giving Birth to Thought], the second part of *Escrita da certeza: Por un feminismo optimista* [Written from Certainty: For an Optimistic Feminism]. This second part consists of three articles: "*Maternidade biológica*" [Biological Maternity], "*Maternidade social*" [Social Maternity] and "Parir o pensamento." In my opinion Queizán follows the general line of the theories expressed earlier, especially those of the French school and of Firestone. For the author, what is essential is to rise above a "uterine feminism," referring to matters related to the reproductive organs, contraception and abortion. This so-called uterine feminism, Queizán emphasizes, refers to "ao pechado, o íntimo, o privado: a casa, cova, caverna na que estamos 'condenadas' polo noso nacemento" [the enclosed, the intimate, the private: the house, cave, cavern to which we are condemned by our childbirth] and the satisfaction of the maternal role as both exclusive to women and lacking any social recognition. In its place is privileged "clitoral feminism," the power of the woman over herself and her surroundings. Such a concept designates the acquisition of a state of being which is complete and unconditioned by maternity, since that symbolizes "o externo, o público ... unha visión de luz fora da matriz, fora de madre ... Para deixar de ser 'naturaleza' dominada..." [the external, the public ... a vision of light beyond the womb, beyond the mother ... so as to cease to be 'nature' dominated] ("Festa da Palabra Silenciada" 54–55).[7]

Like Beauvoir, Irigaray and Kristeva, Queizán affirms that female sexuality has always been associated with procreation and masochism. The woman-mother has to suffer, sacrificing herself for everyone else, in order to demonstrate her value as mother, while her own sexuality and pleasure have always occupied a secondary place. Under such a system, the woman, passive object in the process of procreation, possesses the biological maternity, while the man, active subject, enjoys social paternity. In Queizán's opinion, therefore, maternity is a patriarchal imposition, indicating that in society a matrophagia is produced by means of which the genealogy is masculine. Hence, the mother is converted into the passive carrier of patriarchal values (*Escrita* 57–59).

For Queizán, the mother is both biological and psychological mother, given that in representing maternity as something "natural," the woman is a mother by "instinct." Queizán therefore criticizes the myth of "maternal love," supposed to be innate in woman, as converting maternity into an objective which, when not achieved, produces frustration in the woman (*Escrita* 60). Such a myth was already being questioned by Beauvoir in 1949, when she placed in doubt the presumed naturalness of maternal behaviors, proposing their inclusion in the cultural ambit. In this manner Beauvoir attempts to separate women's biological aspect from the social (Juliano 46). Similarly, Queizán critiques the presentation of mothers as culpable for the traumas, complexes and problems that might arise in their offspring (*Escrita* 61). Nevertheless, Queizán, like Firestone, considers that, since women are objects for motherhood in the patriarchal system, they should assume control of their own body and make the decisions about the "product." In this way, the separation of sexuality from procreation acquires relevance in the women's liberation movement: they discover sexual pleasure and assume control of procreation through contraception and abortion, becoming mistresses of their own uteruses and sexual organs. (*Escrita* 73–75).[8]

Scientific advances that enable infertile women to become mothers are equally a form of control over the uterus, given that they avail themselves of the topic of "unhappiness" of those women who are unable to be mothers. Firestone had already warned: "[O]ften there is a more serious error: results of the *misuse* of technology are very often attributed to the use of technology *per se* ... fertility control, artificial reproduction, cybernation, in themselves, are liberating—*unless* they are improperly used" (186–87). In an analogous manner, Queizán informs us that the unwarranted use of such techniques could be prejudicial, even though the intention of the idea may be positive. Man-doctor assumes a role of demiurge, trying to ensure that the "unsatisfied" woman can become a mother. By means of the new techniques of reproduction, the woman can be separated from her "natural" condition as regards maternity (*Evidencias* 84).

Queizán is not as radical as Firestone, even though she mentions aspects that recall that author's theories: "[C]on seguridade, dentro de pouco ese proceso [la fusión de un óvulo y un espermatozoide] poderá continuar nunha incubadora, en placentas artificiais, fóra do útero, fóra do corpo das mulleres" [Certainly, within a short time that process [the fusion of an ovum and a spermatozoa] might continue in an incubator, in artificial placentas, outside the uterus, outside the bodies of women] (*Escrita* 91). Furthermore, she is a follower of Rich's opinion, considering the use of such techniques as an option: "Non se trata, desde o meu punto de vista, de estar en contra das técnicas que poden axudar a moitas mulleres" [From my point of view this is not about being against techniques that can help many women] (*Escrita* 73).

New reproductive technologies assist the woman to separate herself from nature. According to Queizán, the woman should have the right to aspire to a social maternity, which is the valorization that should take precedence, passing from a biological and natural maternity to one that is legal and autonomous. Queizán argues that consideration of the social mother does take place in the case of women with a certain economic independence, it being linked to female autonomy. Moreover, she adds that there exist diverse types of mother who do not correspond to patriarchal principles: mothers who are genetic, legal, (uterine) bearers and substitute mothers — ovular and uterine — making possible a denomination of "symbolic mother" (*Escrita* 84).

The critical and investigative vision of maternity that is finally offered is evident in Queizán's narrative and is particularly evident in her novel *Ten o seu punto a fresca rosa*. Through the title of the work itself, which is taken from an extract of a poem by Eduardo Pondal in his work *Queixumes dos pinos* (1886) [Lamentations of the Pines],[9] Queizán anticipates one of the central themes of the novel, pedophilia, since it begins with the story of a father who feels sexually attracted to his adopted daughter.[10]

Queizán's novel, situated in the Galician city of Vigo in the seventies and eighties, *Ten o seu punto a fresca rosa* has as its background the formation of the feminist and revolutionary movements of the 1970s. Within this context, Queizán interweaves the stories of three women and their families who are linked by love and death. The majority of the narration is realized through the eyes and thoughts of Charo Santoro, Petra Seixo y Lucía Castro, protagonists of different social class, education and sexual preference, which permits Queizán to explore diverse types of family and maternity through the relationship they share with María Torras, an adolescent of twelve years. Conceived by *in vitro* fertilization, María, natural daughter of Charo Santoro, is given in adoption to Lucía and her husband, Antonio, when she is one year old.

In this way, the various types of maternity that are represented in the novel, the biological motherhood of Charo and the legal motherhood of Lucía, enable Queizán to analyze in a fictitious manner the behaviors expressed in her essay *Escrita da certeza*. The prototype of the self-affirming woman, who does not need motherhood to feel fulfilled, is incarnated in the character of Charo, a surgeon in a Vigo hospital. Very involved in her position as "unha profesional seria e moi considerada" [a serious and well-respected professional] (*Ten* 61), it does not worry her that she is single and without issue. Nevertheless, she unexpectedly begins a relationship with Petra, a nurse, which is strengthened after a year when Petra begins to float the possibility of having a "normal family" by means of a child. To please Petra, Charo decides to become a mother and agrees to submit herself to *in vitro* artificial insemination.

In contraposition to Charo, the author filters her criticism of social opinion that a childless woman is a frustrated and incomplete woman, via Lucía, who is sterile and a member of Vigo high society. Lucía, the second wife of Antonio, fleshes out the role of the perfect and subservient wife who, enmeshed in her dream world of luxury, is incapable of seeing the sexual abuse to which María has been submitted to since babyhood by Antonio. Coming from a wealthy family, Lucía's own childhood has been characterized by the absence of her mother, who loves to travel. Such absence causes Lucía to want a "normal" family, and she decides that because she is unable to have children she will adopt a baby in order to fulfill the roles of housewife and Antonio's devoted spouse. A religious woman, prototype of all that a woman should be in the so-called normal family, Lucía feels increasingly distanced from Antonio, maintaining her relationship with him out of habit.

Hence, through Lucía, Queizán also shows the sexual repression of women, given that Antonio likes submissive women like Lucía. As he detests women who control their own sexuality and demonstrate their own independence, he becomes obsessed with young girls. According to him feminists like his ex-wife Reme, are crazy women who have "reunións pornográficas" [pornographic gatherings] (*Ten* 93), a term under which he sums up Reme's readings on women's search for pleasure in their sexual relations. Antonio's relationship with his second wife is only possible because of his constant foreign travels, made necessary through his work in the factory inherited from his father. He has traveled to third world countries in Asia and the Americas, where he was able to give free rein to the pedophiliac inclinations he needed to satisfy before María's arrival.

Queizán shows her unfavorable opinion of the erroneous use of the science of reproduction for patriarchal ends through the character of Doctor Luna. Luna is presented as the typical seducer/doctor who falls for Charo at first sight, inviting her to dinner after the interview that takes place to evaluate Charo's suitability for insemination. Charo agrees, realizing that the dinner will influence the doctor's final decision. A pioneer of methods of artificial insemination, Luna has been involved in innumerable births. For this reason he considers himself to be a scientific father, since "[a] súa intervención no útero das mulleres levouno a considerarse un xerador de vida" [his intervention in the uterus of the woman leads him to consider himself a creator of life] (149). For him the women are mere objects "[s]eres reducidas a úteros, vaxinas, circuítos húmidos por onde desfilan os espermatozoides" [beings reduced to wombs, vaginas, moist circuits in which the sperm circulate] (149). Offended by Charo's rejection of his sexual advances he decides to inseminate Charo with his own semen, exchanged for that of the anonymous donor. As a result, María is born and from this moment Luna decides to use his own semen in all inseminations, since "[s]entira unha potestade descoñecida, un vigor viril cando colleu aquela nena no colo" [he had experienced a hitherto unrealized feeling of power, a virile vigor when he held that baby girl in his lap] (151). Feeling that he has the right to usurp God's place, Luna enjoys his position of power as the paternal demiurge. Moreover he becomes a defender of the anti-abortion campaign, not for moral or religious considerations, but because he is repelled by the waste of both ova and spermatozoa. For him, the natural state of woman is pregnancy, given that the mission a woman must fulfill in this world is to preserve the species (153).

As can be deduced, in *Ten* the concept of the family as linked intrinsically to maternity is questioned. There are various versions of what each protagonist considers to be a normal family. In the relationship between Antonio and Lucía, although he has no desire for another child (he has a daughter from his previous marriage), Antonio accepts the adoption in order to please Lucía, who is sterile: "Accedeu por compracer á muller que se sentía frustrada por non parir" [he acceded to please his wife who felt frustration at her inability to give birth] (22). In the relationship between Charo and Petra, María is "un capricho de Petra que quixo ser unha pioneira no das parellas de feito que agora estaban tan de moda" [a whim of Petra's, who wanted to be a pioneer in those de facto couples that were now so fashionable] (66). Finally, in Luna's imaginary relationship with Charo, María, the biological daughter of both, is the piece that was lacking to make their union complete. Luna refuses to see the social changes that artificial childbirth can achieve, allowing single women to be mothers, or that lesbian or gay couples can become parents. Eleven years later, he decides to contact Charo again and arranges to meet her in Galicia. When Luna proposes marriage in order to form a "normal family," given that he is Maria's biological father, Charo, appalled, confesses that she is a lesbian and that she would never marry him. From that moment, Luna loses his sanity and, resuming his role as God, murders María in the Monte de Castro, a park in the city of Vigo. Hence, in all three cases, María represents the object that accords with the image of the perfect family, although in each case she constitutes a different type of "object."

It is evident that through her text, Queizán demythifies traditional concepts of maternity, as much biological as social, and criticizes the man who considers himself to be the demiurge, represented in Doctor Luna. She does not present maternity as a barrier for women, but rather as a right of choice and, in this case, of realization of that choice. The fact that one of the protagonists, Charo, decides to have a child by artificial insemination demonstrates not only her independence, but also her control over her own body. Nevertheless, Queizán also outlines the dangers that accompany these technological procedures.

Just as in Queizán's work, in which the emphasis falls on those families who turn to adoption or *in vitro* conception, Moure presents maternity as the exclusive decision of the woman, resulting in a one-parent family in the two works that are the objects of this analysis, *A xeira das árbores* [*The Day of the Women-Tree*] (2004) y *Herba moura [Love Herb]* (2005). *A xeira* is structured around the distinctive avatars of quotidian existence in one, single day in the life of Clara, a single woman with three children. In addition to being a mother, Clara is an independent worker and housewife. Through her, Moure deconstructs all the clichés that surround the mother and the working woman, presenting diverse points of view. Hence, in the text, in addition to the perspective of the principal narrator, Clara, she intertwines other distinct views divided between her boss, an anonymous man, her friend Lola and one of her children. In general, they are masculine points of view, which bring forth relative theories of language as a patriarchal construct that does not permit female expression.

Availing herself of the symbol of the tree, Clara declares herself a woman who is now living the life she has always wanted and for which it was necessary to break with her past: "[E]la era árbore e precisaba ter raíces propias para florecer e dar froito. Por iso rompera co pasado, porque era árbore..." [[S]he was a tree and she needed her own roots in order to flourish and bear fruit. That is why she had broken with her past, because she was a tree] (*A xeira* 110). Through this metaphoric tree, Clara emphasizes her liberty because "separárase da árbore que a xestara para ter as súas propias raíces e crecer contra o chan, desafiando á lei da gravidade" [she had separated herself from the tree that had given birth to her in order to have her own roots and to grow away from the ground, defying the law of gravity] (111). In contrast to her mother, Clara tries to be happy with the exhausting life she has created for herself, clinging strongly to it like the roots of a tree in the earth: "[A]s árbores teñen raíces que as atan á terra e a misión de crecer para arriba, seguindo á luz, desafiando os principios da caída libre dos corpos, nunha xeira sufocante que se prolonga de sol a sol" [trees have roots that they attach to the earth and a mission to grow, following the light, defying the principles of the free fall of bodies in a suffocating journey that extends from sunrise to sunset] (127). The symbolic roots are Clara's three children, from three different fathers and all wanted: "[C]ando menos, desexados pola súa nai" [at least wanted by their mother] (61). Consequently, in *A xeira* there is a clear vision of maternity as a revindication of feminine matters and as a fruit of their own decision-making. Devoted to her children and independent, Clara does not need a husband to get ahead; in fact, in her third pregnancy, Clara simply needed "un home que estivera de paso" [a man who would be there in passing], requiring only that "o ser xestado a amase" [the conceived being should love her] (75).

In contradicting an established order that makes women invisible, she converts herself into a target of criticism. In this respect it is sufficient to highlight the masculine point of view through her boss, who considers her status as single mother of a numerous family "erro descomunal" [a gigantic error] (35), and a block on Clara's promising professional life: "[E]la deu en entregarse á maternidade cunha intensidade que nin Deus, ou mellor, que nin a Virxe María" [she gave herself over to maternity with an intensity greater than either God, or better, the Virgin Mary] (34). Moreover, masculine clichés make their appearance on the subject of the sexuality of the single woman; her boss considers Clara to be a woman who does not have to answer to anybody, being "tan dispoñible, sen marido a quen renderlle contas, debe pasalo de medo" [so available, without a husband to answer to, that she must be really enjoying herself] (35), words that imply the lack of morality of a woman who freely enjoys her sexuality.

As regards *Herba moura*, Moure presents the extraordinary story of three women through whom she defends the passions against the rationalism movement represented by the seventeenth-century philosopher René Descartes. Two of the characters are also from the seventeenth century: Queen Christina of Sweden and the botanist, healer, matron and witch, Hélène Jans. These two characters are historical figures, women who left a real trace in the life of the French philosopher. The third woman is from the twenty-first century: the doctoral candidate Einés Andrade, who is researching Hélène's life. The novel counterposes the human being who is filled with passion and feeling, against the precepts of the rationalist philosophy of which Descartes is the visible head. Cristina, Hélène and Einés all share the gift of wisdom, which gives Moure the opportunity to propose diverse forms of alternative knowledge, thereby showing the necessity for woman to construct her own universe, neither more nor less valid than the masculine (Mesas Gomez 2). In the same manner Moure situates the reader in two opposed positions with regard to knowledge: on the one side is the canonical, rational and masculine; on the other is the alternative, which is anonymous, informal, empirical, intuitive and feminine (Vilavedra, "Herba" 332).

In *Herba*, maternity is seen as a decision appropriate to woman, who shows her independence in all senses. It is for this reason that two of the characters take no account of male opinions as to the conception of a child, or simply relegate the role of the man to one of anonymity, consciously planned motherhood being a matter for the mother. The lower social class character, Hélène, who shows a degree of knowledge unusual for a woman of her time and belongs to a collective of women punished in that period, the healers, or "witches," maintains a relationship with Descartes. Hélène decides that she wants to be a mother without discussing it with Descartes. As fruit of this relationship, Francine is born and, just five years later, dies of scarlet fever.

For her part, Einés is the last descendant of a family of women: "[U]nha caste de mulleres impetuosas, mulleres de armas tomar, que son aquelas contra as que non se deben tomar nunca as armas" [a caste of impetuous women, women who take up arms, who are the ones against whom nobody should ever take up arms] (378). Einés was born in 1969, the year on which man stepped on the moon, and received as a gift of her aunts at her baptism the surname Andrade. The name is the only thing of men that her aunts desire for Einés, since "ningún home a vai recofiecer como propia" [not one man will recognize her as his] (339). The reason for such a choice comes from the stereotypes of those who are objects, women: "[O]s homes din que nós somos volubles, alborotadoras, suspicaces, pusilánimes e medosas... Que a nena sexa firme, tranquila, sincera, forte e atrevida coma un home, ... que as virtudes das mulleres xa llas aprenderemos nós, que para iso as temos todas" [men say that we are voluble, disruptive, suspicious, pusillanimous and frightened ... so that the girl shall be firm, tranquil, sincere, strong and daring as a man, we shall teach her the strengths of women since for this purpose we all have them] (350). Furthermore, the circumstances that surround Einés's conception are very imprecise, not only for the reader but also for Einés's own family, who do not believe that Livia, her mother, has had a carnal experience. In fact, they attribute the conception to a magical event, since Livia, supposedly pregnant to an unknown man, shows no changes in her anatomy during the gestation, thus reinforcing the idea that a man is not necessary in order to conceive, a subversion of the patriarchal myth of the Immaculate Conception. In fact, Moure tends to represent maternity from a magical point of view, as a unique experience of female nature. In the same manner, in *Herba*, Hélène, described as a woman "beleza rotunda, maternal e morna" [of warm, rotund, maternal beauty] (236), makes use of magical acts on the day her baby is conceived, including predicting the sex of the child:

> [F]ixérame tres cruces sobre o ventre: unha para apartar a morte, outra para escorrentar os malos agoiros, e unha terceira para satisfacer un desexo oculto. Empaguceime de Herba de namorar, *Armaria pubigera*.... Tomada dun só grolo, sen aire, na lúa crecente, non hai quen a resista... a terceira cruz que fixera sobre o ventre ... era para conseguir preñar dunha nena e non dun neno, que posto que iamos estar soas na vida, mellor nos iría de sermos iguais...
>
> [I made three crosses on my belly: one to keep death away, another to send the bad auguries flying and a third to satisfy a hidden desire. I anointed myself with the love herb *Armaria pubigera*.... Taken in a single draught, without breathing, under a crescent moon, nobody can resist it ... the third cross that I made on my belly ... was to ensure that I was pregnant with a daughter and not a son, given that, as we would be alone in life, it would be better if we were equal] [193, 196].

Maternity as a magic act, exclusive to woman, reinforces the relationship between woman and nature, which is the basis of Moure's thought.

Finally, Moure, like Queizán criticizes the patriarchal concept of maternity as essential to the realization of womanhood. In this respect, the character of Queen Christina becomes key in *Herba*, given that it is through her that Moure channels her criticism of this aspect of maternity. Christina is defined as "unha muller definitivamente non moi agraciada, con aire de peixe e un pouco marimacho, insegura, irascible, unha muller que sempre se sentiu fóra de sitio, coma árbore chantada en xardín alleo, nun lugar onde non lle correspondía" [a woman definitively lacking in graces, with the air of a fish out of water and somewhat mannish, insecure, irascible, a woman who always felt out of place, like a tree planted in a foreign garden, in a place where it did not belong] (238). Christina is a clever woman, promiscuous and bisexual, whose privileged situation as Queen of Sweden is no impediment to her achieving all that she really desires. Through Christina, Moure affirms that identity between woman and mother is a fallacy, given that they do not constitute interchangeable categories. She considers that maternity is not a project through which women can achieve a "complete" existence, describing such belief in *A palabra* as one of the "máis fortes mitos da nosa cultura, mito recente e burgués onde os haxa" [strongest myths of our culture, a myth recent and bourgeois wherever it is found] (29–30). It is relevant that Christina's abdication is motivated by her refusal to be a mother or to live under the traditional parameters of the Swedish court, which esteemed "o negocio dunha raíña ten que ser reinar, o que inclúe parir novos reis, e non divertirse, nin experimentar sensacións prohibidas, nin moito menos estudar ou escribir. É que o de escribir tamén ten pecado!" [the business of a queen as being to reign, which includes giving birth to new kings and not to entertain herself or experience prohibited feelings, even less to study or write, because writing can also contain sin!] (*Herba* 29).

In light of the detailed analysis of her narrative works it is possible to appreciate Moure's fervent belief in the linking of the mother with nature: a nexus which becomes transparent in the diverse aspects discussed, such as maternity and the woman "tree." Moure attributes this linking with a positive valorization that should be revindicated in order that the woman can "write her history," silenced by the patriarchy and, moreover, reclaim a language that does not render women invisible.

In conclusion, the vision of maternity expressed by Queizan in *Ten o seu punto a fresca rosa* (2000), reflects her affinity with the concept of the dichotomy social maternity/biological maternity, adumbrated by theorists like Beauvoir, Kristeva, Irigaray and Rich, who criticize the idea of a sexual life uniquely linked to maternity and procreation, with the consequent subordination of female sexuality. Through a constellation of feminine characters, Queizán effects a demythification of the traditional concepts of maternity, as much biological as social, in order to proclaim maternity as a right of choice and achievement and not as an obstacle. Queizán subverts all the clichés that surround maternity, such as belief in the existence of the "maternal instinct" or the supposed frustration experienced by a woman who cannot become a mother. Finally, Queizán demonstrates her opinion about the techniques of assisted reproduction, positioning herself unfavorably as respects the erroneous use of science for patriarchal ends.

From the theme of maternity, Queizán continues on to an analysis of the concept of the family. She presents diverse types of nuclear families who do not correspond to the traditional prototype: a family consisting of two lesbians, Charo and Petra; that formed by Lucía and Antonio, who seek to adopt a baby due to Lucía's sterility, and the imaginary relationship of Doctor Luna and Charo. In the three families, María, biological daughter of Charo, adopted as baby by Lucía and Antonio, is the fundamental basis for the consolidation of the families.

As regards Moure, in the analysis of *Herba moura*, she has defined the importance of the maternal genealogy and of maternity, and the imperious necessity to create a new language that defines the feminine reality in all its aspects. Like Queizán, Moure rejects the patriarchal equivalence between woman and mother, which she shows to be a fallacy. Nevertheless, she also presents maternity as a magical and sacred event, in *Herba,* or as a choice that should be attainable by a woman independently of the man, as in *A xeira das árbores*. Therefore, in spite of the divergent positions of both writers, both Queizán and Moure explore the distinct conceptions of maternity that reformulate the idea of family, showing numerous similarities of opinion. It is because the work of both writers creates a solid base and a militant project in constant evolution, that it serves as a model to follow for the younger narrators of today.

## Notes

1. This article was kindly translated by Dr. Gwyn Fox.
2. Until 1975 few authors cultivated the narrative genre. These writers are María Xosé Queizán, with *A orella no buraco* (1965) [An Ear in the Knothole], Xohana Torres with *Adiós María* (1971) [Goodbye María], Dora Vázquez with *Bertantiñá* [Woman from Bergantiños (A Coruña: Galicia, 1971) and Maruxa Fernández Fernández with *Lembranzas e pantasias* (1974) [Memories and Fantasies] (Blanco, *Libros* 35–36).
3. In the Galician feminist movement, as has occurred in the wider national context, two distinct stages are evident: a first phase, from the end of the nineteenth century to the outbreak of the Civil War, and a second, which has been evident since the end of the 1970s. During this second feminist phase three basic evolutionary stages have developed. The first was the moment

of incorporation, which essentially situates itself around the symbolic date of 1975, denominated the International Year of the Woman. A second, rapid growth period occurred between the end of the '70s and the beginning of the '80s. Finally, a third stage of transformation has extended into the '90s and their transition to the twenty-first century (Blanco, *O contradiscurso* 132).

4. Literary production by Galician women writers is not always ruled by the criterion "generational," as occurs in the collected history of Galician literature. Owing to the scarcity that characterizes such production in general, the division into "generations" usually pertains only to a confluence of women writers in a specific period, without proximity of style necessarily taking precedence. In this concrete case, I use the concept "generation" or generational to define the importance of historical context in the works published by the writers who are the object of this present study. María Xosé Queizán began to publish during the later Francoist period, while Teresa Moure began her literary contributions in the twenty-first century.

5. During the course of this project of investigation, I have carried out two interviews that remain unedited: one personal interview with Queizán, in February 2008 and the other, which Moure kindly sent to me in electronic form, also at the beginning of 2008.

6. The work of Luce Irigaray and Julia Kristeva follows different paths from de Beauvoir's theories. Influenced by the differentialist tendency of the second wave of French feminism, Irigaray and Kristeva centre themselves more than Beauvoir in questions of sexual differentiation and maternity (Tidd 120).

7. Queizán uses these new concepts, "uterine feminism" and "clitoral feminism," in a similar matter to certain aspects evident in writings from 1971 concerning the clitoral woman and the vaginal woman, by *Rivolta Femminile*, an Italian feminist group born in Rome in July 1970 (Blanco, *El contradiscurso* 255).

8. However, Firestone shows her reticence in her analysis of patriarchal control over the woman's body when considering that, although through the contraceptive pill a woman can control her fertility, science sees women as inferior beings, more suitable than the male to become "guinea pigs" (188).

9. Eduardo Pondal (1835–1917), author of *Queixumes dos pinos* (1886) and of the lyrics of the Galician national anthem, is one of the principal representatives of the *Rexurdimento* [*Resurgence*], a movement that developed at the end of the nineteenth century that signifies the rebirth of Galician as a literary language.

10. In her essay *Misoxinia e racismo na poesía de Eduardo Pondal* (1998) (*Misogyny and Racism in the Poetry of Eduardo Pondal*), Queizán has developed a detailed analysis of Pondal's works, paying particular attention to an incitement to pedophilia in certain poems, in which she notes an insistence on the part of the poetic voice that it is necessary to deflower girls when they are very young (*Misoxinia* 70–73).

## Works Cited

Beauvoir, Simone de. *The Second Sex*. Trans. H. M. Parshley. 1949. New York: Penguin, 1983.
Blanco, Carmen. *El contradiscurso de las mujeres*. Trans. Olga Novo. Vigo: Nigra Ensaio, 1997.
\_\_\_\_\_. *Libros de mulleres (para unha bibliografía de escritoras en lingua galega: 1863–1992)*. Vigo: Edicións do Cumio, 1994.
\_\_\_\_\_. *O contradiscurso das mulleres*. Vigo: Nigra, 1995.
Chodorow, Nancy, and Susan Contratto. "The Fantasy of the Perfect Mother."n In *Rethinking the Family: Some Feminist Questions*, eds. Barrie Thorne y Marilyn Yalom. New York: Longman, 1982, pp. 54–75.
Firestone, Shulamith. 1970. *The Dialectic of Sex: The Case for Feminist Revolution*. London: Women's, 1979.
Grosz, Elizabeth. *Sexual Subversions: Three French Feminists*. Sydney: Allen and Unwin, 1989.
Hirsch, Marianne. *The Mother/Daughter Plot: Narrative, Psychoanalysis, Feminism*. Bloomington: Indiana University Press, 1989.

Irigaray, Luce, and Sylvère Lotringer, eds. *Why Different: A Culture of Two Subjects*. Trans. Camille Collins. New York: Semiotext(e), 2000.
Juliano, Dolores. *Excluidas y marginales: una aproximación antropológica*. Madrid: Cátedra, 2004.
Kristeva, Julia. *Desire in Language: A Semiotic Approach to Literature and Art*, ed. and trans. Leon Roudiez. New York: Columbia University Press, 1980.
Mellor, Mary. *Feminismo y ecología*. 1997. México D.F.: Siglo XXI, 2000.
Mesas Gómez, Lidia. "Teresa Moure. Herba moura." *Ub.es*. Lletra de dona. Centre Dona i Literatura. Sin fecha. Accessed online, July 7, 2009, pp.1–3.
Moure, Teresa. *Herba moura*. Vigo: Xerais, 2005.
\_\_\_\_\_. *A palabra das fillas de Eva*. Vigo: Galaxia, 2004.
\_\_\_\_\_. *A xeira das árbores*. Santiago de Compostela: Sotelo Blanco, 2004.
Pondal, Eduardo. *Queixumes dos pinos*. 1886. A Coruña: eDixital, 2002.
Queizán, María Xosé. Entrevista personal. 22 febrero 2008. Unpublished.
\_\_\_\_\_. *Escrita da certeza. Por un feminismo optimista*. A Coruña: Espiral Maior, 1995.
\_\_\_\_\_. "*Festa da Palabra Silenciada*: Independencia, insumisión e solidariedade." *Andaina* 6 (1993): 54–55.
\_\_\_\_\_. *Misoxinia e racismo na poesía de Pondal*. Santiago de Compostela: Laiovento, 1998.
\_\_\_\_\_. *Ten o seu punto a fresca rosa*. Vigo: Xerais, 2000.
Rich, Adrienne. *Of Woman Born: Motherhood as Experience and Institution*. 1976. Toronto: Bantam, 1981.
Tidd, Ursula. *Simone de Beauvoir*. London: Routledge, 2004.
Vilavedra, Dolores. "Herba moura." *Lectora:. Revista de dones i textualitat* 11 (2005): 331–33.

# 5

# Feminism and Motherhood in the Police Novels of Alicia Giménez Bartlett

## RENEÉ CRAIG-ODDERS

Alicia Giménez Bartlett, the author of the best-selling Petra Delicado series in Spain, has suggested that the stereotype of women as inherently good has contributed to the scarcity of female protagonists in crime novels. Consequently, the most powerful female role in crime fiction traditionally has been reserved for the one "bad" *femme fatale* character whose function it is to challenge and to emasculate men and to lure them into criminal acts and danger. Traditionally, only this archetype or other stereotypical roles have been reserved for females: "the woman in the crime novel was usually the victim, the mobster's girlfriend to whom he gave a fur coat and who he told to shut-up, the *femme fatale* that always stayed in the background or the long suffering wife of the cop."[1] In addition to the desire to create a positive female protagonist in the Petra Delicado series who broke with that mold, Giménez Bartlett also wanted to disassociate her from the traditionally nonviolent realm of other female detectives. Specifically, she wanted to create "a female protagonist who was a detective and was in charge, something new and agreeable, with female killers who had ideas, none of those women who poisoned food" ("La novela"). Giménez Bartlett is also alluding here to the otherwise peaceful country domain of various matronly, amateur female detectives like Miss Marple. By contrast, Inspector Petra Delicado is a twice-divorced, childless, forty-something former lawyer who operates in the urban environment of Barcelona in which she encounters multiple female criminals as hardened and violent as their male counterparts. Currently, the Petra Delicado series is comprised of eight novels: *Ritos de muerte* [Death Rites] (1996), *Día de perros* [Dog Day] (1997), *Mensajeros de la oscuridad* [Messengers of Darkness], *Muer-*

*tos de papel* [Prime Time Suspect] (2000), *Serpientes en el paraíso* [Snakes in Paradise], *Un barco cargado de arroz* [A Ship Filled with Rice] (2004), *Nido vacío* [Empty Nest] (2006), and *El silencio de los claustros* [The Silence of the Cloisters] (2009). Within the context of the procedural genre, the female protagonist with a male subordinate is a rarity and, in Spain, the Petra Delicado series remains the only pairing of this type.[2]

In the years since its inception, the series has received quite a bit of critical attention and, as anticipated by the author, many critics have explored whether it advances a feminist or a conservative agenda.[3] Given the emergence of the series in the late 1990s and the contemporary context in which both the Petra Delicado character and her author live, it is not surprising that various critics have affirmed elements of the detective's characterization consistent with post feminist ideology. Both the character and her author came of age during the late 1960s and early 1970s, which has been termed the beginning of the Second Demographic Transition (SDT) in Northern and Western Europe by Dirk van de Kaa. During this time fertility decline and postponement were accompanied by a transformation in norms, values, and attitudes regarding family life and childbearing.[4] These demographic changes, particularly as they apply to women's roles and choices, are clearly evidenced throughout the Petra Delicado series.

In addition to the historical context of the Delicado series, however, one must also keep in mind that the police procedural is perhaps the most ideologically conservative subgenre of crime fiction inasmuch as its subject is the realistic depiction of law enforcement. The police system is an institutional pillar of male-dominated society. Petra is a police officer and before that she was a lawyer. Both of these chosen professions evidence that she is clearly a product of a patriarchal society and imply that she recognizes its legitimacy. At the same time, however, as a woman confronted with the constraints it imposes, she is often at odds with much of what she encounters both personally and professionally.

Petra's personal rejection of motherhood can be viewed, initially, as a response to the traditional societal expectations imposed on women. The sole intent to buck societal expectations, however, belies the intensity of her frequent, judgmental scorn of mothers and, indeed, other women in general throughout the series. As we will explore later, her evolving stance toward motherhood and her continuing derision of other women throughout the series parallel ideological and demographic shifts in society and conform to an ultimately conservative agenda.

Although her detective character would have to operate in the male-dominated police system, Giménez Bartlett has said that from the outset she was cautious about falling too easily into what she terms "feminist determin-

# 5

# Feminism and Motherhood in the Police Novels of Alicia Giménez Bartlett

## Reneé Craig-Odders

Alicia Giménez Bartlett, the author of the best-selling Petra Delicado series in Spain, has suggested that the stereotype of women as inherently good has contributed to the scarcity of female protagonists in crime novels. Consequently, the most powerful female role in crime fiction traditionally has been reserved for the one "bad" *femme fatale* character whose function it is to challenge and to emasculate men and to lure them into criminal acts and danger. Traditionally, only this archetype or other stereotypical roles have been reserved for females: "the woman in the crime novel was usually the victim, the mobster's girlfriend to whom he gave a fur coat and who he told to shut-up, the *femme fatale* that always stayed in the background or the long suffering wife of the cop."[1] In addition to the desire to create a positive female protagonist in the Petra Delicado series who broke with that mold, Giménez Bartlett also wanted to disassociate her from the traditionally nonviolent realm of other female detectives. Specifically, she wanted to create "a female protagonist who was a detective and was in charge, something new and agreeable, with female killers who had ideas, none of those women who poisoned food" ("La novela"). Giménez Bartlett is also alluding here to the otherwise peaceful country domain of various matronly, amateur female detectives like Miss Marple. By contrast, Inspector Petra Delicado is a twice-divorced, childless, forty-something former lawyer who operates in the urban environment of Barcelona in which she encounters multiple female criminals as hardened and violent as their male counterparts. Currently, the Petra Delicado series is comprised of eight novels: *Ritos de muerte* [Death Rites] (1996), *Día de perros* [Dog Day] (1997), *Mensajeros de la oscuridad* [Messengers of Darkness], *Muer-*

*tos de papel* [Prime Time Suspect] (2000), *Serpientes en el paraíso* [Snakes in Paradise], *Un barco cargado de arroz* [A Ship Filled with Rice] (2004), *Nido vacío* [Empty Nest] (2006), and *El silencio de los claustros* [The Silence of the Cloisters] (2009). Within the context of the procedural genre, the female protagonist with a male subordinate is a rarity and, in Spain, the Petra Delicado series remains the only pairing of this type.[2]

In the years since its inception, the series has received quite a bit of critical attention and, as anticipated by the author, many critics have explored whether it advances a feminist or a conservative agenda.[3] Given the emergence of the series in the late 1990s and the contemporary context in which both the Petra Delicado character and her author live, it is not surprising that various critics have affirmed elements of the detective's characterization consistent with post feminist ideology. Both the character and her author came of age during the late 1960s and early 1970s, which has been termed the beginning of the Second Demographic Transition (SDT) in Northern and Western Europe by Dirk van de Kaa. During this time fertility decline and postponement were accompanied by a transformation in norms, values, and attitudes regarding family life and childbearing.[4] These demographic changes, particularly as they apply to women's roles and choices, are clearly evidenced throughout the Petra Delicado series.

In addition to the historical context of the Delicado series, however, one must also keep in mind that the police procedural is perhaps the most ideologically conservative subgenre of crime fiction inasmuch as its subject is the realistic depiction of law enforcement. The police system is an institutional pillar of male-dominated society. Petra is a police officer and before that she was a lawyer. Both of these chosen professions evidence that she is clearly a product of a patriarchal society and imply that she recognizes its legitimacy. At the same time, however, as a woman confronted with the constraints it imposes, she is often at odds with much of what she encounters both personally and professionally.

Petra's personal rejection of motherhood can be viewed, initially, as a response to the traditional societal expectations imposed on women. The sole intent to buck societal expectations, however, belies the intensity of her frequent, judgmental scorn of mothers and, indeed, other women in general throughout the series. As we will explore later, her evolving stance toward motherhood and her continuing derision of other women throughout the series parallel ideological and demographic shifts in society and conform to an ultimately conservative agenda.

Although her detective character would have to operate in the male-dominated police system, Giménez Bartlett has said that from the outset she was cautious about falling too easily into what she terms "feminist determinism" and thereby implies that she did not necessarily have a feminist agenda in writing the series ("La novela"). Not surprisingly, the reviews that the series initially received in Spain reveal that literary critics indeed had expected that such an agenda would be central to the series and were quite unprepared to address the novelty. When *Ritos de muerte* was published in 1996, one critic wrote that Giménez Bartlett had succeeded not only in creating "a pair of realistic and psychologically rich characters" but, also, that she had done so within "the context of a feminist theme (*in the best sense of the word*) that hasn't been used much in crime fiction" (Arnaiz).[5] As noted, the first of the Petra Delicado novels was published in the late 1990s; an era according to many cultural critics marked by a movement away from what many perceived as the more rigorous feminism of the 1980s in the United States, Great Britain, Spain and other westernized nations. In her well-known study of the feminist hard-boiled fiction of the 1980s of American writers like Sue Grafton and Sara Paretsky, Sandra Tomc has identified an aggressive critique of the patriarchy and its institutions, which included the feminist detective's rejection of the police force in these novels. By the 1990s, however, Tomc finds a number of crime stories like *Prime Suspect* that completely contrast with earlier crime fiction by women in that they "bizarrely combine an aggressive critique of patriarchy with a narrative that highlights the virtues of submission and conformity." With regard to American feminist crime stories of this era, Tomc argues that they reflect changes in feminism in the late 1980s and "tend to find their political rationale in contradiction itself, marking out a program made up simultaneously of vilification and acceptance" (47). Jeremy G. Butler has made similar observations about the American TV series *Cagney and Lacey* which, despite the ideological backpedaling involved in the recasting of the role of detective Christine Cagney, went on to establish itself as one of the most progressively feminist programs on television. Butler affirmed that the exploration of the contradictions inherent between the institutionalized masculinity of the police and the presence of femininity was central to programs such as *Cagney and Lacey*, and *Prime Suspect*. In the case of *Cagney and Lacey*, the dramatic resolution usually endorsed the compassionate compromise made by the female characters between being a good police officer and being a "real" woman. We recall, for example, that the Lacey character was married with children. In *Prime Suspect*, the fascination of Tennison as a character was the powerful and compelling focus on the internal and external confrontations and contradictions faced by a leading female character who was in most circumstances a police officer first and a woman second.

    I would suggest that similar contradictory aspects of the characterization of Petra Delicado identified by various critics are neither unexpected nor ironic. Notwithstanding the choice to write within the confines of the conservative procedural genre, Giménez Bartlett has created a complex multidimensional female character whose plausibility resonates with millions of readers in numerous countries — including women who describe themselves as feminists and those who do not. That is to say that while some critics have found "bizarre" the simultaneous vilification and acceptance of the patriarchy in crime fiction written by women, in actuality it is not. It may be incongruous, paradoxical or even at times hypocritical but there is nothing peculiar about it. Rather, it is quite the opposite, exceedingly ordinary and true to life. This is a primary aspect of crime fiction. Like other popular culture texts, crime fiction participates in the production of what critics like Joke Hermes, call cultural citizenship, inviting us, as readers, "into new types of collectivities that stretch far beyond national borders" (1). Hermes defines cultural citizenship as "the process of bonding and community building, and reflection on that bonding, that is implied in partaking of the text-related practices of reading, consuming, celebrating, and criticizing offered in the realm of (popular) culture" (10). Popular culture "makes the presence known of those who are not in positions of direct political or economic power" thereby serving as a counterforce that ultimately provides an alternative sense of community which is not provided by social institutions such as political parties, trade unions, sports clubs or the family (11).[6]

The immense popularity of the Petra Delicado series clearly points to this collectivity of readers. This is due in no small part to the fact that the series so precisely reflects the changing demographics of contemporary Spain, particularly as it relates to women's experiences.

When we first meet the forty-something Petra Delicado in the 1996 *Ritos de muerte*, she has never been in charge of investigating a case and seems wholly unsuitable for the job. Due to short staffing, she is suddenly called from her routine job as document librarian and assigned to investigate what soon turns out to be a series of rapes of fragile young women. Petra's literal emergence from the department of documentation housed in the basement of the station house casts her stereotypically as in the dark and clueless. She comes from a well-to-do family from whom she is largely alienated and her working class colleagues consider her an intellectual. Indeed, her comments and thoughts about many of the people she meets while on the job reinforce this portrayal as somewhat of an outsider and a snob. She is twice divorced, childless, and arguably rather self-centered. Throughout the series she has multiple affairs, and while she doesn't want to give up her independence, she spends much time obsessing about her relationships with men and wondering about the choices she has made — including whether or not to have children. She and the partner she is assigned, Fermín Garzón, initially appear to be wholly incompatible. Fermín, who is in his late fifties, is a strict, by-the-book type of flatfoot. While always respectful of Petra's authority, he makes it known from the start that he disapproves of her methods of interrogation and frequently questions her tendency to psychoanalyze the victims and the suspects. At first, in fact, it seems that it would be more appropriate for Fermín to lead the investigation. Petra is slow to realize Fermín's value perhaps, in part, because she has a history of unsuccessful relationships with men. It was the domination of her first husband which she compares to a parent/child relationship that eventually compelled her to escape that life and become a detective. Despite her multiple love interests, in retrospect, it becomes very clear that the most important relationship Petra has throughout the series is with Fermín who embodies the norm within the police system; the epitome of male-dominance that she must confront. The evolution of this friendship is testimony to their eventual acceptance of difference and tolerance and, more importantly, to their growing mutual respect as Petra evolves as a detective and Fermín as a partner.

Both Petra and Fermín are cast as loners in all but the later novels in the series, *Nido vacío* and *El silencio de los claustros*. In the first installment, *Ritos de muerte,* we learn that Fermín has lived in a boarding house since the death of his wife principally because he is completely without domestic skills. Petra, on the other hand, purchases a house in this first novel. Inasmuch as the movement from the public to the domestic sphere is associated with post feminism, one might be tempted to focus on the purchase and refurbishment of the house as indicative of Petra's self-imposed re-assignment to domestic space and, therefore, her displacement from the classically male detective role. This space, however, does not constitute confinement for her but rather escape from her former marital shared space. Furthermore, her complete lack of domesticity is highlighted continually. Despite initial fantasies about dedicating herself to domestic tasks, the general disarray and lack of food in the house soon forces her to hire someone else to clean and cook. While she clearly envisions her home as a retreat, during the investigations she is generally foiled in her attempts to utilize it to that end. Instead, she sometimes ends up conducting police business there. The storyline of the 2004 novel *Un barco cargado de arroz* effectively summarizes the incongruity between Petra's apparent fantasy of domestic bliss and her actual personal and professional aspirations. Here she invites Fermín to stay with her when his son comes to visit with his homosexual lover. The male presence functions as sort of a trial run as Petra grapples with the idea of cohabitating with her insistent lover, Ricard. On the one hand, she does assume the domestic role in part here. On the other hand, Ricard's arrival at the moment that Fermín is preparing an omelet for her is evidence of his newly acquired domesticity—learned largely at the insistence of Petra—and it constitutes some attempt on her part to reform the patriarchy on the local level. Fermín's domesticity also contrasts importantly with Ricard to whom she refers to as "un desastre doméstico" [a domestic disaster] (173). Later, as she attempts to host the perfect going away party for Fermín's son, we see this ambiguity with regard to Petra's identity resurface. While ostensibly her real purpose in giving the party is to facilitate Fermín's tolerance of homosexuality, she is not immune to her colleague's appreciation of her domestic skills:

> ¡Qué casa tan coqueta, Petra! Ya sabía que no tendrías los ceniceros a tope de colillas y revistas caídas por el suelo como los policías de películas, pero un gusto tan exquisito se sale de lo común.
> Lamenté que Ricard no estuviera presente para oír aquel comentario.
> [What a cute house, Petra! I already knew you wouldn't have dirty ashtrays and magazines all over the floor like the cops in movies, but such exquisite taste really goes beyond.
> I was sorry that Richard wasn't there to hear that remark] [243].[7]

In the midst of the conflicting aspirations evinced here, Petra's domestic bubble bursts in the most unpleasant manner when she is called away from the party to identify a body at the morgue. This scene typifies Petra's experiences as she readily sacrifices these fleeting moments of domestic bliss in favor of professional responsibilities.

Like her male counterparts, Petra spends the great majority of her time in public spaces; she is a frequent visitor to the bar across the street from the precinct and she identifies herself as belonging in an urban environment. Her home is located in a neighborhood of old houses not far from downtown. The purchase of it represents part of the process of re-inventing herself after her second divorce. This neighborhood, with which Petra identifies, also contrasts sharply, for example, with the suburban setting of *Serpientes en el paraíso* where she is appalled at the spectacle of the antiseptic, homogenized environment which she calls "una realidad creada artificialmente que nada tenía que ver con la fealdad, el ruido o la contaminación del entorno real" [an artificially created reality that had nothing to do with the ugliness, noise or pollution of the real one].[8]

As a female positioned in the superior role, Petra's stance on feminism is certainly a problematic aspect of her characterization, which initially places her as within, rather than against, the patriarchal institution. Early in the series she does explicitly deny that she is a feminist. Yet, there are multiple instances later in the series that contradict this assertion as she reflects on the relevancy of the feminist movement to her reality. By the fourth installment, *Muertos de papel*, she explicitly comments on the failure of young women to acknowledge the efforts of the older generation with regard to the freedoms they enjoy:

En fin, encontraba toda esta caída de los tabúes tradicionales francamente estimulante. Pero no era sólo cuestión de imagen: si alguna vez me había entretenido en leer los artículos, me sorprendieron sistemáticamente un lenguaje y unos planteamientos pletóricos de libertad. Cosas como: "Es tímido tu chico en la cama? Veinte modos de espabilarlo" demostraban que las mujeres jóvenes actuales estaban mucho más liberadas de lo que llegaría jamás a estarlo cualquier mujer de mi generación. Así es la vida, pensé, actualmente se vive como juego aquello por lo que nosotras habíamos organizado una revolución.

[All in all, I found the whole falling away of traditional taboos frankly stimulating. But it wasn't just a question of image: if now and then I had entertained myself reading some articles, I was surprised by the language and approaches overflowing with freedom. Things like: "Is your guy shy in bed? Twenty ways to wake him up" showed that young women today were much freer than any woman of my generation would ever be. Such is life, I thought, what we had organized a revolution for was now just a game] [40–41].[9]

The existence of the post-feminist perspective among many women in contemporary Spain to which Petra alludes here has been affirmed by several recent sociological studies. In a 2004 interview, the well-known Spanish feminist, Lidia Falcón affirmed the existence of a backlash against feminist ideals in Spain, especially among women between the ages of eighteen and thirty:

> there has been a very important reversal of feminist ideas among the younger generations, fundamentally because the worse problems the older generation faced have been resolved. All the propagandizing from the politicians has helped this along, the schools and the media assuring us that we're all equal. Because of that, when women face real problems: work, salary, promotion, childbirth, relationship difficulties, childcare, there is a huge sense of frustration and uncertainty because none of the expectations they've had since childhood are met.[10]

Margaret Andrews and Anny Brooksbank Jones have noted two primary commonly held objections to feminism in contemporary society. The first is the stigmatization of feminists as marginalized activists and the second is the notion that feminism is now superannuated, "that it has nothing more to offer young women who have grown up with the notion that they enjoy unprecedented equality with men in law" (235). Petra, however, implies that she is not one of these women as she clearly allies herself with the older generation. Nevertheless, she does experience the dilemma throughout the series of reconciling her professional aspirations with both her own feminine identity and the traditional/conservative values imposed upon her. This is very much in line with the situation of many women in contemporary Spain as described by Falcón. In summarizing the current state of the feminist movement in Spain, Falcón laments that women have not realized the dream of feminizing the patriarchy but, in order to succeed, are relegated to learning to operate within the same, male-dominated system:

This is the corruption of the desired recognition of equality. At the moment, men are winning the battle by way of imposing their own criteria and women are imitating them because it's the only way to survive in a world that favors masculine values. What's lacking in feminism is the force to impregnate society with values like solidarity, understanding and peace. Meanwhile, women who want to succeed in their profession and open doors in society are forced to behave like men or be penalized by remaining marginalized ["Ha estado"].

Returning now to Petra's rejection of motherhood, clearly this choice for independence is part of her response to the traditional societal expectations imposed on women but it can also be seen as part of her participation in the post-feminist backlash that she supposedly laments. There is a complete indictment of maternity evidenced in the series with characters like the domineering mother in *Ritos de muerte* for whom Petra has no sympathy and who is shown to be ultimately responsible for the crimes committed by her son. Rape and murder are portrayed here, as Nina Molinaro has shown, as gendered crimes where the real victims are not the dead women but the mother dominated male criminal and his girlfriend/adopted sister (who is also the victim of a "bad" woman). In the same novel, there is a motif of dead geraniums that functions to reiterate Petra's rejection of the maternal role. Here, her total disinterest in the poor state of the geraniums implies that she is devoid of maternal instinct (as she appears to be in other examples throughout the series). The subtext here is that, as a woman, wouldn't she naturally be interested in the flowers (e.g., the domestic)? In contrast, both her second ex-husband Pepe and her partner Fermín take an active role in attempting to revive the geraniums and Petra is resentful of the male bonding engendered by this mutual interest. Tellingly, the geraniums resurface in a dream wherein Petra imagines herself fertilizing and reviving them with the pulverized genitals of the rapist. Thus, she symbolically puts herself in the male/aggressor role, not the traditional female/maternal one. It is certainly not coincidental either that the rapist marks all of the victims with an impression of a flower thereby branding them as females/victims. Ironically, it is this branding iron that leads Petra to him. As she gains power and closes in on the criminal, the geraniums begin to revive.

This demystification of motherhood seen here, to use Giménez Bartlett's term, is carried to an extreme in her 2001 short story "La voz de la sangre" wherein the victims and the killer are all female prostitutes and the motive for the crime is revenge against a bad mother who abandoned the killer at birth and whom she finds years later running a brothel. After six months of working in the brothel, she goes back one night with the intent to kill her mother but is unable to go through with it. Unfortunately, she encounters one of the other prostitutes on her way out and suddenly loses control and kills her and the others too. When she thinks back on the case, Petra's condemnation of the mother is completely unsympathetic:

> la funesta Agripinia, auténtica ogra del cuento, se retorcía como una hydra furiosa cuando supo de la pequeña tragedia griega que se había montado a su costa.... Y es que el asunto de la sangre y la consanguinidad, la maternidad, la filialidad y demás lazos hemoglobínicos no deja de estar demasiado mitificado.
>
> [the fatal Agripinia, the real ogre of the story, writhed like a furious hydra when she learned of the little Greek tragedy that had played out at her expense.... And the thing is that the business about blood relationships, maternity, daughterly behavior and all other blood ties is always over mythified] [Giménez-Bartlett "La voz"].[11]

Fermín's reply to this "¡Bueno, inspectora!, ¿qué quiere que le diga? Una madre es una madre" [Well, Inspector, what do you want me to say? A mother is a mother] echoes Petra's disturbing, post feminist perspective on motherhood as an individual choice which some women make and for which they must pay a price as it rests on the notion that neither the government nor society can nor should offer any support to parents for the common good of raising the next generation" ("La voz" VII). In fairness, there is a moment when Petra interrogates the ex-husband of one of the victims and her rough treatment of him leads Fermín to question whether her motive is to solve the case or to get a medal for her "feminismo radical" [radical feminism] ("La voz" III). Despite this, the story is a sad commentary on women as their own worst enemies and Petra's voice doesn't dissent from the others.[12]

The vilification of the mother figure is prevalent also in the much later *Nido vacío*. The title alludes to the absence of the two young girls that Petra is searching for throughout and also suggests the motive of the childless director of the agency responsible for protecting the girls who Petra ultimately holds responsible for the murders committed by one of the girls. The girls are also victims of unbelievably bad biological mothers who would allow their sexual exploitation in the child pornography ring that Petra discovers. Another mother figure portrayed negatively here is the wife of Petra's love interest Marco; Laura, whom Petra assesses as stereotypically self-absorbed, highly stressed and cold. Petra is especially judgmental of Laura's maternal instinct to protect her young daughter by limiting her involvement with the police after she witnesses a crime. On top of that, this behavior, deemed unreasonable by him, adds to Marcos' growing disaffection for Laura and subsequent attraction to her polar opposite: Petra.

In complete contrast to these examples, there are other moments where Petra questions her own choices regarding maternity. In *Serpientes en el paraíso*, for example, she laments her career choice and the loss of not having had children: "¿Qué extraña tendencia autopunitiva me había llevado hasta la frontera desde la que se divisa la sima negra del alma humana? Debería haberme encontrado en un pequeño lugar seguro adonde solo llegaran las risas de mis propios hijos, ocho o diez" [What strange self punishing tendency had brought me to the border of the black abyss of the human soul? I should have found myself a safe, little place where only the laughter of my own eight or ten children could be heard] (278). Her related obsession with the angelic child of one of the suspects with whom she oversteps the limits of a professional relationship, however, only serves to blind her judgment and delay the resolution of the case thereby tipping the balance again away from motherhood as a positive state. Mothers, it seems, will inevitably allow their emotions to muddle their rational thinking.

While rejecting the traditional role of motherhood, Petra's character does evince other traditionally feminine aspects. One that undoubtedly rings true for many female readers is her apparent desire to conform to a feminine ideal that she recognizes as oppressive. Throughout the series, she utilizes the traditionally feminine to disassociate herself from the sordidness of the criminal world. At the conclusion of the case in *Ritos de muerte*, for example, she takes solace in watching some models on television.

Similarly, in *Muertos de papel*, wherein the reader is immediately informed that the case will be one in which "la imágen, el aspecto, la influencia en los otros y la consideración pública de un personaje eran el centro de la cuestión" [the image, the aspect, the influence one had on others and the public perception of the person were at the center of the question] the novel ends with what appears to be Petra's preoccupation with precisely the same thing as she visits the beauty salon, goes shopping for new clothes and dresses up only to have a simple dinner with Fermín: "Me había puesto tan elegante porque necesitaba limpiar de mí los últimos restos de delito, de muerte, de sospecha y culpabilidad. Y oler bien, también necesitaba oler bien" [I had made myself up so elegantly because I needed to wash myself of the remains of the crime, of death, of suspicion, and of guilt. And to smell good, I also needed to smell good] (8, 314).

Readers are also witness to Petra's dilemma regarding the reconciliation of a romantic relationship with her aspirations of self-realization. She is fully aware that this was impossible to attain in either of her marriages — the first in which she felt she was married to a father figure and the second in which she played the maternal role to her younger husband — yet she continually entertains the fantasy of it. Indeed, her constant musings about whether she should sacrifice her independence and privacy and co-habitate with her insistent lover in *Un barco cargado de arroz* disrupt the mystery narrative, in effect, overshadowing it to the point that the resolution of the detective's relationship not only parallels the resolution of the crime but is the more engaging mystery.

Rather than constituting a narrative weakness, this undermining of the generic convention deliberately draws the focus to the reality of contemporary women like Petra.

The foregoing certainly illustrates that the series evinces some of the same type of ideological backpedaling and simultaneous exploration of the inherent contradictions between the police force and the female protagonist that Tomc and others have identified in crime fiction from the late '80s and early '90s. Like the Tennison character of the 1990s television series *Prime Suspect*, considered by Tomc to be a prime example of the post-feminist detective, Petra often exhibits contradictory behaviors as she seemingly aspires to be accepted within the police force. Nevertheless, until the problematic epilogue of *Nido vacío*, Petra does manage to avoid a symbolic initiation as one of the boys (unlike the Tennison character as Tomc notes). The endings of the earlier novels are void of any kind of congratulatory or celebratory event with her superiors or even her colleagues. Petra typically keeps her distance from all but Fermín. Until *Nido vacío*, the endings also reaffirm her rejection of the domestic, taking place either in a bar with a commiserating drink with Fermín or involving some version of a flight fantasy. The ending of *Un barco de arroz* is testimony to this. When asked what her dream would be (her "*barco cargado de arroz*"), Petra doesn't wax poetic on any equalitarian society or express any aspirations as a member of the male dominated police force. Instead, her reticence to be subsumed into that institution is reaffirmed by her failure to complete the necessary paperwork throughout the case — it is Fermín who does that — and also by her casual mention that Coronas, her superior, did not congratulate them for solving the case. Furthermore, her admission that she would have liked to be a biologist, living alone in the jungle and devoted to the study of some animal allies her with that icon of the female lone wolf — Jane Goodall. Petra undeniably must make compromises on both a personal and professional level but, even though both she and Fermín laugh off her pipedream, the fact that she rides off into the sunset with a new, younger lover at the end represents a final expression of freedom and escape.

For better or for worse, all of that changes in *Nido vacío*, the seventh installment in the series which might well be just as appropriately titled *The One Where Everyone Gets Married*. In an extended epilogue that can only be described as matrimonial overkill, Petra, Fermín and their younger colleague Yolanda all renounce their membership in what Petra now sarcastically refers to as "un selecto club de solitarios" [a selective singles club] (385). Petra's wedding celebrates her expressed desired to give up what she had always held most dear "la libertad, la independencia, la tranquilidad" [freedom, independence, tranquility] in favor of an institution which she now prefers not to ponder too deeply: "Pero en fin, allí estábamos dispuestos a ratificar una vez más que la convivencia amorosa es posible. Preferí, sin embargo, no llevar los pensamientos al plano teórico; el matrimonio es lo que es y yo había decidido intentarlo de nuevo" [But, in the end, there we were ready to confirm once again that loving coexistence is possible. Nevertheless, I preferred not to carry my thoughts to the theoretical level; marriage is what it is and I had decided to try it again] (385, 387). Her new husband Marcos is an architect who comes complete with two previous divorces and four children to whom Petra now becomes a willing stepmother. At the wedding, Sonia, one of the younger officers, even presents the happy couple with a set of baby dishes and Petra's sister inquires as to whether the couple will have children. Petra's response, however, indicates that she has no such plans. Nevertheless, she does happily assuage the worries of Marcos' youngest daughter when she informs her of his intent to expand Petra's house to accommodate them all. In light of the multiple opportunities the detective has had throughout the series to observe the many challenges of parenthood together with the outright vilification of the other maternal figures in the novel, Petra's notions about her future stepmother role are startlingly facile and ironic:

> Todo era diferente en este tercer matrimonio: me unía a un hombre en estricto plano de igualdad. No sería de él ni hija ni madre. Tendría, además una legión de vástagos postizos a los que ni siquiera sabía aún cómo tratar. Pensaba, en cualquier caso, que la primera regla de oro que debía imperar en mi nueva vida era seguir siendo yo misma, si es que eso tiene algún sentido en realidad.
>
> [Everything was different with this third marriage: I was joining myself to a man on a strictly equal level. I would be neither his daughter nor his mother. I would also have a legion of false offspring whom I had no idea whatsoever how to treat. I was thinking, in any case, that the first golden rule that should prevail in my new life was to continue being myself, that is, if that makes any sense in reality] (390).[13]

The implausibility of this plan is evinced only seconds later by Petra's own thoughts regarding Garzón's recent marriage; "Buena razón lleva quien afirma que todos cambiamos irresmisiblemente tras el matrimonio" [Whoever affirmed that we all change irremissably after marriage was right] (391). This change she then ascribes to a rather odd combination of destiny and free will; "si somos inteligentes debemos concluir que la esencia de la vida es la aceptación de lo que viene, pero nunca una aceptación resignada y doliente, sino la que queda después de estar bien seguros de haber intentado ejercer hasta el último minuto nuestra voluntad" [if we're smart, we should conclude that the essence of life is the acceptance of what is to come, but never a resigned and painful acceptance but, rather, one that comes after being very sure that we've tried to exercise our own will until the very end] (391).

At the same time that Petra marries for the third time and takes an entirely new family into her personal space, the congratulatory speech that her boss makes at the wedding indicates she may have become subsumed into that institution too:

> Nuestra querida Petra Delicado se nos ha casado.... No les voy a negar que al principio me inquieté porque pensé que podría dejarnos; pero cuando me aseguró que continuaría en la policía me serené. Debo de ser masoquista, la verdad, porque no hay mujer en el mundo que me ponga más nervioso: es peleona, protestona, anárquica, cabezota, sarcástica y, en el colmo de las virtudes, y ustedes perdonarán la expresión, tocapelotas.... Sin embargo, todos la apreciamos. Yo diría más: creo que todos estamos un poco enamorados de Petra, y la razón de tal enamoramiento es que ella representa la esencia de lo que es una mujer.
>
> [Our dear Petra Delicado has gone and gotten married on us.... I'm not going to deny that at first I was upset because I thought she would leave us, but, when she assured me she would stay with the police, I calmed down. I must be a masochist, truthfully, because there's no other woman in the world who makes me so nervous: she's argumentative, oppositional, old-fashioned, head-strong, sarcastic, and on top of all those virtues, you'll pardon the expression, she's a ball buster.... Nevertheless, we all appreciate her. And, I'll add that I think we're all a little bit in love with Petra, and the reason for that is that she represents the essence of what a woman is] [393].

It seems that all the men are in love with Petra now. Even Ricard, the boyfriend she left in *Un barco cargado de arroz* returns here hoping for another chance with her. Unfortunately, Petra gives him false hope when she confesses that she has changed and can no longer sustain her ideal of solitariness due to her own weakness: "La soledad ya no me parece una panacea, pero sólo porque me he vuelto más débil" [Solitariness doesn't seem like a panacea to me any longer, but only because I've become weaker] (326). Equally as unsettling as Petra having established herself now as the much loved bad girl of the police force is her continuing poor treatment or perception of almost all of the other women in the novel including her younger subordinates Yolanda and Sonia. In the case of her female colleagues, Petra generally treats them like children as when she chastises Sonia for commenting on the bride's social standing at Fermín's wedding. When Marco's questions this, Petra explains it as all part of the job: "Ser inspectora de policía tiene una vertiente de maestra rural, ya te acostumbrarás" [Being a police inspector is a bit like being a rural school teacher, you'll get used to it] (383). In contrast, Petra has nothing but praise for Fermín's intended, Beatriz, despite the fact that from the reader's perspective she makes no discernable contributions to society. She does exhibit the utmost decorum and move in the right social circles, however. In addition to these questionable merits, Petra also notices with affectionate dismay the positive influence Beatriz is already exercising on Fermín's wardrobe.

*El silencio de los claustros*, the eighth installment in the series, begins just as Petra is about to pass the one-year mark in her new role as stepmother to Marcos' four children. Here, she is called to the convent where one of Marcos' children attends classes to investigate a murder. Petra is immediately faced with the problem of what to do with Marina, her six year old stepdaughter, when she is called to the scene of the crime. In consultation with Marcos, it is decided that Marina can stay home alone waiting for Marcos while Petra goes off to work. The promise she makes to herself not to think about "los innumerable peligros que una casa encierra" [the innumerable dangers of the house] puts a handy, albeit questionable, end to the only parental scheduling predicament she will face in the novel (13). As a stepparent, Petra does worry about whether the children will like her and how she can possibly fulfill the roles of detective, wife and stepmother adequately: "Quiero atrapar a un asesino ladrón de momias, y ser amable con los compañeros de trabajo y una esposa excelente ... y, por si no fuera bastante quiero ser una madrastra que no tenga nada que ver con la de Blancanieves" [I want to catch the killer who stole the mummy and be friendly with my colleagues as well as be an excellent wife ... and, if it's not too much to ask, I want to be a stepmother who is nothing like Snow White's] (97). She further laments that while there may be other women out there that can do it all, she isn't one of them and her job is particularly incompatible with these new roles: "Sin duda existen mujeres que son excelentes esposas y madres, buenas físicas nucleares y que en sus ratos libres cooperan con una ONG, pero no era mi caso. Una policía vivía al instante, en la incertidumbre.... Una policía no puede imponerse rutinas" [Doubtless there are women who are excellent wives and mothers, good nuclear physicists and who in their free time volunteer with a non-profit agency, but that wasn't me. A police officer lives in the moment, in uncertainty.... A police officer can't have routines] (97). The wholly negative portrayal of the children's biological mothers, generally voiced by the children or Marcos, placates Petra's worries to some degree as when Marina attempts to comfort her by telling her that her older brother's mother "es una histérica" [is an hysteric] (94). That assessment, reportedly, came from Marina's own mother when Marcos and she were married. It is but one of several such remarks voiced by Petra and others that once again position her as the superior woman and her life choices as the right ones and echoes the voices of many women today who participate in what those in the U.S. refer to as the "mommy wars." This disharmony intensifies when Fermín takes it upon himself to satisfy the children's curiosity about police work and takes them to the station house. Petra must then deal with their mother's anger. As luck would have it, the boy's mother calls when no one is home and leaves a threatening message. Once again, Marina attempts to quell Petra's concern: "Me parece que ya te dije que la madre de los chicos es una histérica" [I think I already told you that their mother is an hysteric] (144). When Marina's mother calls, Petra hangs up on her despite the fact that she knows it was a poor decision on Fermín's part to take the children there. Petra then blames the whole fiasco on Marcos' failure to anticipate and thereby pre-empt his ex-wives' reactions. Finally, Marcos apologizes to Petra, indicating that she certainly shouldn't be expected to assume any actual parenting role: "Lo que creo es que llevas razón, mis ex-esposas son un incordio. Y los niños también, quizá no debieran venir tanto por aquí" [What I think is that you're right, my ex-wives are an inconvenience. And the kids too — perhaps they shouldn't come around so often] (170). In a later conversation with Fermín, Petra reveals that despite her best intentions, she hasn't really changed at all: "pero yo tenía la ilusión de que el matrimonio me ayudaría a cambiar ciertas cosas, como por ejemplo el orden de las prioridades vitales, aunque no ha sido así" [but I had the idea that marriage would help me change some things, like the my priorities, for example, but it hasn't] (321).

Sally Munt has written "[the] peculiar attraction of a crime novel is its ability to appease sometimes contradictory desires, which presumably can placate the feminine and provoke the feminist in all of us" (207). The Petra Delicado series clearly exemplifies what Munt refers to as the "contradictory positioning of liberal feminism, straddling ideological allegiances between bourgeois centre and the oppositional impetus of feminism" (204). The difficulty then is in constructing the female detective in such a way so as not to alienate the average reader while at the same challenging their perceptions and attitudes. The question remains whether this is the case with the Petra Delicado series. Although the novels may not evidence a sustained critique of the patriarchy, as others have noted, Petra consistently gives voice to the questions and doubts that many women have with regard to what it means to live, function, and behave in contemporary society. On the other hand, the renouncing of her independent ideals and her marriage in *Nido vacío* may certainly have provoked disappointment among feminist readers. Without a doubt, having to call home to announce you won't be home for dinner or having to eat the dinner you don't want because your husband has prepared it as Petra does in *El silencio de los claustros* is far from the freedoms she enjoyed in the earlier novels.

Munt also argues that socialist feminist crime novels often sacrifice pleasure for political correctness and affirms "sometimes these texts are just too serious, failing to deliver suspense or resolution satisfactorily, degenerating into pedantic political primers" (205). Despite the absence of a superior alternative offered in the narrative, or, perhaps because of it, the notion that we may recognize ourselves in characters like Petra Delicado, reminds us as readers of the work yet to be done. The issue is not whether the series is one which critics like Tomc find disturbing due to its "lack of commitment to any of its arguments," (e.g., its post-feminist stance), instead, the series constitutes what Hermes has called a "hybrid mix of politics and pleasure" (75). In the context of cultural citizenship, the reading of detective novels is a form of agency and criticism of the system also. The sense of empowerment that readers gain from recognizing "cracks in dominant culture' is paradoxical because it ultimately results in a "continuing allegiance to that system" (77). Yet, as Hermes notes, "cultural citizenship is structured as a domain of pre-political consideration, of unease with states of being, rather than as a monument to specific rights, duties, or identities" (77). So, the question as to how to reconcile the contradictions inherent between the institutionalized masculinity of the police force and the presence of a female detective in the Petra Delicado series might well be answered by another question. Is it necessary to do so in order that the series function on the level of creating cultural citizenship? The series, with all of its contradictions, at a minimum, does engage us in meaningful debate about society. As a final word regarding Petra's ongoing role as a professional and her new roles as a wife and mother, the series reflects the contemporary divide among women regarding their choices relating to work and motherhood and it reveals that society has a long way to go towards the realization of equality for and among women.

## Notes

1. See "La novela negra, espejo de los cambios sociales," elmundo.es, 21 January 2005: n.p. Translation mine. All other quotations from this source are given parenthetically.

2. There are other well-known male/female police pairs, like Lorenzo Silva's Vila and Chamorro from the Bevilacqua series but in these the female is the subordinate officer.

3. See Godsland, Molinaro and Thompson-Casado. Shelley Godsland, for example, notes that Petra repeatedly denies that she is a feminist and that she rejects the relevancy of the feminist movement to her reality. Ultimately, she finds the character evocative of Faludi and Greer's perception of the post-feminist as a "commercially motivated and commercially constructed individual" (89). In contrast, in her study of *Ritos de muerte*, Nina Molinaro borrows Kathleen Gregory Klein's term and views the novel as a uniquely Spanish manifestation of a feminocentric text (one which does not necessarily need a feminist detective but, in its foregrounding of gender, leads to the questioning of partriarchist assumptions). At the same time, however, she notes that the novel "articulates a man's world that polarizes men (and women who act like men) against women, in part because the police procedural prescribes solidarity within the police force, a rule which Petra follows and, to some extent, desires." (111). Finally Kathleen Thompson-Casado falls somewhere in the middle; recognizing that while the series does not evince a sustained critique of the patriarchy, its somewhat watered down representation of female agency may appeal to more conservative readers who might reject the latter. This brand of feminism, she argues, should not be discounted as it may in fact function to "empower readers to question personal as well as social issues" (79).

4. The authors of "Childbearing Trends and Policies in Europe" outline the process of the Second Demographic Transition (SDT) as described by Ron Lesthaeghe and Dirk van de Kaa. In addition to the decline and postponement of fertility, they note that in most of Europe there has been an increase in the acceptance of intimate relationships among un-partnered individuals,

as well as an acceptance of non-family living arrangements and of childlessness, and a positive evaluation of cohabitation as a premarital stage and as an alternative to marriage. They also note that non-marital childbearing has also become widely accepted, especially within stable cohabiting unions, whereas childbearing to single mothers is still mostly regarded as undesirable. At the same time, the authors note that the family has not become an obsolete institution:
> On the contrary, family life — though in more diverse forms — continues to be highly and almost universally valued, and parenthood remains at the top of many people's life priorities. What has changed is the motivation for parenthood. Childbearing is less frequently seen as a "duty towards society" or as an inescapable destiny, and it has increasingly become a result of a planned decision of each couple, who in their decision-making process may consider various potential positive and negative effects of parenthood on their relationship, lifestyle, and economic well-being. Parenthood increasingly serves individual self-fulfillment and private joy, but it is also taken very seriously, and there is a considerable emphasis on responsible parenthood and the wellbeing of the children. Without a doubt, these changes in norms and values do not take place in isolation from broader economic and social developments; increasing prosperity, rising educational levels, and the rapid spread of labour force participation among women are among the factors that typically accompany the Second Demographic Transition [see Frejka, Tomas, et al., 10].

5. See "El futuro del crimen," elmundo.es, June 29, 1996: n.p. Translation mine.

6. Hoping to find "the critical energy so lacking in what used to be the women's movement in the Netherlands, Joke Hermes, a self-identified member of the "erstwhile feminist elite," documents the conservativeness (e.g., post-feminist attitude) of contemporary crime fiction readers in the Netherlands. Hermes also notes that a similar condition exists in academic feminism: "Discourses of emancipation, however important in individual cases, do not have the critical or political purchase that they used to have. From the framework of fragmented identities, it is difficult, if not impossible, to go back to the older certainties of emancipation, however much power differences continue to structure both global and national and also everyday social relations" (63). While admittedly anecdotal, Hermes' interviews with a number of self-described feminist readers of crime fiction reveal "a domestication of feminism that is shocking not so much for its deradicalization of the issues involved (such as violence against women, or how women still and often have to fight for respect and acknowledgment in the workplace), but for its acceptance of a status quo that should, but is not highly likely to, change at short notice" (64).

7. Alicia Giménez Bartlett, *Un barco cargado de arroz* (Barcelona: Planeta, 2004), p. 243. All translations are mine. Page numbers for all subsequent quotations from this edition are given parenthetically.

8. Alicia Giménez Bartlett, *Serpientes en el paraíso* (Barcelona: Planeta, 2002), p. 18. All translations are mine. Page numbers for all other quotations from this edition are given parenthetically.

9. Alicia Giménez Bartlett, *Muertos de papel* (Barcelona: Plaza y Janés, 2000), pp. 40–41. All translations are mine. Page numbers for all other quotations from this edition are given parenthetically.

10. See "Ha estado con nosotros Lidia Falcón," elmundo.es, October 29, 2004: n.p. All translations are mine.

11. Alicia Giménez Bartlett, "La voz de la sangre," elmundo.es, 5–11 August, 2001, part I, n.p. Translation mine.

12. The authors of "Spain: Short on children and short on family policies," point to this perception in contemporary society and argue that "what Spanish society needs most is enhanced awareness of the nature of reproduction as an element of social balance in which all its members – public authorities, employers, individuals – are implicated and whose cost should not be borne exclusively by families, and certainly not solely by women who decide to be mothers." See Margarita Delgado, Gerardo Meil and Francisco Zamora López, *Demographic Research* 19.27: 1100.

13. Alicia Giménez Bartlett, *Nido vacío* (Barcelona: Planeta, 2009), 390. All translations are mine. Page numbers for all other quotations from this edition are given parenthetically.

## Works Cited

Andrews, Margaret, and Anny Brooksbank Jones. "Re-Registering Spanish Feminists." In *Contemporary Spanish Cultural Studies*, eds. Barry Jordan and Rikki Morgan-Tamosunas. London: Arnold, 2000, 233–40.
Arnaiz, Joaquin. "El futuro del crimen."*elmundo.es*, 29 June, 1996: n. pag. Web. 20 August 2007.
Brooksbank Jones, Anny. *Women in Contemporary Spain*. Manchester: Manchester UP, 1997.
Butler, Jeremy G. "Police Programs." *The Museum of Broadcast Communications*. N.p. n.d. n. pag. Web. 16 August 2010.
Delgado, Margarita, Gerardo Meil and Francisco Zamora López. "Spain: Short on Children and Short on Family Policies." *Demographic Research* 19.27 (July 1, 2008): 1059–1104. Accessed August 17, 2010.
Frejka, Tomas, Tomáš Sobotka, Jan M. Hoem and Laurent Toulemon. "Summary and General Conclusions: Childbearing Trends and Policies in Europe." *Demographic Research* 19.2 (July 1, 2008): 5–14. Accessed August 17, 2010.
Giménez-Bartlett, Alicia. *Un barco cargado de arroz*. Barcelona: Planeta, 2004.
_____. *Día de perros*. Barcelona: Grijalbo, 1997.
_____. "Ha estado con nosotros Lidia Falcón." elmundo.es, October 29, 2004, n.p. Accessed August 17, 2010.
_____. "La voz de la sangre." elmundo.es, August 5–11, 2001. el mundolibro.com, 5 August 2001: n.p. Accessed August 17, 2010.
_____. *Mensajeros de la oscuridad*. Barcelona: Plaza y Janés, 1999.
_____. *Muertos de papel*. Barcelona: Plaza y Janés, 2000.
_____. *Nido vacío*. Barcelona: Planeta, 2007.
_____. *Ritos de muerte*. Barcelona: Grijalbo, 1996.
_____. *Serpientes en el paraíso*. Barcelona: Planeta, 2002.
_____. *El silencio de los claustros*. Barcelona: Planeta, 2009.
Godsland, Shelley. "From Feminism to Postfeminism in Women's Detective Fiction: The Case of Maria-Antònia Oliver and Alicia Giménez-Bartlett." *Letras Femeninas* 28 (2002): 84–99.
Hermes, Joke. *Re-Reading Popular Culture*. Malden, MA: Blackwell, 2005.
Humm, Maggie. *Border Traffic: Strategies of Contemporary Women Writers*. Manchester and New York: Manchester University Press, 1991.
Klein, Kathleen Gregory. "Habeas Corpus: Feminism and Detective Fiction." *Feminism in Women's Detective Fiction*, ed. Glenwood Irons. Toronto: University of Toronto Press, 1995, pp. 171–189.
_____. *The Woman Detective: Gender and Genre*. Urbana and Chicago: University of Illinois Press, 1988.
Molinaro, Nina L. "Writing the Wrong Rites? Rape and Women's Detective Fiction in Spain." *Letras Femeninas* 28 (2002): 100–117.
Munt, Sally R. *Murder by the Book? Feminism and the Crime Novel*. London: Routledge, 1994.
"La novela negra, espejo de los cambios sociales." elmundo.es, 21 January 2005: n.p. Accessed December 10, 2007.
"Serpientes en el paraíso, el nuevo caso de la inspectora Petra Delicado." elmundo.es, September 17, 2002, n.p. Accessed August 17, 2010.
Tomc, Sandra. "Questing Women: The Feminist Mystery after Feminism." *Feminism in Women's Detective Fiction*, ed. Glenwood Irons. Toronto: University of Toronto Press, 1995, pp. 46–63.
Thompson-Casado, Kathleen. "Petra Delicado; A Suitable Detective for a Feminist?" *Letras Femeninas* 28 (2002): 71–83.
van de Kaa, Dirk J. "Europe's Second Demographic Transition." *Population Bulletin* 42: 1 (1987).

# 6

## Charting the New Nuclear Family in Pedro Almodóvar's *Los abrazos rotos*

SAMUEL AMAGO

> *"If there is something that characterizes the end of the twentieth century it's the rupture of the traditional family. Now you can form families with other members, other ties, other biological relations that need to be respected."*
> — Pedro Almodóvar (qtd. in D'Lugo *Pedro Almodóvar* 103)

From the consolidation of Francisco Franco's authoritarian regime in the early 1940s through his death in 1975, the Spanish family, which was always an important institution in traditional Spanish society, became enshrined in the dictator's ideological "reformation" of the country. Basic legislation made the family "one of the 'organic' institutions of the state, and between 1945 and 1958, the position of male head of the family (*cabeza de familia*) was given legal status" (Rodgers 175). In Franco's Spain the family was "the primary site where ideological issues [could] be displaced and naturalized [...proclaiming] the family as a legitimate site for effective political action, mobilizing 'the people' around universal issues of morality, generation, and gender that cut across class lines" (Kinder 72). Because of its symbolic and legal association with the Spanish nation, the family was to become a field of ideological contestation in oppositional cultural representations. In her classic book *Blood Cinema*, Marsha Kinder demonstrates how the new Spanish cinema subverted Francoist ideologies of the family through the ideological reinscription of popular cinematic forms (Hollywood melodrama and Italian neorealism) and a critical deployment of the Oedipal narrative (197–275) as methods of addressing "political issues and historical events that were repressed from filmic representation during the Francoist era" (197). Dissident filmmakers attacked

Franco's family-centered ideology through cinematic representations of patricide, incest, and family violence. Some of the foundational works of fiction and film of the Franco period depicted a Spanish family in decadence and decay.[1]

The family remains a central feature of contemporary Spanish life, and, as the chapters of this collection variously attest, it continues to enjoy a rich and wide-ranging presence in the country's narrative culture. The present essay explores how the family functions allegorically in the recent work of Spain's most commercially and critically successful filmmaker, Pedro Almodóvar. Following a brief overview of the importance of families to his earlier oeuvre, I shall propose that *Los abrazos rotos* (2009) represents a radical departure for the director that suggests perhaps a new direction in his cinematic representation of this most honored of Spanish cultural institutions. Further, the film's cartographic imagery, its emphasis on technologies of representation — especially the X-ray — and its extreme reflexivity and intertextuality invite the viewer to read the film from a national historical perspective. I argue that these techniques function as a cinematic archeology of recent Spanish history — and of Almodóvar's own trajectory as a director — through which the director reflects critically the ongoing cultural and juridical processes known in Spain as the movement to recover historical memory. By triangulating *Los abrazos rotos* within the interrelated conceptual axes of national cinema, the aesthetics of cinematic reflexivity, and the genealogical conceit that plays out through its narrative, we can discern how historical inquiry is central to Almodóvar's allegorical rehabilitation of democratic Spain and, as such, that the film represents perhaps a resolution of what Teresa Vilarós famously called the country's *mono del desencanto*.

Mark Allinson notes "families are ubiquitous in Almodóvar's films, whether they be the conventional nuclear family (often including elderly grandparents), highly unconventional families or groups of friends who function as families" (63). But while they are ever-present in his filmography, more traditional family formulations have tended to appear as "oppressive, uncaring and frequently in the process of breaking down" (63). Allinson observes that fathers in particular have a propensity to fare poorly: "They tend to be either repressive patriarchs or absentees" (63). Indeed, both *¿Qué he hecho yo para merecer esto?!* (1984) and *Volver* (2006) feature the early murder of the father, while a paternal figure is significantly absent in *Todo sobre mi madre* (1999), *La mala eduación* (2004), *Tacones lejanos* (1991), and *Hable con ella* (2002).

Continuing in this vein, in an important study, Anne Hardcastle has explained how deviancy plays a central role in Almodóvar's representations of the family. This deviancy, however, is seldom negative, but rather has tended to hold the constructive potential for proposing democratic alternatives to retrograde Francoist family traditions. Hardcastle notes, "the tension between deviance and systemic norms goes beyond a restructuring of the Francoist patriarchal family to represent a change from the hierarchical family of the fascist state towards flexible interactions between an individual and a community (family) that is in many ways a model for democracy" (80). Using *Tacones lejanos* (1991) as a case in point, Hardcastle demonstrates how in many of Almodóvar's films the family that was so important to Francoist discourse becomes "a model for a modern, democratic Spain that allows for deviance within a balanced, tolerant community" (82). Deviance from more traditional norms, family structures and comportment thus becomes a means rather than an end, as Almodóvar is able to use non-traditional representations of the family to "expose the rigid, repressive contexts that either compel deviance as a form of resistance or unjustly label any non-conformity as deviance" (90).

Hardcastle maintains that in many of his films, Almodóvar spreads "deviance among the main characters, so that the ultimate critical target is not any individual, but rather rigid structures of behavior in family interactions" (80). She concludes that within the filmmaker's interpretation of the family dynamic, "widespread deviance [...] serves as a restructuring tool for his fictional families as well as a Spanish national family, both struggling to break free from the rigid legacy of the Francoist family's patriarchy and fascism and searching for alternate relationships based in the equality and tolerance of democracy" (91). In other words, in many of Almodóvar's films, family deviancy is a method of engaging critically with a historically repressive Spanish patriarchy.

Pedro Almodóvar's most recent film, *Los abrazos rotos*, would seem at first to continue the trend of family deviancy, since broken, sometimes deviant, families appear throughout the narrative: Lena's (Penélope Cruz) father suffers violently and dies from cancer, Ray X (Rubén Ochandiano) is not only estranged from his father Ernesto Martel (José Luis Gómez), but he has himself also been divorced twice, is estranged from his own son, and he only recently appears to have embraced his homosexuality, while the protagonist Mateo Blanco (Lluís Homar) does not know that his production assistant's son, Diego (Tamar Novas), is also his son. In keeping with the general contours of Almodóvarian family dynamics, an oppressive, violent, or simply absent father is central to all of these various examples of patriarchal or familial dysfunction. As the director suggested in a much earlier interview, "fathers are not very present in my films. I don't know why.... This is something I just feel. When I'm writing about relatives, I just put in mothers" (qtd. in *Blood Cinema* 253). To this end, Paul Julian Smith remarks that the characters in Almodóvar's films "are akin to Spaniards of the Transition, miraculous orphans deprived of a dreaded and ridiculed Father, whom they would prefer to disavow" (*Desire Unlimited* 19).[2]

The daddy problems in *Los abrazos rotos* serve a diegetic function, setting the stage for the development of the plot: after her father's death, Lena is forced into a relationship with Martel, who then takes his place as her authoritarian surrogate father/lover. He stands metaphorically as a decrepit violent patriarchy that would keep Lena at home, ostensibly caring for her yet under the real threat of phallic violence, which is reinforced by the colorful Warhol prints of guns and knives appearing throughout his house. And later, it is ostensibly his son Ray X's desire to tell the story about his own repressive father after his death, and his appearance at Mateo Blanco's door that triggers Mateo's own return to his past, a past he has strenuously and willfully sought to forget. In this way, if we consider the fact that the bulk of the film narrative is comprised of Harry's narration of his past to his son Diego, *Los abrazos rotos* is at its core a historical film that deals with the piecing together of a lost or repressed family history through memory. *Los abrazos rotos* is "Todo sobre mi padre."

If *Todo sobre mi madre* and *Volver* can be understood as Almodóvar's melodramatic meditations on motherhood, community solidarity, and maternity, *Los abrazos rotos* constitutes a contrasting reflection on paternity that draws upon the tradition of film noir.[3] What is noteworthy about the film, however, is that while it contains images of a violent and severe patriarchy in the figure of Martel, it also envisions a progressive reintegration of the nuclear family through Mateo and Diego's mutual recognition of each other as father and son, and, after Judit's (Blanca Portillo) reconciliation with Mateo, a reconstitution of the biological family unit consisting of mother, father and child. Indeed, the last scene of the film significantly features Judit, Diego, and Harry, animatedly engaged in their collaboration on what will be the true director's cut of the film, "Chicas y maletas," that Martel had destroyed.

Keeping in mind the fact that so many of Almodóvar's film narratives envisage the *disintegration* of traditional forms of family—which we notice especially in the conspicuous absence of positive father figures, and in the fact that several fathers are murdered or killed early in several films—the conclusion of *Los abrazos rotos* is somewhat radical—and indeed deviant—in that it figures quite explicitly and purposefully the *re-formation* of a well adjusted nuclear family comprised, in quite traditional fashion, of a biological father, a biological mother and their son. The fact that the film ends with this image of a reunited heteronormative family is all the more strange if we take into account the fact that only a few months after the release of *Los abrazos rotos*, Almodóvar was appearing in the media for critical comments he made regarding the Vatican's stance on family values. In an interview published in the

German daily *Die Zeit*, the director held that "Es una locura no reconocer de qué modo viven millones de personas. Benedicto XVI debe reconocer también a las familias que son diferentes" [It's crazy not to recognize the way in which millions of people are living today. Benedict XVI should also recognize different families] (*El País*),[4] adding that present-day families are also comprised of "padres separados, travestis, transexuales y monjas enfermas de sida" [separated parents, transvestites, transsexuals, and nuns suffering from AIDS] (*El País*). These and other statements are clearly inspired by his filmography. He continues, "Ruedo películas desde hace más de 20 años y en ellas una familia siempre es un grupo de personas en cuyo núcleo hay una esencia de la que todos se ocupan" [I've been shooting films for more than 20 years and in my work a family is always a group of people brought together by some essential issue that matters to them] (*El País*). The director's public comments echo his earlier statements on family that I have included as an epigraph to this essay. But of the seventeen films he has made over the last thirty years, *Los abrazos rotos* is the first in which a nuclear family appears in this kind of traditional configuration as the positive outcome of narrative development.

It is here that I arrive at my animating questions: Is Almodóvar proposing a return or reformation of the traditional family? Has the director come full circle, to a point in which a heterosexual family unit can now be "normal" in an Almodóvar film? Has the director worked through the family issues that were so central to his previous films, so that there may now exist a caring comprehending father figure? Indeed, Mateo Blanco acts as an exemplary father throughout the film. He shows compassionate concern for Judit's son Diego long before he knows he is his son, he takes the boy under his wing as his screenwriting partner, and when Diego is hospitalized after inadvertently mixing drugs at a club Mateo nurses him back to health and covers for Diego while his mother Judit is abroad. Does this "ideal father-son bonding" (Kinder "Restoring" 33) suggest the return of a progressive Spanish patriarchy? In terms of narrative structure, the answer would seem to be yes, since the film ends with familial *integration*, offering a picture of family unity achieved through the protagonists' shared appreciation for film as an art form. And while previously Almodóvar's "film families struggle against repressive, inflexible social codes that enforce power hierarchies, punish deviance, and link social/familial life to a legacy of fascist control" (Hardcastle 82), in *Los abrazos rotos* oppressive societal pressures are conspicuously absent. The only oppression is embodied in the figure of Martel, who stands conspicuously as a representative of multinational capital. That is, the villain of this film is neither the working class father of *¿Qué he hecho yo para merecer esto?!*, nor the lecherous stepdad of *Volver*. Nor is he an absent authoritarian figure against whose influence any number of protagonists struggle in the earlier films. Martel is the powerful Latin American businessman, voyeur, and maleficent producer of "Chicas y maletas," the film within the film. Almodóvar establishes Martel's link to capital early in the film through mise-en-scène: an image of Martel's Madrid office tower appears behind a close-up of his firm's name, with the word Capital appearing prominently in the foreground. Martel, the director would seem to suggest, is Capital, the new bad guy for late capitalist democratic Spain.

Given its indebtedness to film noir, the film narrative relies upon the antithetical balance of opposing forces: Martel, as the bad father figure, is contrasted with Mateo as good father figure. Aside from the fact that they are both literally fathers, these two male characters are held together symmetrically through their romantic relationships with Lena, whose body becomes the object and intermediary of their battle to possess her. She is also the central object/actor of their films: Mateo's camera seeks to document her, committing her image to film, while Martel at the same time has his son Ernesto Jr. (later Ray X) shoot a documentary of the making of "Chicas y maletas" in order to surveil her.

Lena's body as locus for both filmic/video representation and site of violence is poetically transcribed in a sequence shot at the hospital after Martel—in the film's most overtly noir scene—has pushed her down the stairs. Here Almodóvar pauses narrative development while the camera lingers on several X-Ray images of Lena's bones and skull, thus rendering her insides apparent to the viewer while her physician purportedly documents possible fractures. The X-Ray motif is echoed in the persona of Martel's son, who has chosen for himself the "nombre artístico," Ray X. This emphasis on the X-ray as a motif in the film points to its importance to the viewer's interpretation of the plot. Before returning to my discussion of the Spanish family in the film, I should like to outline briefly some of the historical and theoretical issues that complement Almodóvar's use of X-ray imagery in order to relate it to his reformulation of the family trope. As Jose van Dijck elaborates in *The Transparent Body*, quoting Lisa Cartwright, the X-ray was historically a socially transgressive instrument that "exposed the private interior of women to the gaze of medicine and the public at large" (van Dijck 89).[5] The X-ray was later associated with the idea of a "photography of death," in which the viewer was able to apprehend in the image his or her own mortality:

> Perhaps more than penetrating the flesh to reveal agents of disease, and more than baring the secrets of the heart, Röntgen's new device allowed people to steal a glance at their future fate as a skeleton. The shadows of bones on skiagraphs were strongly associated with mortality; death was imprinted in the living body and X-rays made it visible to the naked eye [van Dijck 93].

Van Dijck elaborates that from its invention by the German physicist Wilhelm Röntgen in 1895, the X-ray was not only perceived as a penetrating technology — making the flesh transparent — but it was "also thought to have predictive qualities: literally foreshadowing man's deadly destination and turning the body into a transcendent object" (94). In the case of *Los abrazos rotos*, the X-ray images that appear so prominently and deliberately after Lena's fall down the stairs serve several purposes. The images not only represent Lena's bones (although we do not see any clear signs of breaking) but also function to prefigure her violent death by car accident in Lanzarote. Further, the X-ray pictures of Lena's skeleton represent the idea of forensic archeology, as they evoke emblematically the unearthing of bones. Indeed, we recall that when the film begins, Lena is already dead, so that these X-rays at once remind the viewer that she is dead (at the present time of Mateo's remembering) while also predicting her future death (from the past point of historical reference). As it is deployed in Almodóvar's film, the X-ray functions to blur the temporality of Lena's life and death, a temporality already rendered opaque by the film's complex narrative structure. Simultaneously, and more abstractly, the X-ray also suggests the photographic erosion of Lena's subjectivity, since by definition the technology works to diminish the cognitive distinction between interior and exterior, rendering — to borrow a phrase from Akira Lippit — her "interiority as photographic phenomenon" ("Phenomenologies" 76).

The X-ray, as representation, offers an illusion of transparency that has important epistemological ramifications. As Lippit details, "the surface of the X-ray opens onto an impossible topography, a space that cannot be occupied by either the subject or object, or rather, a space in which the subject and object are dissolved into a phantasmatic hybrid or emulsion — an *atopos*" ("Phenomenologies" 80). In *Los abrazos rotos*, the impossible topography of the X-ray points to Lena's uncertain ontological status in the film, as she is both alive (in the past) and dead (in the present) yet constantly *made present* in the film through Mateo's memory, the archival footage shot by Ray X in which she appears, and within the film "Chicas y maletas." Lena is literally a ghost made present through the imaging qualities of film and memory.

The X-ray as technology promises the erasure of the dividing line between inside and outside, between the body's limits and its interiority. This uneasy relationship between interior and exterior in fact embodies one of the central paradoxes of *Los abrazos rotos*: we at once see everything of Lena's body, her face, her hair adorned with a variety of wigs, her body dressed in an array of dresses, her bare breasts, even X-rays of her bones, yet at the film's conclusion we are left with very little sense as to who she really is. In this respect she is not only ghostly but also a pathetic figure — a classic noir heroine/victim — who is never able to transcend a somewhat passive role that alternates between photographic and amorous object of Mateo's lenses and of Martel's violent attentions. Lena stands as the film's thematic and structural core, the center of the love triangle upon which the entire flashback narrative relies, but we do not know what makes her tick, even though we are allowed to see her from just about every perspective, including an internal one. It is perhaps more tragic, then, that the film's resolution — in which the nuclear family is reconstituted — relies on her violent death, the breaking of her body, and the dissolution of her self. Almodóvar's new nuclear family is built upon Lena's corpse. Indeed, we recall that Mateo's emergence from the hospital after the accident that has claimed Lena's life is rendered as a full shot of Judit, Mateo and a young Diego standing at the top of the stairs, preparing to descend hand in hand. Mateo survives his ordeal, but after her death Lena becomes a ghost, a phantasm, perceived only through the imaging powers of video and film stock.

In a review of the film Marsha Kinder recalls the final scene: "Mateo, Judit, and Diego sit together in front of a small screen, like a family watching television, enjoying the restored version of the movie" ("Restoring" 34). Yet, they are not *like* a family at all. The three actors represent the very definition of the traditional biological family. If, following Hardcastle, the long pattern of family deviancy in Almodóvar's films suggests a way to restructure a Spanish family "struggling to break free from the rigid legacy of the Francoist family's patriarchy and fascism and searching for alternate relationships based in the equality and tolerance of democracy" (91), what does it mean when the family is structured as a man, a woman, and their biological son? Indeed, given the tradition of family deviancy in Almodóvar's films, what is particularly noteworthy about *Los abrazos rotos* is its apparently *traditional* emphasis on the reformation of a heteronormative family structure. It would seem, in fact, that the only thing deviant about the family appearing at the end of *Los abrazos rotos* is the fact that its existence and functionality are perhaps purely *ad hoc* and therefore dependent on the recovery of the film within the film. The path to family reconstruction is certainly not normal, but in the end we are indeed left with a reconstituted nuclear family. Divorced from official Francoist ideology and Catholic dogma, Mateo Blanco, Diego and Judit function together as an economic unit whose functionality depends on the context of filmmaking. With the death of Martel, the evil capitalist financier, they are able to confront their past, reconcile, and put their movie back together again. Yet, more important than the actual reformation of the nuclear family in *Los abrazos rotos* is the process through which it is reformed: it is through the protagonists' attention to history, to uncovering the past, that makes possible this happy — if problematic — denouement.

It has become nearly impossible to discuss contemporary Spanish culture without referring to the country's authoritarian history and its "miraculous" transition to democracy. And while Almodóvar, especially early in his career, has been widely quoted as insisting that he approaches his moviemaking as if Franco had never existed (Vernon 28), the broader patterns of his filmography would suggest otherwise (Vilarós). What is noteworthy about *Los abrazos rotos* and his earlier *La mala educación*, however, is how both films portray a fictional director very similar to Almodóvar himself who is reflexively engaged in uncovering and understanding the past. This process is thematized in the photography of *Los abrazos rotos*, which draws heavily upon visual contrasts between light and dark. The film's opening and closing scenes, for example, draw attention to light. In the opening title sequence lighting assistants gauge the illumination and orientation of Lena's lighting double relative to the camera, while the final scene foregrounds the movement from light to darkness, as the light filter closes gradually until we only see the brightness of the characters' faces before the fade to total black. The focused light of the monitor in front of Mateo, Judit, and Diego illuminates them as a reconstituted nuclear family unit.

The film's final fade to black at once emphasizes the blindness of the film's central character, while also bringing to bear the question of light as a motif. Earlier in the film, while Mateo and Diego view Ray X's video footage of the accident, an important topic of their discussion is the lighting that made the shooting of the video possible. We also recall the projector in Martel's living room where he views the documentary video shot by his son during the filming of "Chicas y maletas." Blue, green and red are not the primary colors of *painting* but rather are the constituent colors of *light*. The projector, positioned to cast light upon the screen, pointed directly at the camera — and, thus, upon us, the viewers — is part of the apparatus that constitutes cinema itself as a medium of representation and constitutes yet another aspect of the film's reflexive attention to its own status as imaging technology.

The alternating discourse of light and darkness in the film at once points to the generic lineage of *Los abrazos rotos*— inspired as Almodóvar is by the tradition of film noir — while also pointing to the director's concern with uncovering or laying bare the means of cinematic production and representation. This attention to the cinematic apparatus can be associated also with the idea of history put forward in the film, whose plot centers on the shedding light on the past, of making secrets visible or known to its characters and to the audience. The emphasis on light and lighting technologies is linked to the corollary prominence of a variety of other modes of representation and imaging — the X-ray, photography, cartography, video, Braille, painting, silkscreen, DVD, television — all of which point to the various modes of representation through which we represent and make sense of reality. These visual technologies, almost all of which depend upon light for their proper function, reinforce the crucial link between representation and recognition, imaging and knowing in *Los abrazos rotos*.

In *Los abrazos rotos*, representation, reflexivity, and the family motif coalesce in order to visualize the construction of a post-authoritarian Spanish nuclear family. In contrast to the earlier *La mala educación*, *Los abrazos rotos* offers a sunnier ending that hints perhaps that Almodóvar has worked through the terrible issues — family and otherwise — that made *La mala eduación* such a challenging film. *La mala educación* is a dark meditation on subterfuge, violence, and murder that ends ambiguously, while *Los abrazos rotos* would seem to offer a more optimistic perspective on how the shedding of *light* on the past can actually allow a reflexive protagonist to move forward, to work through trauma in order to arrive at a functional present, prepared also for a promising future. In this respect, the film is ultimately optimistic in that it demonstrates how critical historical self-reflection can lead to understanding, recognition, knowledge, and unity.

Keeping in mind the democratic potential that Hardcastle finds in Almodóvar's deviant family narratives, I want to conclude by suggesting that in *Los abrazos rotos* the reconstruction of the Spanish family is also democratic, even as it diverges from the previous pattern of family representations in Almodóvar's films. The movie's *re-formation* of the Spanish family through Judit, Mateo and Diego is purposefully enacted alongside the simultaneous reconstruction of recent Spanish history, and in this way the film calls to mind the ongoing political, social, and cultural efforts to recover historical memory in post–Transition Spain. In the final analysis, *Los abrazos rotos* is a memory text that emphasizes reflexively the importance of shedding light — even when it takes the form of a penetrating, sometimes damaging radiation of the X-ray — on the past and of coming to terms with its traumas. Just as the various modes of representation seen in the film stand for other things, so the final image of Mateo, Judit and Diego would seem to stand for a new Spanish family, damaged by its traumatic past but unified, reformed, reconstructed, refigured, and prepared to move forward into an uncertain post–Transition future.

Marvin D'Lugo has mapped Almodóvar's representation of the central moral instructions of traditional Spanish life — the family, the Church, the law — and elaborated how the director challenges those traditional values through his filmography. In particular, D'Lugo's comments on Almodóvar's use of the police in particular are instructive to my conclusion. Tracing the images of cops from the director's earliest feature length *Pepi, Luci, Bom y otras chicas del montón* (1980) D'Lugo points out that after *¿Qué he hecho yo...?!* the characterization of the police begins to change from "the enforcers of those repressive social and moral codes" (49) to more sensitive empathetic characters who "affirm the very values that historically [they] had blocked and suppressed" (49). D'Lugo concludes that "in positioning the law to witness and valorize murder, gay love, or any of the other countless acts that defy the 'earthly' and 'celestial' powers of the old Spain, Almodóvar's cinema continues to engage its audience in the project of imaging Spain's present by rewriting the social and moral logic of its past" (64). *Los abrazos rotos* marks a similar shift or evolution of the filmmaker's representation of paternal authority in which the understanding sympathetic father, quite in opposition to nearly all fathers in all previous Almodóvar films, is brought into the Almodovarian fold where he becomes, for the first time, a positive presence.

*La mala educación* and *Los abrazos rotos* owe more to the tradition of film noir than to the melodramatic forms that structure Almodóvar's other films. Both films are historical, and both are the director's most self-reflexive films to date. But the questions remain: Why film noir for these rigorously self-reflexive films? What does film noir allow a director to do with historical material? And how does the family figure into these films? Film noir, much like the X-ray, relies on a dual representational scheme that depends on the contrast between black and white, seeing and not seeing, which, in turn, evokes the central motif of the noir worldview: the unseen, unseemly underworld that remains hidden from public view. In an essay on noir and the X-ray, Hugh Manon writes "it is important to account for *chiaroscuro* not solely in terms of affect or mood, but as representing a specific kind of optical structure — the structure of the X-ray — as well as a particular brand of criminal deception" (2). In other words, the lighting schemes that give film noir its distinctive look not only resemble the X-ray, but "they also spell out in visual terms the *noir* criminal's goal of outward suspicion" (2–3). Manon suggests that the "more than meets the eye" cliché that is often associated with the film noir functions not only "as a fuel for paranoia but also more pointedly as an invitation to *see oneself not seeing*" (3). That is, the noir visual style reminds the viewer that the "x-ray-like insight is precisely what average people lack and helps to pinpoint *noir*'s overarching investment in a fantasy of public obliviousness" (3). In *Los abrazos rotos* Almodóvar makes the idea of historical obliviousness visible by laying bare the cinematic apparatus, emphasizing process over final product, and, ultimately, by bringing those techniques to bear on a historical theme. Taken together, *Los abrazos rotos* and *La mala educación* would seem to indicate that when Spain is the country in question, film noir is perhaps *the* genre for historical representation.

In *Los abrazos rotos* Almodóvar establishes a parallel between medical imaging and his own reflexive approach to filmmaking. Further theorizing the X-ray and its importance as representational technology, Lippit has remarked that:

> Given the combined internal and external views of an object made possible in an x-ray image, the viewer is forced to occupy an impossible vantage point — at once

inside and outside. Accordingly, the stability of both the perceiving subject and the perceived object are called into question. The x-ray collapses, as it were, the metaphysical foundation of the senses, the essential dualism that separates interiority from exteriority. In the x-ray, only a faintly perceptible line recalls the former separation of the dimensions of interiority and exteriority, subject and object ["X-ray Files" 6].

The self-reflexive film functions in much the same way, by revealing the traces of a diegetic visible exteriority (plot or story, broadly defined) while rendering transparent its own constituent parts (discourse, apparatus). This kind of film shows itself showing — or images itself imaging — in order to force the viewer to reevaluate his or her status vis-à-vis the film. Much like the metapictures W. J. T. Mitchell analyzes in *Picture Theory*, the self-reflexive film endeavors to explain what films are, and thus to stage the "self-knowledge" of movies (Mitchell 57). In this way, a film like *Los abrazos rotos* is phantasmatic, to use Lippit's term, in that it represents an impossible topography that at once maps itself *and* its own coming into being, so that both appear superimposed upon each other. In much the same way, the Spanish family, as it is reconstituted and imagined in this film, is diagnosed and imaged as through an X-ray. *Los abrazos rotos* functions as an X-ray in which the viewer may perceive a diachronic representation of the historical Spanish family as it has traversed not only the long twentieth century in Spain but also Almodóvar's oeuvre. The director's references to his own work in the film are not merely nostalgia, but instead point to the movement and evolution of the themes and forms of his work as he has progressed as a filmmaker. It is fitting, then, that the most dominant intertextual reference in the film is to *Mujeres al borde de un ataque de nervios* (1988), the film that first gave Almodóvar massive global recognition and established him as Spain's most recognizable auteur.

Mateo, Judit and Diego's voyage to family unity is by no means traditional. Diego is the result of a long-ago Caribbean fling between Mateo and Judit, while out of jealousy Judit betrays Mateo by allowing Martel to sabotage his movie. Judit is thus obliquely responsible for Mateo's blindness and Lena's death. Yet the three central characters emerge from their narrative travails united and ostensibly happy. What makes possible this reformation of a new nuclear family is their shared sensitivity to the importance of acknowledging the past. Shedding light on their past — and, by extension, on Spain's past — leads to their reconciliation and reconstruction of a nuclear family. The allegorical reading of the film family that I am proposing here is supported by the numerous maps of Spain that are visible on the walls of Mateo's office and by the Spanish tourism poster that appears behind Lena as she and Martel confer with Mateo after her injury from the spill down the stairs. These images of Spain engage the viewer in what Tom Conley has called the "locational imagining" that is constitutive of map reading and movie going. Conley posits that in representing maps within their diegesis, "the cinemas turn their places — themes or commonplaces, non-places, any-places-whatsoever, or the locations in which they are shot — into critical spaces" (212) so that "the perception of space [...] calls being into question" (212). In *Los abrazos rotos*, these geographical reminders of the idea of Spain can also be interpreted as highly recognizable global trademarks that brand two of Spain's most marketable and profitable exports: Penélope Cruz and Pedro Almodóvar. But when viewed alongside the film's self-conscious emphasis on memory, history and historical inquiry — the shedding of light on purposefully forgotten events of the past and a concomitant reconciliation — the film acquires a broader allegorical relevance. Pedro Almodóvar made his name as a filmmaker during the 1980s and indeed became known in the critical literature as a synecdoche for a Spanish Transition that sought legitimacy through its own purposeful rejection of the country's past. But the mature Pedro Almodóvar of *Los abrazos rotos* would now seem to stand for a democratic Spain that is more fully engaged with the uncomfortable task of recovering its historical memory and thus acknowledging the violent legacy that belies the rosy picture of its miraculous move into late capitalist modernity. It is instructive, then, that the last moving images that Mateo and Lena view before their tragic accident — these will be literally the final media pictures that Mateo ever sees — are comprised of the scene in Rosellini's groundbreaking historical film, *Viaggio in Italia* (1955), in which its main characters assist in the exhumation of two Pompeian lovers locked in their own final embrace.

Almodóvar's interfilmic quotation of *Viaggio in Italia* is an appropriate method of signaling his film's historical pretensions. As Dudley Andrew writes apropos of the former film, "*Viaggio in Italia* alerts [its protagonists] and us to the possibilities of exchange between past and present, through the manner by which we look and through our response to being looked at, that is, being measured by a living past" (177). Thus, historical memory is a motif that can be unearthed even in the cinematic work of one of Spain's most popular and unapologetically apolitical filmmakers. As Vilarós, D'Lugo, and others have shown, Almodóvar's films have always reflected the time and place of their making, from the exuberance of the 1980s *movida* to the uneven modernization of the 1990s. And now, it would appear that the memory fever that has gripped contemporary Spain manifests itself in the historical framing of *Los abrazos rotos* and the earlier *La mala eduación*. As Spaniards have seen, beginning in 2000 with the unearthing of Franco's mass graves and the ongoing national debate about the recovery of historical memory there, the country's violent, repressive past continues to haunt it, even as it moves forward into the twenty-first century as one of Europe's more spectacular economic and political successes.[6] As Francisco Ferrándiz notes, the exhumations that began and Prioranza del Bierzo and that have continued throughout the country "have thrown into the face of Spanish society a series of uncomfortable and dramatic images of skeletons bearing the imprint of violent death" (312). These exhumations have allowed Spaniards to reevaluate the past through media coverage, reorder national space through commemorative landmarks and rituals, and redraw collective memory through testimony.

*La mala educación* — whose reflexive approach to the reconstruction of a complex past links it structurally and thematically to *Los abrazos rotos* — ends without atonement or forgiveness. There is no working through of its characters' painful memories. The earlier film's protagonist may close the door on the past — obtain closure, even — but what Enrique Goded (Fele Martínez) carries forward with him is an unresolved, hopelessly complex historical consciousness. It is not surprising then, that that film should end in the 1980s as Spain marched happily and obliviously along through its Transition. The lack of real historical reflexivity, the film suggests, made those years a noir fantasy of national obliviousness made possible only by a collective "borradura histórica" (Vilarós 56). *Los abrazos rotos*, on the other hand, envisions a director who has finally acknowledged the importance of confronting his past while recognizing its importance to his own movement into the future. The complex temporal and structural framing of *Los abrazos rotos* draws attention to Almodóvar's new concern with the representation of personal and national historical realities through cinema. At the film's conclusion, Mateo, Judit, and Diego look forward to the reconstruction of Mateo's film at the same time that Mateo comes to terms with Lena's memory. If Lena is Spain — battered, bruised, violated, and ultimately killed — this new nuclear family would seem to represent present-day Spaniards who have, along with Almodóvar himself, perhaps only now begun to revisit their recent history and to acknowledge the skeletons hiding in their collective closet. At the end of the film, as the screen begins its fade to black, Mateo utters the final words of *Los abrazos rotos*: "las películas hay que acabarlas. Aunque sea a ciegas" [films have got to be completed, even if it's blindly]. We might reformulate his statement to reflect the archeological aims of Almodóvar's meta-noir films: historical memory must be faced, even if it's blindly. The only path to recovery for the Spanish family is through responsible and reflexive historical inquiry.

## Notes

1. As Roberta Johnson notes in her book on Carmen Laforet, the concept of family generations is generally useful to novelists and filmmakers because "the family paradigm [not only]

provide[s] a compact microcosm for dealing with a particular society, [but] it [also] lends itself readily to the universalizing dimensions of archetype and myth" (140).

2. Much like his earlier film, *La mala educación*, *Los abrazos rotos* is far too complex to summarize succinctly. In general terms, however, the film centers on a blind film director, Mateo Blanco, who now makes a living as a screenwriter. Over the course of the film he recounts to his assistant's son, Diego, the story of a passionate love affair he had with his lead actress, Lena, in the 1980s. The story is told through a series of flashbacks through which he appears to come to terms with his traumatic past.

3. Manuela, in *Todo sobre mi madre*, has been discussed by many critics in terms of her role as a mother figure (Acevedo-Muñoz, Maddison, Kinder, Martin-Márquez, Smith, Sobrer, Sofair, Zecchi) who "carries the story of the Motherland to Spain's metropolitan centers of Madrid and Barcelona, where she embodies Almodóvar's new super-maternal stereotype for a globalized Spain" (Kinder "Brain Dead" 17). As part of the symbolic geographies of the earlier film, several critics have also analyzed Barcelona itself "as a maternal figure, welcoming the reborn Manuela into the world through her embrace" (Martin-Márquez 2004: 505). Related to the idea of Barcelona as a maternal entity is the journey by train signaling her new beginning in a new city, and a long tunnel which seems to recall a birth canal (Kinder 2004: 17; Martin-Márquez 2004: 504; Acevedo-Muñoz 2004: 29).

4. All translations are my own.

5. That Lena will be the primary object of the film's gaze is clear from the first image, in which the viewer is offered a voyeuristic privileged view of first her body double and then her in the video viewfinder. The black and white tones of that first image suggest a connection with the X-ray images that the viewer sees after she has been pushed down the stairs by Martel.

6. As of this writing, with nearly 20 percent unemployment and a burst housing bubble Spain's economic future would seem to be less than sunny. Perhaps this explains in part Almodóvar's use of the financier Martel as the bad guy.

## WORKS CITED

Acevedo-Muñoz, Ernesto R. "The Body and Spain: Pedro Almodóvar's *All About My Mother*." *Quarterly Review of Film and Video* 21 (2004): 25–38.
Allinson, Mark. *A Spanish Labyrinth*. London: I.B. Tauris, 2008.
"Almodóvar: 'Una familia puede estar formada por transexuales, travestis…'" *El País*, June 8, 2009. <elpais.com>.
Andrew, Dudley. "Film and History." In *The Oxford Guide to Film Studies*, eds. Richard Dyer, E. Ann Kaplan, and Paul Willemen. Oxford: Oxford University Press, 1998, pp. 176–89.
Dijck, Jose van. *The Transparent Body: A Cultural Analysis of Medical Imaging*. Seattle: University of Washington Press, 2005.
D'Lugo, Marvin. "Almodóvar's City of Desire." *Quarterly Review of Film and Video* 13.4 (1991): 47–65.
Ferrándiz, Francisco. "The Intimacy of Defeat: Exhumations in Contemporary Spain." In *Unearthing Franco's Legacy: Mass Graves and the Recovery of Historical Memory in Spain*, eds. Carlos Jerez Farrán and Samuel Amago. Notre Dame, IN: University of Notre Dame Press, 2010, pp. 304–25.
Hardcastle, Anne E. "Family Therapy and Spanish Difference/Deviance in Almodovar's *Tacones lejanos*." In *Spanishness in the Spanish Novel and Cinema of the 20th–21st Century*, ed. Cristina Sanchez Conejero. Newcastle, UK: Cambridge Scholars, 2007, pp. 79–92.
Johnson, Roberta. *Carmen Laforet*. Boston: Twayne, 1981.
Kinder, Marsha. *Blood Cinema: The Reconstruction of National Identity in Spain*. Berkeley: University of California Press, 1993.
\_\_\_\_\_. "Reinventing the Motherland: Almodóvar's Brain-Dead Trilogy." *Film Quarterly* 58 (2004): 9–25.
\_\_\_\_\_. "Restoring *Broken Embraces*." *Film Quarterly* 63.3 (2010): 28–34.

Lippit, Akira Mizuta. "Phenomenologies of the Surface: Radiation-Body-Image." *Collecting Visible Evidence*, eds. Jane M. Gaines and Michael Renov. Minneapolis: University of Minnesota Press, 1999, pp. 65–83.

———. "The X-Ray Files: Alien-ated Bodies in Contemporary Art." *Afterimage* 22.5 (1994): 6.

Maddison, Stephen. "All About Women: Pedro Almodóvar and the Heterosocial Dynamic." *Textual Practice* 14.2 (2000): 265–84.

Manon, Hugh S. "X-Ray Visions: Radiography, *Chiaroscuro*, and the Fantasy of Unsuspicion in *Film Noir*." *Film Criticism* 32.2 (2007-08): 2–27.

Martin-Márquez, Susan. "Pedro Almodóvar's Maternal Transplants: From *Matador* to *All About My Mother*." *Bulletin of Hispanic Studies* 81 (2004): 497–509.

Mitchell, W J. T. *Picture Theory: Essays on Verbal and Visual Representation*. Chicago: University of Chicago Press, 1994.

Rodgers, Eamonn. *Encyclopedia of Contemporary Spanish Culture*. London and New York: Routledge, 2002.

Smith, Paul Julian. *Desire Unlimited: The Cinema of Pedro Almodóvar*, 2d ed. London: Verso, 2000.

———. "Silicone and Sentiment." *Sight & Sound,* September 1999, <http://www.bfi.org.uk/sightandsound/issue/199909/>.

Sobrer, Josep Miquel. "*La gran encisera*: Three Odes to Barcelona, and a Film." *Catalan Review* 18.1-2 (2004): 121–28.

Sofair, Michael. "Reviews: All About My Mother." *Film Quarterly* 55. 2 (2001): 40–47.

Vernon, Kathleen M. "Melodrama Against Itself: Pedro Almodóvar's 'What Have I Done to Deserve This?'" *Film Quarterly* 46.3 (1993): 28–40.

Vilarós, Teresa. *El mono del desencanto: Una crítica cultural de la transición española (1973–1993)*. Madrid: Siglo XXI, 1998.

Zecchi, Barbara. All About Mothers: Pronatalist Discourses in Contemporary Spanish Cinema." *College Literature* 32.1 (2005): 146–64.

# 7

# Recovering Gender
## *Motherhood and Female Identity in* El pájaro de la felicidad *and* Gary Cooper que estás en los cielos

Diana M. Barnes

The sharp decline in Spain's birth rate from one of the highest in the world to one of the lowest within a few short years following Francisco Franco's death in 1975 demonstrates the empowerment of Spanish women to make choices about maternity in modern Spain. Carmen Martín Gaite describes the climate during Franco's dictatorship in which motherhood was made compulsory: "Mediante préstamos a la nupcialidad y los famosos subsidios y leyes de protección a las familias numerosas, Franco se había propuesto remediar el estrago demográfico de aquel millón de muertos.... Y la mujer tenía que ser la primera en pagar el pato" [With loans to the married couple and those famous subsidies and laws protecting large families, Franco proposed to remedy the demographic ravages of war that left a million dead.... And it was the women who were the first to bear that burden] (52).[1] With Franco's death came rapid sociopolitical changes that profoundly impacted the familial status of women.

In two films directed by Pilar Miró, the social and psychological complexities of these changes and their implications for personal choice play out on screen as the main characters redefine their prescribed gender behavior and their relationship with motherhood at different stages of Spain's political Transition. This essay considers self re-definition through exile, geographical and psychological, by examining the roles of female protagonists in *Gary Cooper que estás en los cielos* (1980) and *El pájaro de la felicidad* (1993) against the backdrop of post–Franco Spain. Both films present single female protagonists struggling to achieve autonomy void of the determinants established in a society in which gender roles were strictly defined.[2] The films' thematic representation of the family highlights the gap between the "Franco mother" and the "post–Franco daughter," and more specifically, the deliberate distancing of the daughters from a generation of domestic impositions that they choose to reject. In *El pájaro* Carmen, the protagonist, reconsiders the choices she has made in her life about her role as mother, daughter, wife and lover as she revisits her past and isolates herself from her present. Her quest begins after she is sexually attacked by a group of thugs on the street. After the attack Carmen seeks solace and solitude through inner-exile, emigration and sexual experimentation as she resolves her past and embraces her present in a new emotional and physical territory. She eventually retreats to a remote oceanside village in southern Spain and falls into a sexual relationship with her son's wife. Finally, ironically, Carmen embraces motherhood to care for her grandson.

In *Gary Cooper*, the protagonist, Andrea, a tough-minded, chain-smoking television director, faces her own mortality after she is diagnosed with a potentially deadly cancer. Andrea confronts present and past relationships as she comes to terms with her own fragility. She begins her journey evaluating her identity relative to her disease, and to the people in her life both past and present. Andrea is seen during the three-day period in which the movie's timeline develops, racing through busy streets in her car, traveling metaphorically away from the influence of death, to resolve unfinished business in her past and present. Andrea confronts her relationships with the men in her life, with her mother and finally, with herself. Andrea locates herself physically and emotionally away from the influences of the familiar to find empowerment of choice and self-reconciliation through personal and physical traveling.

In both movies the women are physically violated. Andrea's assault takes the form of a malignant uterine mole that mimics pregnancy. Self-redefinition begins in both films with the protagonists reflecting their history against male influences in their lives. Both women acknowledge unresolved personal, generational and political differences between themselves and their mothers, and both evaluate their ambivalent and, at times, ironic relationship with maternity. Mercedes Sampietro plays the lead role in both films. Jaume Martí-Olivella points out that the two films, and others directed by Miró during this time period "inscribe the political through the personal ... and ... are films that share a confessional tone, a poetic visual style, and the specular gesture of inscribing Miró's own private story in social contexts of general and collective significance" (228).

*Gary Cooper*, produced while Spain was in the throes of its political Transition, highlights the recovery and advent of new civil liberties for women.

The shift toward democracy and women's rights was just beginning and Andrea's character is represented in the sexist society still prevalent in 1980s Spain when only 27 percent of the work force was comprised of women. Journalist and novelist Rosa Montero describes the social ambiance: "The influence of Catholicism, for which sexual difference is divinely ordained, plus the legacy of eight centuries of Arab occupation laid the foundations for a sexism that the Franco period would only aggravate" (381). Miró herself is representative of the "new" woman post–Franco, and elements of her life parallel Andrea's.[3] Both are television directors, suffer from a life-threatening condition, and exhibit strong personalities.[4] Besides their physical ailments, Jesús Angulo sees a lot of Miró in Andrea's character: "Seca, autoritaria, exigente, en ocasiones excesivamente dura, su figura responde a la descripción que muchos de sus colaboradores han hecho de ella" [Dry, authoritative, demanding, on occasion excessively tough, her character corresponds to the way many of her collaborators have described her] (22). Angulo observes similarities that Miró's protagonists share. He points out that neither Carmen nor Andrea tell the people closest to them about their feelings of fear and anger. The elements of silence as well as anger are characteristic to both protagonists' demeanors. It is through their silence that they speak, and through their anger that they find grounds to act.

In her discussion of anger in feminist and maternal terms, Marianne Hirsch writes that a woman's anger frees her of her cultural duties prescribed by society: "A mother cannot articulate anger *as a mother*; to do so she must step out of a culturally circumscribed role which commands mothers to be caring and nurturing to others, even at the expense of themselves" (170). Various emotions are evident in Carmen's character, but a contemplative anger is the most prevalent. Anger can be a point of departure, according to Hirsch: "To be angry, moreover, is to create a space of separation, to isolate oneself temporarily; such breaks in connection, such disruptions of relationships again challenge the role that not only psychoanalysis, but also culture itself assigns to mothers" (170). In Carmen's case, the culture that influenced her and her country for almost 40 years defined motherhood as a sacred requirement ordained not only by the Church, but enforced by the government as well.

After she is raped at the beginning of *El pájaro*, Carmen's anger motivates her to leave her live-in boyfriend and move into a hotel temporarily to a neutral and impersonal space. In this way she begins to separate from what is traditional to her. Before she breaks from her past altogether, she returns to her childhood home in Catalonia, simultaneously finding comfort in the bucolic scenery, and confrontation with her mother as she defends the decisions that directed her life away from family and motherhood. It is not her mother who welcomes her home with open arms rather, it is Carmen's connection to the land. In a compelling series of scenes in *El pájaro* Carmen lies down in the fertile fields of her family's property and contemplates the landscape. She surrounds herself with earthly familiarity to feel the solace of the land. The scenes play out to the melancholic music of Jordi Savall and mark a turning point in the storyline when the protagonist exiles herself from the nurturing reassurance of her land to relocate south to Almería, where nothing is familiar. Carmen travels away from a personal and political past toward a redefinition of who she is as a mature woman in a still young post–Franco society. Her self-imposed physical and psychological exile from all that is and was familiar — her partner, workplace, family — allows her to relocate to a place of liberation from old pains to begin again, however difficult. In his book *Authoritarian Spain 1939–1975: Literature and Inner Exile*, Paul Ilie describes exile: "Territorial exile, as everyone agrees, is experienced emotionally as an unexpected and absurd shock." The paradox of this initial shock is that its "painful and unacceptable wound is fleeting and healed eventually by time" (61).

Carmen's rape may have been pivotal in prompting her to resolve her past with her present, but she had long before broken out of the confines of motherhood. The night she is attacked, Carmen is leaving her estranged son's apartment. It was their first encounter in a number of years, and his invitation to dinner came with a request for money. Carmen is not "maternal" toward her son or her new grandson. She had left her son and his father years before and had distanced herself from her only child. Carmen's rejection of motherhood is apparent also in her absolute lack of "maternal instincts" when Nani, her son's wife, asks her to hold her grandson for the first time. Carmen does not know what to do with the infant and is clearly uncomfortable with him in her arms.

Carmen is already an enigma in Francoist Spain. Viewers realize quickly that the protagonist, who was developed specifically for film 17 years after Franco's death, is not born of the dictator's ideologies. This is evident particularly when she rejects her role as mother and wife, and further, when she focuses inward as subject rather than outward upon the needs of those around her. The development of the plot reaffirms this, as Angulo points out that Carmen is the subject around which every other character revolves. There are no subplots that stand on their own: "la protagonista se ve rodeada de una serie de personajes sin ninguna entidad propia. Absolutamente todos ellos no existen más que en función de Carmen, como desencadenantes de una serie de reacciones por su parte" [The protagonist is surrounded by a range of characters with no entity of their own. Absolutely none of them exist except in relation to Carmen, as descendents of a series of reactions on her part] (30).

Carmen, representative of the rising number of professional women joining the workforce of the 1980s, is financially independent and is afforded the opportunity to focus on her own needs. But Miro's professional female characters are not typical of the majority of Spanish women at the time, as pointed out in *Contemporary Spanish Cinema*:

> The reduction of financial worries and the logistical difficulties of domestic arrangements permit these women and the films they protagonise to focus attention on the psychological and philosophical problems associated with a range of female experiences, but they fail to address the more pragmatic obstacles to female autonomy, which are the reality for the vast majority of women [129–130].

Carmen is subjected to the same social expectations as other women who grew up during Franco's era, reduced during the rape scene to a one-dimensional being: woman/sexual object as the perpetrator shoves her against her car while another man holds her so she can not fight back. Carmen keeps her eyes on her attacker's face but doesn't call out. Another member of the gang, impatient and anxious, yells "vámonos ya, puede ser tu madre" [Let's go already, she could be your mother] (*El pájaro* 6) as though she were hardly worth the effort. Interestingly, in the written script, the line is "pero, macho; es una tía vieja, un deshecho ... te estás follando a tu madre. ¡Venga!" [but, man; she's an old lady, not worth it, ... you're fucking your mother. Come on!] (*El pájaro* 6). Although the filmed scene plays out slightly differently in dialogue than the script, it is telling that as a "mother" she should be rejected as old and untouchable. It is the last thing said in this scene, leaving Carmen with the label of "mother," physically violated and left in the dark with no purse, no identification, alone. The combination of factors may be interpreted as symbolic of what woman as object, is to Transitional, post–Franco Spain, whose emblematic "woman-mother" was rejected along with Francoist dogma and eventually transformed. While Franco's Spain charged women with the social obligation of upholding post–Civil War ideologies through procreation and strict Catholic rituals, she produced one of the highest birth rates in Europe.

The ambivalence of the term "mother" at the end of this scene represents the paradoxical situation in which Carmen finds herself. Even though she has rejected motherhood, gained financial independence, and fulfilled her social responsibility by supporting her son financially, she is still demeaned as a "mother" by one man and chastised as a mother by another. Carmen's son Enrique relays his feelings to her in the following scene: "Dejé de veros porque siempre estabáis ocupados. Dejé de escribirte porque nunca me contestabas. Me fui de casa mucho después de darme cuenta de que era un estorbo" [I stopped seeing you because you were always busy. I stopped writing to you because you never answered me. I left home long after I realized I was a nuisance] (*El pájaro* 4).

Not only had Carmen rejected her own maternal role with her son, but also later, at her mother's table, she rejects her position in the family by opposing her mother's ideologies first by arguing with her, and then through silence. Throughout the movie, the element of silence is present in distinct forms. First, after the rape scene, Carmen returns to her apartment and finds it empty. She does not go to the police and report her attack, and she does not discuss it with her live-in boyfriend Fernando. Unaware that she has been violated, Fernando leaves her to attend a party, and she wanders silently around her rambling apartment, the sequence of scenes set off by close-up shots of her determined gaze. In the apartment, Carmen pulls a book off a shelf to read the underlined words of a poem written by Ángel González. She reads "Si yo fuese Dios y tuviese el secreto, haría un ser exacto a ti" [If I were God and privy to the secret I would make a being exactly like you] (González 137).[4] Perhaps the lines were highlighted in honor of a lover, but in this instance, I believe Carmen looks for her own redemption, "ti" being her other self, the one she will recreate. The remainder of the poem, unread in the movie, ends: "Escucho tu silencio. Oigo constelaciones: existes. Creo en ti. Eres. Me basta" [I listen to your silence. I hear constellations: you exist. I believe in you. You are. That's enough for me] (González 137).

This "other" self that Carmen knows to exist, listens to and desires to evolve into, is born as a resolution to the conflict of the plot through abjection of self brought on by the violation she experiences. Abjection, a feeling of degradation and humiliation, are not uncommon symptoms of rape, and are part of a wide range of emotions rape victims may experience (*The Female Fear* 41). Julia Kristeva, in *Powers of Horror: An Essay on Abjection*, identifies abjection as an "inescapable boomerang, a vortex of summons and repulsion [that] places the one haunted by it literally beside himself" (1). Carmen is beside herself figuratively as she struggles to come to terms with who she is in her own eyes rather than through family or social arrangement. Through her own silence Carmen identifies her aloneness, her singleness, with retrospective gazes, not necessarily reflective through mirror images of herself, but rather inward gazes.

In her article "La mirada de la mujer y la mujer mirada: En torno al cine de Pilar Miró" Begoña Siles examines the melancholic gaze in both *El pájaro* and *Gary Cooper* through Freud's treatment of melancholy as a symptom of pain. Siles suggests that Miró's plots in general address Freud's analysis of profoundly painful states of mood: "Los personajes que transitan por la narración sienten ese abismo de tristeza, ese dolor incomunicable que les agrieta por dentro hasta hacerles perder el gusto por cualquier palabra, por cualquier acto, inclusive, el gusto por la vida" [The characters who travel through the narrative feel this abyss of sadness, this incommunicable pain that rips them apart inside to the point that they lose their desire for any word, any act, even for life itself] (7). Siles attributes Carmen's deep sadness to the attack she suffered, and Andrea's to the cancer growing in her uterus, suggesting that all of Miró's works have, as a common thread, this same melancholic overtone prompted by a profound negative experience: "Todas estas experiencias quiebran la existencia controlada y plácida en la que vivían los personajes de la obra de Pilar Miró. La herida abierta vislumbra la fragilidad de la vida y empuja a los sujetos hacia la penumbra de lo inexplicable" [All of these experiences shatter the placid and controlled existence within which the characters in Pilar Miro's films lived. The open wound sheds light on the fragility of life and pushes the subjects toward the semidarkness of the inexplicable] (Siles 7).

The "penumbra" [semidarkness] and the "inexplicable" [inexplicable] to which Siles refers, is a place with which Carmen does not identify. The night she is attacked she writes a letter to Fernando from her hotel room, confirming the break in their relationship: "Quiero buscar a mi marido, quizás a mis padres.... Seguramente debería buscarme a mí. Perdida en mi trabajo intentando sobrevivir" [I want to look for my husband, maybe my parents.... Surely I should look for myself, lost in my work trying to survive] (*El pájaro*). Her writing is interjected with camera shots of Carmen's expression of sad contemplation as she puts words to paper, preparing to outline a commitment she is making to herself. Indeed, as the plot unfolds, Carmen fulfills all of the designs, beginning with a trip home to see her parents, and finally, conquering loneliness by embracing it, and redesigning her identity. Still, it is through rejection and abjection that Carmen reaches resolution.

In Ripoll, the home of her youth, Carmen is faced with what is most familiar to her, knowing what her family's expectations are for her. It is in this setting where silence is used as an undertone to set the mood of many of the scenes. Whether forced upon her because of the impossibility of communication, as in the case with her mother, or by design because the small, country town provides a peaceful venue for her to contemplate her future. It is from this quiet juncture that Carmen begins to find inroads to a new identity for herself on her own terms and in her own language. This point of departure for Carmen allows her to construct a new set of parameters within which gender acknowledgement is absolutely original. This is one of the most powerful feminist paradigms that the movie demonstrates as Carmen is free of the cultural ramifications of gender-fixing. Simply put, she no longer hears the rote conscriptions that restricted her for so many years.

The confrontation at Carmen's home between mother and daughter is notable on several levels. There is no point of agreement between the two, no real communication. In fact, they speak different languages, representative of generational differences between the mother, who spouts Francoist rhetoric in Castilian, and her daughter, who speaks to her parents mostly in Catalan, the language of her mother's youth. The clash between the mother and daughter is symbolic of the fissure between two female generations indoctrinated by different social and political influences. Carmen's mother complied with her civil duties to raise her children according to the government's strict social code and to tend to her house, home and husband. Montero describes the phenomena:

> The fact that the social and cultural advances gained by women in Europe over the last fifty years (since the Second World War) have, in the case of Spain, been compressed into the last two decades and has created a very special situation. First, as we have seen with regard to women entering employment, there are two Spains: the 50+ age group ... tends to have much more traditional values and lifestyles [382].

Considering the 1995 date of publication of *Spanish Cultural Studies*, a more accurate age group to date would be a 60+ age group. Further, an additional demarcation between the two groupings can be divided amongst professional and university graduates.

Carmen, a member of the under–60 age group, represents the grouping of women who abandoned their mother's Spain to forge new ground for women. Carmen's mother laments that she misses the days when strict rules defined the role of the mother. The mother and daughter are at political and personal odds, with the mother complaining about the new socialist regime that came into power after Franco's death. Carmen defends her position as an independent woman who has rejected her identity as "mother."

> Carmen — Estudié, aprendía, trabajé, me casé, tuve un hijo. Y viví hasta ahora de mi esfuerzo.
> Madre — De momento no tienes marido, ni hijo, ni nadie. Algo harías mal.
> Carmen — Muchas cosas... O bien. Depende de como se mire.

> [Carmen: I studied, I learned, I worked, I got married, I had a son. I lived up until now by my own efforts.
> Madre: As of now you have no husband, no son, no one. You did something wrong.
> Carmen: A lot of things... Or well. It depends on how one looks at it] [El *pájaro* 29].

Here, even more so than in *Gary Cooper*, the clash of gender-culture becomes relevant to what Martí-Olivella refers as Miró's "making the private into a public story" (215) in that the far-reaching Francoist agenda that guided Carmen's mother ruptured with the Dictator's death. Carmen's rejection of the dogma of her mother's generation has broken a sacred mother/daughter bond. That is, the private implications of Carmen's rejection of not only motherhood itself, but of her mother as well, fracture the very public political agenda of the Franco era.

Nancy Chodorow, in *The Reproduction of Mothering*, refers to mothering as a phenomenon that "occurs through social structurally induced psychological processes. It is neither a product of biology nor of intentional role-training" (7). Changes in social structure specific to gender organization within Spanish culture before and after Franco's death, retarded (in terms of Franco's ideology) Carmen's desire and ability to mother. She has to redefine who she is before she can acknowledge the maternal aspects of her gender. Chodorow explains, "women, as mothers, produce daughters with mothering capacities and the desire to mother. These capacities and needs are built into and grow out of the mother-daughter relationship itself" (7). Since Carmen has no relationship with her mother, she has none of what Chodorow considers to be a "social structurally induced psychological process" (7).

Carmen rejects her past with a sense of finality after spending long afternoons roaming her family's property with her father, with whom she speaks Catalan and with whom she mainly converses about the natural regenerating features of earth and specifically, the land he harvests for trees and fruits. These are conversations about rebirth that are fit for a man; talk about farming and soil are not traditionally women's talk, but symbolic that Carmen's relationship with her father allows her to contemplate regeneration at a basic level rather than within the gender-specific discourse that defines her relationship with her mother. It is in this quiet setting, between Carmen and her father, amongst the fruits of his labor, that she is liberated from a painful past.

Until that point, we see Carmen identified as woman/mother/victim, and now she will disassociate herself from those labels and elemental constructs of womanhood described in *Elemental Passions* by Luce Irigaray as a dependency upon men that dates to the divine:

> Because of this dependency, woman is submitted to all kinds of trials: she undergoes multiple and contradictory identifications, she suffers transformations of which she is not aware, since she has no identity, especially no divine identity.... Quite apart from any explicit violence on the part of men (incest, rape, prostitution, assault, enslavement) woman is subjected to a loss of identity which turns love into a duty, a pathology, an alienation for her [2].

Irigaray suggests that in order to self-identify, women work toward becoming men's equals. In opposing her mother, this is precisely what Carmen strives for, and is paradoxically able to achieve in her relationship with her father on neutral ground of discerning discourse. The paradox arises because the father at once embodies (literally) the fundamental patriarchal family construction that Carmen wholly rejects, while providing her with a place for her own self-achievement void of those same constructs. While Carmen leaves her family home with her childhood and adolescent memories, she takes with her what she has achieved as an adult, and what allows her to function independently; her work as an art restorer.

The portrayal of both Carmen in *El pájaro* and Andrea in *Gary Cooper* as strong female subjects, provide spectators with a film structured differently than the traditional Hollywood product, home of the male gaze described by Laura Mulvey.[5] In her chapter "Woman as Image, Man as Bearer of the Look," Mulvey writes, "In a world ordered by sexual imbalance, pleasure in looking has been split between active/male and passive/female" (62).

In both films, through prolonged camera shots of Sampietro's face, at times expressionless, the spectator sees the personality of the character disappear as her expression becomes serious and thoughtful, as though her thoughts are drifting, traveling to some far off place. Close-up, lengthy camera shots of the actress's face show closed-mouth expressions of anger and melancholy. The lingering camera shot is symbolic of a silence that for decades was imposed upon women in a society where their voice was heard only within a domestic setting and even then, only when allowed. It also shuts down verbal communication from the actress to the audience, leading the spectators to understand that she is traveling internally, thoughtfully to a place of emotional exile. Ilie describes exile as a state of mind: "To live apart is to adhere to values that do not partake in the prevailing values; he who perceives this moral difference and who responds to it emotionally lives in exile" (2). First Andrea, and then thirteen years later Carmen, remove themselves from the "prevailing values" to a place of inner sanction that is at once physical and emotional. Ilie points out that exile is not limited to physical displacement: "It is also a set of feelings and beliefs that isolate the expelled group from the majority" (2). Ilie writes this in regard to Spain's shifting migration patterns and exile trends during and following the Civil War, but the premise also informs the idea that through exile, Carmen and Andrea reject the enduring conditions that influenced gender behavior within the family and the workplace.

As evidenced by Miró's films, and explained in an article by Isolina Ballesteros, in her article "El desplazamiento del centro y la despersión de los márgenes" [Displacement of the Center and Dispersion of the Margins], the representation of women in film began to change post–Franco:

> empieza a abandonar en las pantallas el pasivo papel de objeto de la mirada masculina, y pasa a ser sujeto de la acción (y de la dirección cinematográfica), se aleja del asignado espacio de lo doméstico y se hace visible en el exterior; cuestiona su función en períodos históricos señalados y se presenta como víctima principal de la represión franquista, dando relevancia a temas, hasta ahora tabús, como el divorcio o el aborto.
>
> [she begins to abandon the on-screen passive role of the object of the male gaze, and becomes a subject of the action (and of cinematographic direction), distancing

herself from the assigned domestic space to become visible on the outside; she questions her function in pointed political periods presenting herself as the principal victim of Francoist repression, giving relevance to themes, and even taboos, such as divorce and abortion] [4].

In *Gary Cooper* Andrea's subjectivity extends this change in representation to an appearance that could be considered androgynous. Throughout the film Andrea strives to be treated, as Irigaray has suggested, as an equal to men: "Ha adoptado una estética masculina que simboliza poder en el espacio público y protesta contra las definiciones restrictivas de la feminidad" [She has adopted a masculine aesthetic that symbolizes power in a public space and protests the restrictive definitions of femininity] (Ballesteros *La mirada* 34). Miró re-identifies femininity by stripping her character of any overt feminine behavior or presentation prescribed by Franco society. Thus, the Miró paradigm trumps the Franco paradigm with a purpose so that femininity is redefined through an active desire to reject Francoist ideals, particularly specific to maternal requirements. It is with long, silent stretches of unfocused gazes aimed introspectively that Andrea achieves a self-awareness and internal self-identification. Rikki Morgan suggests that this silence, conveyed by Andrea's refusal to communicate her fears to those around her, stems from "a tacit denunciation of the inadequacy of the language of patriarchy to express her feelings" (190). Morgan also acknowledges that Andrea defines who she is through "her relationship with other people" (180), and recognizes the irony of Andrea's need to self-identify through others "since she remains dependent on others for recognition and confirmation of that image" (184). Morgan examines this within the context of "Sartre's argument that, as individuals simultaneously struggle to establish their own consciousness and self-image as dominant, they are also dependent for confirmation of their dominance on conscious recognition by others: 'I can know myself only through the mediation of the other'" (184). Morgan cites Sartre's contention that in an effort to project a specific image to others, the true self may be lost or replaced or concealed by a false image. She asserts "such behavior constitutes an abdication of responsibility to the real self ... and thus poses an obstacle to Being-for-Itself" (182). In other words, by reflecting her identity off of others, Andrea risks losing what is basic to her identity because her identity is dependent upon others' input. However, both Carmen and Andrea exhibit a desire to locate "individualness" within. Perhaps by experiencing the influence of death in her own life, Miró has projected upon both of her female protagonists the same "individualness" she may have felt facing the ultimate solitude of death, thereby stripping them of their socially/culturally prescribed maternal identifiers in order to exist in a solitary position.

It is meaningful that Andrea's cancer is in her uterus and mimics pregnancy, manifested physically in exaggerated signs of morning sickness. Before her cancerous mole was discovered, Andrea believed she was pregnant, and had decided to keep the baby. When she chooses motherhood, it is not available to her. The biological and cultural conscriptions that identify her woman-gender are denied to her. Influenced by death, Andrea views her life from a point unreachable by the rest of the population. The two factors, death and gender, allow for the birth of a character who is of an atypical female gender and mindset. Morgan emphasizes the influence of urgency and the role that the theme of death plays in the film. She points out that the television production that Andrea directs is *Huis Clos* and that it is based on Sartre's theories on consciousness. One might consider as well that Andrea's character contains parallel elements to that of Pablo Ibbieta in Sartre's short story "The Wall" (1939). In the short story Pablo experiences a profound philosophical evolution of his conscious ability to identify and interpret the world around him acknowledging his impending death by a firing squad of Spanish Nationalists during the Spanish Civil War. In Pablo's case, rather than sharing in the collective fear of the others sentenced to die with him, he reevaluates reality altogether in the most basic terms. He spends his last night contemplating his relationship to the world and deconstructing what he once considered familiar. Pablo talks about the beauty of the sky as seen from his small holding cell after he is given his death sentence: "But it wasn't like it had been: the night before I could see a great piece of sky from my monastery cell and each hour of the day brought me a different memory.... But now I could watch the sky as much as I pleased, it no longer evoked anything in me. I liked that better" (Sartre 7). Pablo is stripped of what he believed to be his identity. He becomes uncommunicative and finds objects absurd, as though no longer attached to the constraints of worldly acknowledgment.

While Morgan suggests that Andrea is uncommunicative because patriarchal discourse is inadequate to convey her feelings and thoughts (178), I believe that while that plays to the feminine aspect of the conflict her cancer produces, moreover she is silent because words become too strictly associated with prescribed meaning in general and because in a sense, words just do not matter anymore. Communicating even with her boyfriend is ineffective. For example, when Andrea tries to explain her medical condition to Mario, he misinterprets what she is trying to say and offers to accompany her to London for an abortion. Mario and Andrea more than ever fail to communicate. When he believes he has the right to make decisions regarding the consequences of Andrea's maternity, *simplifying* her condition to pregnancy, the differences between the two are compounded. He functions in a man's world, the public sphere of the workplace. He is alive, feeling a great distance between himself and his own mortality. With death all around him in the stories he covers and even a terrorist death threat against him, Mario becomes more certain of his "aliveness" because his threat is not internal or fixed to a certain hour. He is extroverted and communicative, in control of his voice and supposedly, of his future.

Andrea, on the other hand, faced by her own death, feels vulnerable to it, less powerful in its grip. This is indicated by her unwillingness to communicate, an indication that her fight is over. She has, although not to the same degree as Sartre's Pablo, given in to the possibility of her own mortality. This is apparent particularly when she examines her naked body in front of the mirror, asking of it: "¿Te vas a morir? ¿Te vas a hacer esa cabronada? [Are you going to die? Are you going to fucking do that?] (*Gary Cooper*). The camera moves slowly, following her hand as it moves across her body and down below her navel. The shots portray her body, through close-up, contained views, asexually, identifying her gender without erotic sexuality as she passes her hand above the area where her cancer is growing. The question she poses, in the reflexive, indicates her own close involvement with the consequences, but is paradoxical because the question itself is aimed at her body, portrayed hygienically but not without gender identifiers. Andrea addresses her body as though it were detached, viewing it externally and considering its gender.

While Andrea's character is presented purposefully away from the emblematic Spanish woman-figure of the Franco era, the male characters of the movie enhance her lack of emblematic "Spanishness" by being presented in typical masculine fashion. Mario, for example, along with other male roles in the film, represents "typical" male personality traits. He has an affair with a woman while considering reuniting with Andrea. Julio, another male character in the movie, complains that his live-in girlfriend wants him to cut ties with his wife. Both Julio and Mario, the male characters with whom Andrea has had recent sexual relationships, present the popular notion that men are disloyal. The fact that Andrea's character does not represent popular gender culture roles highlights her behavior as unique to a patriarchal point of view. Miró explains her purpose in directing a film in which traditional gender roles and expectations are ruptured: "Tenía necesidad de hacer una cosa de este tipo y ver qué pasaba. En España el cine ha salido de la comedia o de la farsa ... no se consiguen plantear los problemas de un modo serio y haciendo una introspección profunda en nuestra propia manera de ser" [I needed to do something like this to see what would happen. Spanish film has developed out of the comedy or the farce ... it does not present real issues seriously with deep introspection that represent who we are] (Morgan 34).

The real issues put forth by Miró in both films presented in this chapter reflect an evolution of the same character. Both women face personal challenges and both encounter problems communicating with their mothers and with the men in their lives. The scene between Andrea and her mother demonstrates how different the two generations are in their perception of their social roles. When Andrea asks her mother for 120,000 pesetas, her mother directs Andrea to ask her brother for it because she is old and unable to understand money matters, as though her generation wasn't taught such things. When Andrea visits her mother, the older woman scolds her for carrying the wrong purse, wearing the wrong shoes and sporting a necklace that looks foreign. Andrea does not inform her of her pending surgery. Searching for a common ground with her mother, Andrea asks, "Si de verdad creyeras que te vas a morir mañana, ¿qué me dirías?" [If you truly believed you were going to die tomorrow, what would you say to me?] (*Gary Cooper*). The older woman does not answer. Andrea finds no protection or support from her mother. Her attempt to reach an earnest and genuine level of communication with her is remarkable in that it is the first and possibly the only time in the film that Andrea exposes her emotional vulnerability to another person, other than to her former lover at the end of the film. The absolute lack of response from her mother, incapable of sensing her own daughter's desperation, shows the depth of the lack of connection between the two women that transgresses social, political and cultural ground. Andrea's mother peers at her daughter from across the room through her opera glasses instead of moving toward her to literally close the gap between the two women. It is poignant that even with close examination, she recognizes only Andrea's outward appearance.

The familial construct presented by Miró in the two movies evolved considerably from the time that Andrea's mother was a young woman, and portrays the sociopolitical changes during the Spain's Transition and even later. Andrea, in 1980, presents a serious, intelligent, independently capable single woman. Meanwhile, in *El pájaro*, Carmen, at an untraditional age, under untraditional circumstances, mothers her grandson after engaging in a homosexual relationship with her daughter-in-law. The plot development reflected the mood of the country, as well as legislation that changed the way men and women live. With Carmen, Miró sheds light on what would become a landmark law in Spain. In 2005 it became the third country, along with Holland and Belgium, to legalize gay marriage. By the time *El pájaro* was produced, the *Ley de Peligrosidad Social* [Law of Social Danger] had been repealed and the country's first lesbian public demonstration was held in 1987 (Hooper 121). That protest was prompted by the arrests of two gay women for kissing in public. Hooper writes, "That year, on 28 June, lesbian activists staged a 'kiss-in' in the Puerta del Sol, the square which has always been Madrid's rallying point, and it became an annual event" (121).

Martí-Olivella suggests that the homosexual relationship between the older Carmen and young daughter-in-law Nani, in *El pájaro*, undermines the established national patriarchal narrative: "The homoerotic bonding between Carmen and Nani clearly threatens the stability of the fraternal (even the fraticidal/Cainite) model of Spain's national narrative" (*Refiguring Spain* 218). While it is clear that the female-female relationship questioned national gender patterns, it also created a new space for gender questions on a personal level for the character. The homoerotic relationship separates Carmen further from the typified female constructed and thereby construed by masculine identifiers. Carmen, through the lesbian relationship, recreates who she is in terms of gender, not necessarily in terms of sexuality. By experiencing a sexual relationship with another woman, she is free of the patriarchal dominion over her body and is free to self-identify through a new, closer reflection of self.

Considering that, following the homoerotic relationship, Carmen embraces maternity and experiences a selflessness not previously seen in her character, the threat to patriarchal narrative to which Martí-Olivella refers, is played out in a paradoxical development. In a patriarchal society, particularly considering Spain's recent history at the time the film was produced, Carmen is where she is "supposed" to be. She is raising a son, selflessly taking on the enormous task that belongs to her daughter-in-law. The difference is that she is raising her grandson on her own terms, in her own body, self-identified by a woman within a woman's parameters.

In conclusion, as we look more generally at the protagonists in these films we see that Carmen, at the end of *El pájaro*, appears to have achieved her goal. For her, "sola" means without a partner, not without motherhood. Andrea, however, does not fulfill her desire to become a mother, and in fact, the outcome of the film is unresolved. One might draw a metaphor between the collective mood of the country at the outset of the Transition and the unresolved conclusion of *Gary Cooper* and the end of the Transition and the final scene of *El pájaro*. Andrea's future is uncertain, offering more questions for her than answers. Her health is precarious and her personal relationships unsupportive. Andrea looks to a strong male influence from her past for support and comfort, knowing that he unavailable. In the end she is alone and relies upon strangers to save her life as she undergoes a risky surgery.

The women in both films are influenced by an anxiousness caused by a sense of finality in their lives; they express a desire for independence driven by a need to avoid victimization. Carmen states, "procuraré una felicidad sola sin nada que pueda hacerme daño[T18]" [I will endeavor to find happiness alone without anything that can hurt me] (*El pájaro*) and Andrea declares, "quiero no necesitar a nadie para no quedarme decepcionada" [I want to not need anyone so that I am not left deceived] (*Gary Cooper*). Andrea and Carmen guard themselves against phantom or real aggressors metaphorically representative of the patriarchal society in which both women lived. The very portrayal of the protagonists as subject figures in films directed by a woman demonstrates the changes that were taking place in the arts and in society in Spain during Spain's Transition.

## Notes

1. This and all other translations from Spanish to English in this chapter are my own.
2. In his book *The New Spaniards*, 2d ed., John Hooper elaborates upon this, citing the Spanish civil code article 57. He points out that without her husband's approval, a wife cannot "initiate legal proceedings, enter into contracts, or buy and sell goods. She could not even undertake a journey of any length without her husband's approval" (126).
3. Pilar Miró is considered a pioneer for her work in Spain's film industry. An award winning screenwriter, Miró was director of state television as a member of the Ministry of Culture between 1982 and 1986.
4. Pilar Miró suffered from heart disease and had surgery twice during her adult life to replace and repair valves in her heart. Miró died in 1997 from heart problems at age 57.
5. Laura Mulvey's cinematic gaze was a prevalent consideration following the publication of her book in 1975, and was applied widely in literary criticism during this time.

## Works Cited

Angulo, Jesús. "El cine de Pilar Miró." *Nosferatu: Revista de Cine* 28 (September 1988): 18–32.
Ballesteros, Isolina. *Cine (ins)urgente: textos fílmicos y contextos culturales en la España postfranquista*. Madrid: Fundamentos, 2001.
\_\_\_\_\_. "El desplazamiento del centro y la dispersión de los márgenes en dos películas de la transición: *Gary Cooper que estás en los cielos* (1980) *y Deprisa, deprisa* (1980)." *Anuario de cine y literatura en español* (1995): 3–16.
Chodorow, Nancy. *The Reproduction of Motherhood*. Berkeley: University of California Press, 1978.
*¡Cría cuervos!* Dir. Carlos Saura. Perf. Geraldine Chaplin, Ana Torrent. Home Vision Cinema, 1975.
*Gary Cooper, que estás en los cielos...* Dir. Pilar Miró. Perf. Mercedes Sampietro, Jon Finch, Carmen Maura. Cine Español, 1980.
González, Ángel. "Me basta así." *El grupo poético de los años 50: Una antología*, ed. Juan Garcí Hortelano. Madrid: Reimpresiones, 1983, pp. 56–57.
Hirsch, Marianne. *The Mother/Daughter Plot: Narrative, Psychoanalysis, Feminism*. Bloomington: Indiana University Press, 1989.
Hooper, John. *The New Spaniards*, 2d ed. New York: Penguin, 2006.
Ilie, Paul. *Literature and Inner Exile: Authoritarian Spain*. Baltimore: John Hopkins University Press, 1980.
Irigaray, Luce. *Elemental Passions*. Trans. Joanne Collie and Judith Still. New York: Routledge, 1992.
Jordan, Barry, and Rikki Morgan-Tamosunas. *Contemporary Spanish Cinema*. Manchester and New York: Manchester University Press, 1998.
Kristeva, Julia. *Powers of Horror: An Essay on Abjection*. Trans. Leon S. Roudiez. New York: Columbia University Press, 1982.
Marti-Olivella, Jaume. "Regendering Spain's Political Bodies: Nationality and Gender in the Films of Pilar Miró and Arantxa Lazcano." In *Refiguring Spain Cinema/Media/Representation*, ed. Marsha Kinder. Durham, NC, and London: Duke University Press, 1997, pp. 215–238.

Martín Gaite, Carmen. *Usos amorosos de la postguerra española*. Barcelona: Editorial Anagrama, 1987.
Montero, Rosa. "Gender and Sexuality: The Silent Revolution: The Social and Cultural Advances of Women in Democratic Spain." In *Spanish Cultural Studies: An Introduction The Struggle for Modernity*, ed. Helen Graham and Jo Labanyi. Oxford: Oxford University Press, 1995, pp. 381–395.
Morgan, Rikki. "Female Subjectivity in *Gary Cooper que estás en los cielos.*" In *Spanish Cinema: The Auteurist Tradition*, ed. Peter William Evans. New York: Oxford University Press, 1999, pp. 177–193.
Mulvey, Laura. "Visual Pleasure and Narrative Cinema." In *Feminist Film Theory: A Reader*, ed. Sue Thornham. New York: New York University Press, 1999, pp. 57–68.
*El pájaro de la felicidad*. Dir. Pilar Miró. Perf. Mercedes Sampietro, Aitana Sanchez Gijón, Luís Homer, Mari Carmen Prendes. 1993.
Rich, Adrienne. *Of Woman Born: Motherhood as Experience and Institution*. New York: Norton, 1986.
Sartre, Jean-Paul. *The Wall*, 7th ed. New York: New Directions, 1948.
Siles, Begoña. "La Mirada de la Mujer y la Mujer Mirada. En torno al cine de Pilar Miró." *Razón y Palabra* 46 (August-September 2005): 1–20.

# 8

# Picking a Fight with Domestic Violence
## *New Perspectives on Patriarchy in Contemporary Spanish Cinema*

PAUL BEGIN

In spite of the sharp changes in the family brought on by immigration, social and geographic mobility, sharply declining birth rates, the demographic shift of women in terms of education and the workforce, economic pressures, birth control, new legislation and changing attitudes toward divorce and gay marriage, Spaniards are not moving toward a post-family phase in which nuclear families are abandoned in favor of what Anny Brooksbank Jones has (perhaps cynically) labeled "nuclear consumer units" (389). Rather, as we can observe via current debates over gay marriage and adoption, the family is increasingly a question of semantics, one in which the notion of the nuclear family no longer signifies three generations of family members living under the same roof with an abundance of children, which we know was promoted as the dominant model throughout the Franco years, though it was not the only model in practice (Brooksbank Jones 388). And as notions of what constitute the family fluctuate over time so do notions of patriarchy. We could site, for example, the numerous accounts of how shifts in workplace demographics and parenting responsibilities have impacted the way in which we understand patriarchy, with more men being called upon to share responsibilities if not take on entirely the role of primary caregiver.[1] Similarly, as workplace values have changed with regard to male-female relationships so have family expectations in terms of comportment as men and patriarchs. This evolving face of patriarchy has logically impacted or been impacted by representations of patriarchy on screen, particularly in the case of a recent series of Spanish films dealing with the here-and-now of contemporary society. The purpose of this essay is to consider the transformations in patriarchy in light of some of the social changes mentioned above through their representation in three recent films, *La buena estrella* (1997) by Ricardo Franco, *El bola* (Achero Mañas, 2000), and *Te doy mis ojos* (2003) by Icíar Bollaín. More than simply presenting the ways in which these films represent patriarchy, the one specific aim is to evaluate these films as constructs that contribute, consciously or not, directly or indirectly, to a larger social discourse about the changing face of Spanish patriarchy through an engagement with realism.

Before moving forward it will be useful to clarify two issues; first my use of the term realism and second, certain assumptions vis-à-vis the function of cinema within the context of social discourse in Spain. The term realism brings with it a whole host of complex theoretical baggage, and this is clearly not the space to attempt an encompassing definition of realism as it has been used over the years, not only in reference to cinema but also with painting and literature. Raymond Williams, for example, makes it clear that there is no consensus on the use of the term realism. He goes through the historical and contemporary uses of the term (as well as "reality" and "real") and comes up with four basic uses (i–iv), the latter two of which (iii–iv) are of interest here:

> as a description of facing up to things as they really are, and not as we imagine or would like them to be — "let us replace sentimentalism by realism, and dare to uncover those simple and terrible laws which, be they seen or unseen, pervade and govern" (Emerson, 1860); (iv) as a term to describe a method or an attitude in art and literature — at first an exceptional accuracy of representation, later a commitment to describing real events and showing things as they actually exist [R. Williams 258–9].

Christopher Williams, for his part, has set out a number of varying "realist" positions by filmmakers and critics ranging from Eisenstein and Vertov to Rossellini and Hitchcock, only to come to the conclusion that "the only idea on which they seem to agree is that film should in some sense be truthful or tell the truth" (C. Williams 79). Even if the posture is not adopted, time and again, there is an overwhelming tendency to at least speak to a dualist position with relation to realism, that is, a distinction between a spectacular cinema that seeks to entertain (e.g., Hollywood) and a cinema that seeks to reveal/educate/convince through a faithful rendering of reality (e.g., documentary). Thus realism and realist cinema are often used to describe a cinema that is (a) "truthful" insofar as it corresponds the physical elements of reality, or (b) the way in which it "investigates" that reality to reveal larger truths about society and even human behavior that would otherwise go unnoticed, or both. Realist cinema, in this way, does not simply mimic surface appearances but also attempts to reveal social machinations, or as Rossellini once stated, it is an "investigation of reality, forming a relationship with reality" (32). This is, broadly, the way in which the Spanish films in question will be discussed — through their ability to speak to the here and now of contemporary Spanish reality both in terms of replicating the physical and social conditions as well as in their ability to illuminate aspects of Spanish society and human relations within that context.[2]

Embedded in this discussion of realism is an assumption that cinema can, and maybe should, have a social function. Take for example André Bazin's comments regarding the realism of Wyler and Goldwyn's *The Best Years of Our Lives*:

> The nature of the subject, its actuality, its social value called for, in the first place, a quasi documentary of meticulous accuracy. Samuel Goldwyn and Wyler wanted to make a social rather than an artistic film. It was a question of exposing one of the most distressing social problems of post-war America with all the necessary breadth and subtlety through a, no doubt, fictionalized, narrative, though scrupulously truthful and exemplary [qtd. in C. Williams 40].

Here, as elsewhere, Bazin connects the truth function of cinema with its social discourse within the context of clearly fictionalized narrative. It is not a question of mimicking reality, as if to put a reflector up to daily life, but rather one of creating a filmic representation of reality with an almost didactic purpose. In this sense, aestheticism is not set against realism since, as Bazin has famously quipped, "realism in art can only be achieved in one way — through artifice" (1971: 26). In fact, elsewhere Bazin, as one of the great defenders of Italian neorealism, would go so far as to suggest a proper role for cinema when he writes that, "art for art's sake is just as heretical in cinema as elsewhere, probably more so" (2005: 30).

This sense of a responsibility to *create* truth with an eye toward social discourse is itself an attitude that has pervaded much of Spanish cinema dating back, at least, to Javier Bardem's famous statement at the Cinema Conversations of Salamanca in 1955 in which he challenged the industry, and by extension the government, to support and create a cinema that is socially relevant *and* aesthetically viable. Bardem's own films, notably *Muerte de un ciclista* (1955) and *Calle Mayor* (1956), exemplify this dual agenda, taking into account the strict censorship that was imposed in Spain in this period. This notion of creating a relevant and engaged cinema of high aesthetic quality has carried over to a number of contemporary filmmakers and even an industry that actively supports films that mirror and denounce social ills (Quintana 11; Triana-Toribio 157). Filmmakers such as Fernando León de Aranoa, Iciar Bollaín, and Achero Mañas, have all achieved distinction in Spanish cinema through decidedly realist films that deal with issues such as immigration, drug abuse, domestic abuse, the recuperation of historical memory, terrorism, racism and neo-nazism, as well as our current interest: the re-organization of the nuclear family and the subsequent change of the face of patriarchy (and matriarchy for that matter). As Feenstra has noted, these filmmakers are responsible for a corpus of feature-length films with realist tendencies that represent a certain Spanish mindset during this historic period (214). For example, Bollaín's *Te doy mis ojos* received state support while the preface to the script indicates under no uncertain terms that the film would effectively enter into the hot-button current debate in Spain over the problem of domestic abuse (Bollaín and Luna, 15).[3] There is, furthermore, no debate as to whether or not this film engaged the public and made an impact, even if that impact is, ultimately, unquantifiable (Gould Levine 228).

In spite of this commitment to reflect upon social issues in Spanish cinema itself, studies in Hispanic cinemas have tended to place a heavy focus on "important" films and filmmakers, namely Almodóvar, and the vital issues of gender and sexuality.[4] You could say that we are witnessing a complete reorientation, both socially and culturally, toward the way in which we think of sexuality and gender, and human relations in general and our criticism reflects this. And while this in itself deserves our attention, I believe that we are behind in addressing what this shift means in terms of socio-cultural institutions, such as the family, and in this case, patriarchy. Patriarchy, and fatherhood especially, is not a stable cultural ideal over time (Griswold 252). It involves different responsibilities and traits depending on one's culture, socio-economic status, religious convictions, etc. So if, for example, the construction of male identity and masculinity has changed over time, what does this mean for the institution of patriarchy? What is expected of contemporary European fathers and husbands? And what do these current circumstances mean for children's lives, the experience of women, and the relative power between the sexes? In short, if the terms that define masculinity are fluid and in flux, how do we then define patriarchy?

One public site of inquiry is indeed film, and the representation of patriarchy has been a constant in Spanish cinema from the beginning. Though this may simply be the logical consequence of film's natural relationship to society, it is also the case that the family has often played a symbolic role in Spanish cinema over the years. Isolina Ballesteros provides an important overview of the uses and functions of patriarchy within Spanish cinema, noting that in the 1960s films that represented family in a glowing light received state support. On the other hand, directors such as Carlos Saura and José Luis Borau offered monstrous and dysfunctional fathers as well as castrating mothers within a divided, furtive, insane, and perverse familial framework as an allegory to past sociopolitical repression, corruption, and alienation (272). In the 1980s Almodóvar continued to subvert the figure of the traditional patriarch either through his absence, or through elimination for being perverse or ineffective, or by substituting him with the marginalized, homosexual son, as seen in films such as *¿Qué he hecho yo para merecer esto?!* and *Ley del deseo*. Almodóvar's films continue along these lines into the 1990s, paralleling a general trend to present alternative views of the nuclear family and patriarchy specifically. As Ballesteros observes by quoting Massumi, "simultaneously, and following a noticeable tendency in the Western cinema market, an entirely new generation of directors are reproducing, reconstructing, or satirizing the familiar familial formula, always inexistent, which can now only be conceived of as simulacrum in the way in which it claims 'a dangerous similarity to a putative model'" (275).[5] Ballesteros goes on to state, specifically, that if the Francoist family in its diverse filmic representations was already dysfunctional and never really matched the familial model officially propagated by the State and Church, it is no surprise that in the last decade of the twentieth century the idealized nuclear family was viewed as a lost paradise, never to be recovered, and was substituted with an alternative family of choice (275). Ballesteros draws on Baudrillard to affirm this view that nuclear family as it was idealized under Franco is, and in fact was, a thing of the past — that the real ceased to exist long ago only to be replaced by a nostalgia for something that never really existed but which now has the job of covering up the lack of a basic reality (275). It is precisely this lack of a strong patriarchal system that surfaces on screen in many of the films by Almodóvar and even León de Aranoa's *Familia* (1996).

It is certainly the case that there appears in the 1990s a rash of films that present an alternative to the "traditional" family and traditional patriarchy, but this does not necessarily assume that the prior model was nothing more than a construct. It is more likely the case that the so-called traditional model was a general social practice based on a collective ideal, one that has since undergone radical changes, including the social and cultural practices that make up patriarchy. In fact, if we can agree that "official" discourse under Franco attempted to impart a Catholic view of patriarchy, a similar case could be made that the cultural elites are now effectively trying to forge a different perspective through cultural consensus. Whereas films by Saura and Almodóvar have received more critical attention for their formalism and subversion, films by Bollaín, León de Aranoa, and Mañas, tend to present patriarchy is a more practical light, offering alternatives to the given structures.

This attempt to redefine patriarchy can be observed in Ricardo Franco's *La buena estrella*. *La buena estrella* is the story of a butcher, Rafael (Antonio Resines), who drives by and sees Marina (Maribel Verdú) being physically abused by her husband, Daniel (Jordi Mollà). Rafael intervenes and brings Marina home for protection and to recuperate. When it turns out that Marina is pregnant, Rafael becomes a sort of adoptive father who replaces the abusive and drug-dependent Daniel. This presentation of the biological patriarch as abusive and psychologically unhealthy is a linking thread in each of the films that will be examined here. In the case of *La buena estrella*, the comparison between two competing conceptualizations of patriarchy is portended by the opening sequence of the film in which a bull is being dismembered in graphic fashion. It is clearly meant to be symbolic of what is at stake in the social and cultural politics of contemporary Spanish cinema as it relates to patriarchy. The gruesome image of Spain's well-worn national symbol of masculinity is clearly designed to foreshadow the film's demystification of traditional patriarchy through the juxtaposition of two competing models.

The dissection of patriarchy is then carried out through the contrast between the "biological" father, Daniel, and the adoptive father, Rafael. Patriarchy can be both "a biological act but also a cultural enactment" and *La buena estrella* likewise seems keen to divide these into two parts (Griswold 251). Daniel (Jordi Mollà) provides an almost typecast abusive and machista husband, the type that can be found in any number of films, not only Spanish. His character is closely associated with the sort of patriarchy that derives its power from the body. This is underscored at a crucial moment in the film when Marina is forced to choose between the two male figures, there is a somewhat forced, full-frontal shot of Daniel. Jordi Mollà's penis is the focal point of the mid-range shot, and functions as an immediate reminder of certain values that have traditionally been associated with the male patriarch, mainly, to be sexually dominant and virile, reverting back to the bull from the beginning of the film.

Ultimately, after the death of Marina, her daughter Estrella and Rafael form an adoptive family, but in contrast to Daniel, Rafael is impotent. Though Marina attempts to awaken his sexuality, it proves to be impossible. And Rafael, unlike Daniel, does not exhibit jealousy nor does he appear to subscribe to any sort of medieval honor code, in spite of the fact that Marina does betray his trust at a critical juncture. This makes for an interesting (and intentional) contrast between two modes of patriarchy. While it is Daniel who impregnates Marina, it is Rafael who eventually assumes the role of nurturing father and surrogate husband until Marina dies. In short, the film effectively counters what Griswold has called the "demographic regime" of fertility with one of human solidarity (252). The notion that paternity, the ability to sire children and its relation to masculinity, is critical to any definition of patriarchy is contrasted with an image of stability, support, both emotional and logistical, and mutual respect. But is this picture offered in Franco's film far too optimistic? This is, perhaps, where notions of realism and social commitment are helpful.

Ángel Quintana has referred to this brand of contemporary Spanish cinema as timid realism ("realismo tímido") (15). Quintana's account, beginning in the 1990s, describes Spanish cinema as an industry that is more willing to engage in social and political commitment (11). According to Quintana, this preoccupation with "the real" became a stylistic question; it was not a question of interrogating reality as much as one of constantly referring back to the present. He is referring specifically to the films in question here, and this is where he finds the description of timid realism to be apt because of the way in which these films allow the spectator to feel Spanish cinema has discovered the reality of the situation, but that it is ultimately a game with a realist undertone (17). Referring to Bollaín's *Te doy mis ojos* specifically, Quintana criticizes the way in which these films fail to interrogate the ambiguities of reality while diluting the crude reality into a "laboratory of feeling" (19). His view, in summary, is that this approximation to reality can be ascribed to a desire to please the public rather than put for more "experimental" films (Quintana 21).

Although Quintana fails to see some of the important nuances between films such as *Te doy mis ojos*, *Mar adentro*, and *El bola*, several of his observations about contemporary social issue cinema ring true, such as the importance of veracity of place as well as the importance of breaking with the star system in order to create a more naturalistic film (20–1). Some concessions are made, such as the case of Javier Bardem playing Ramón Sampedro in *Mar adentro*. But there is an element of truth in Quintana's suggestion that known actors and actresses will dilute a film's realism (naturalism in this sense). Quintana's critique certainly rings true when considering *La buena estrella*. In this sense there are three issues in particular that bear mentioning in a discussion of the film. The first is the use of professional actors: Maribel Verdú, Antonio Resines, and Jordi Mollà, all three of which are known entities in the Spanish star system. The viewer reactions indicate that these known actors are in fact a distraction from the film as a realist depiction of contemporary society, since spectators tend to focus more on the stars and their performances than the content of the film itself.[6]

Second, as Quintana points out via other films (though he misunderstands *Te doy mis ojos*), the melodramatic plot of *La buena estrella* undercuts its potential for showing the crude reality of Spanish society and converts the film into a crowd-pleasing spectacle.[7] As the anonymous reviews point out, the spectator is distracted from the predominant social ill, i.e., domestic abuse perpetrated by the husband, and is instead focused on the development of the unlikely relationship between the impotent butcher and the female protagonist. The third issue is the sum of the first two, in which the finale, though tidy and cathartic, registers with the spectator as contrived. Ricardo Franco tries to solve the problem of a dysfunctional family dynamic as product of an abusive, addictive patriarch by substituting him with the docile, sex-less Rafael. Yet nothing else is changed, the female protagonist is not empowered in any way while the social conditions remain status quo. Though a more inviting view of patriarchy is offered, it is neither plausible nor practical because it does not offer any structural changes to expose or prevent the continued legacy of physically dependent and often abusive patriarchy. Although Mollà's character is critiqued through ridicule as a type (symbolized by the bull that Franco hopes to butcher), Resines' character is not a plausible solution with which anyone would likely want to identify. His self-less care for Marina first and her daughter later is indeed noble but it is also the stuff of Hollywood. In the end, we learn very little about what it really means to be a single mother attached to an abusive man, nor are we offered very many practical solutions that might better fit contemporary notions of fatherhood and/or husbandry.

*Te doy mis ojos*, on the other hand, differs from Ricardo Franco's account of patriarchy in three fundamental ways: (1) it offers insight into the social code that dictates acceptable behavior from the patriarch; (2) it presents an element of psychological depth to the traditionally dismissive view of the abusive patriarch; (3) it provides an alternative view of patriarchy that is more plausible, even if it also creates a double standard in terms of how we understand patriarchy vis-à-vis national identity. It should be added that *Te doy mis ojos* also operates on an extradiagetic level through its intertextual references to art. Most critical attention has been paid to the female protagonist of this film, and in particular the way in which *Te doy mis ojos* interjects into the hot-button debate on domestic abuse and dysfunctional families. For the next few lines I will be focusing on the dichotomy established in the film between the Spanish father/husband and the contrasting figure of his Scottish brother-in-law.

*Te doy mis ojos* is already widely recognized for its "realist" denunciation of domestic violence in Spain at a time when the issue seemed to have reached a boiling point. Funded in part by the Government of Castilla y León, it is directly connected to the larger push by the media and governments to raise awareness about the issue of domestic abuse while also informing viewers of the complex social and interpersonal dynamics that allow domestic abuse to incubate. Beyond the careful psychological portrait of the abuser and the abused, as well as the socio-historical context, Bollaín and co-writer Alicia Luna also forge a subtle parallel between Pilar's (Laia Marull) abusive husband, Antonio (Luis Tosar), and John (David Mooney), the fiancé/husband of Pilar's sister, Ana (Candelas Peña). With John, Bollaín injects into the film a patriarchal figure in terms of husbandry and fatherhood (albeit surrogate) that contrasts the traditional yet dysfunctional system that entraps Pilar. In opposition to most published reports on Spanish domestic life, John and Ana can be seen as equal partners in their domestic chores, recalling a recent bit of legislation aimed at holding spouses equally responsible for domestic chores.[8] Their marriage is civil not religious. Ana is the breadwinner while John seems to be more in touch with the children, in particular Juan, his nephew. All of these are signs of breaking with past traditions and forging a familial system that is much more secular as opposed to the religious institutions that governed Pilar's marriage. Patriarchy, as far as John is concerned, is a form of shared authority in which masculinity is not compromised through one's involvement with children or through one's egalitarian relationship with one's partner.

Bollaín's careful use of *mise-en-scène* makes the dichotomy clear when Antonio shows up at his mother-in-law's house for his son's birthday. Here Antonio and John are carefully placed into a medium range shot so as to contrast the way in which John engages the children, including Antonio's own son, while Antonio sits sullenly, smoking his cigarette. Antonio feels subverted by John when the latter gives Juan a video-gaming consul that immediately causes the young boy and his friends to forget the soccer ball presented to him by his biological father. This moment seems to crystallize the notion that Antonio's distant and authoritarian presence has been usurped by a male figure that is willing to connect in a more direct way with the children.

The juxtaposition of the abusive, *machista* husband from Spain and the more passive, egalitarian mate from Scotland is maintained elsewhere in the film, creating a type of transnational discourse within *Te doy mis ojos*. In this way, the film continues a trend that can be found in Bollaín's previous films, namely *Hola, ¿estás sola?* (1995) and *Flores de otro mundo* (1999), both of which are notable for the way in which they unite, quite literally, a diverse array of cultures, races, and ethnicities within the context of contemporary Spain. On the one hand, this transnational discourse works toward erasing a notion of essentialism in understanding patriarchy. Much like Franco's *La buena estrella*, Bollaín seems to be making the argument that patriarchy should not have its base in biological fact or preconceived notions of a familial structure, but rather on a nurturing relationship. The paradox is that John represents both another ethnicity and another culture, which creates a sense that the answer to the biological-hereditary system of patriarchy resides outside of Spanish culture. The protagonist's mother, for example, effectively inherited ideas about marriage during the Franco dictatorship that include tolerating physical abuse as part of being married and she is highly unsympathetic to her daughter's attempts to distance herself from Antonio as it separates her son from her biological father. Meanwhile it is Ana who met John while studying abroad and has effectively "imported" him. The notion, if taken this way, is dangerous insofar as it allows the viewer to see domestic violence as a strictly national problem, or worse, a biological one, which therefore cannot necessarily be altered through public demand or governmental intervention.

The more likely reason for Bollaín's treatment of patriarchy is that the director wants to set the problem up as a cultural and historical pattern. The film is intentionally set in Toledo, which in many respects is considered to be the birthplace of Spanish civilization in terms of language and Roman Catholic religious mores. In addition, the use of Toledo as setting creates a sense of claustrophobia given the fact that it is surrounded by the Taugus River, which itself figures into many scenes in the film (Bollaín 14). Pilar, it seems, cannot escape Toledo as a physical space (Antonio prevents her from taking an interview in Madrid by viciously attacking her) or its repressive patriarchal structure. This suffocating reality is confirmed through the incorporation of art in the film, as Bollaín deftly includes paintings to highlight the change in inherent problems vis-à-vis patriarchy in Spanish culture. As Pilar passes through the Church of San Tomé she observes the stern faces of several bygone church leaders and then a painting of Mary, or "La Dolorosa," with whom she seems to identify. The situation vis-à-vis patriarchy thus emerges as a product of historical circumstance and cultural breeding, a cycle that is not easily broken. Linda Gould Levine summarizes in the following way: "Bollaín's textured representation of Antonio's rage and narrow patriarchal mentality, a product of centuries of western culture and religious thought, is significantly clothed in the metaphor of art, despite his dislike of museums and high culture" (224). The net effect is to create, as Gould Levine has so well put it, a sense of entrapment. Bollaín additionally goes to great lengths to reveal the psychology of male abusers akin to Antonio, as we follow him into therapy sessions in which, with the peer context, prescribed roles and even physical abuse are considered a natural outcropping of the male-female relationship.[9] The glimmer of hope seems to reside in Pilar's self-empowerment and with alternative family dynamics, as seen in the relationship between John and Ana. It is within this context that John presents a more viable model of patriarchy as a father figure unburdened by social and historic cultural mores.

Still, it is Achero Mañas' *El bola* that offers the most viable option in terms of alternative forms of patriarchy. Like the films discussed earlier, *El bola* presents patriarchy in binary fashion, through the development of two versions of patriarchy. On the one hand there is the father Mariano (Manuel Morón) and son Pablo (Juan José Ballesta), who represent a more traditional Spanish family and version of patriarchy at various levels — the grandmother (father's side) lives at home; mother cooks, cleans, and cares for mother-in-law; Mariano owns and runs a local hardware shop; Pablo spends his afternoons helping in the family shop; their dress and décor can only be described as typical. More important is the fact that the relationship between Pablo and his father is one of strict hierarchical order. This can be observed from the outset, when Pablo fails to be cordial to a friend of Mariano's he is severely scolded, ostensibly for potentially harming his father's reputation in some minute way. This relationship is in direct contrast to that of José (Alberto Jiménez) and Alfredo (Pablo Galán), in which the family is decidedly more hip and closely knit. The house is decorated and furnished in the Ikea mould and with contemporary art; José makes a living as a tattoo artist; José friends are clearly from an era in which drugs and sex were the norm. For example, he has a close friend die of AIDs in the film. This is most likely a vague nod to the *movida* culture of 1980s. Most importantly, José and Alfredo relate to each other on a more informal and egalitarian level; Alfredo is not disciplined but reasoned with, and it is clear that he is expected to make his own decisions.

In terms of the film's realism, the physical conditions do indeed resemble any typical suburban setting outside of Madrid, though perhaps it could just as easily be any European suburb, with its block and high-rise living, local bars, shops, and schools, and even a theme park within striking distance. In fact, it is perhaps this sense of "this could be anywhere" that gives the film a stronger sense of reality and certainly increases the spectator's investment in the film as a picture of a possible everyday reality. In terms of montage, the dichotomy is carefully developed so as to leave the viewer wondering, at least initially, which family has something to hide, which patriarch is attempting to do what is best for his family and which situation is more conducive to a healthy upbringing and positive social interaction. Alfredo, as the new kid at Pablo's school, enters the film as the sullen rebel, unwilling to play in the others' seemingly inane games. This is confirmed when he and Pablo cut class and go to an amusement park. In short, Mañas sets Alfredo up as the more likely culprit to lead the two astray. But it is also Alfredo who eventually sniffs out the abusive circumstances in Pablo's home and tries to do something about it. It is in fact Alfredo's father—the tattoo artist with a shaved head and stylish gear—who takes Pablo in at great personal risk because of legal implications. Mañas, through a carefully plotted binary is best constructed through the corporal aspect of the film. On the one hand, José brutally attacks his son—beatings that are so difficult to watch that, according to Stephen Holden, "only the most cold-hearted viewer could fail to respond." Mañas here plays with stereotypes knowing that one might more likely expect such violent thrashings from the tattoo artist. In direct contrast to the abuse suffered by Pablo, the film shows José giving his son a tattoo as a sort of coming-of-age gift. It is with the tattoo, ironically, that he is conferring on his son an amount of trust and camaraderie.

A noticeable absence in each of these three films comes in the form of any official institution that would intervene in the case of domestic abuse and provide instruction or support for a shift in cultural values. There are indeed scenes of group therapy in *Te doy mis ojos*, but these are presented to be ineffectual, exactly the same as Pilar's visit to the police, which proved to be not only fruitless but humiliating, since she could not indicate any particular physical damage on her person — psychological damage is not visible to the naked eye, and this does not count in a court of law. *El bola*, meanwhile, takes this issue even further by noting how José's attempt to help young Pablo may actually cost him a great deal of legal trouble. "Official" intervention does not seem to be the end game of these films. Perhaps this is in itself an indication of the agenda of these films, that is, to foster cultural awareness as opposed or in addition to legislation. To wit, as *El bola* closes, Pablo describes the abuse he has suffered, which includes drinking his own urine, to either to social worker or a police officer. We never find out. This is because we are never offered a glimpse of Pablo's interlocutor. In addition, *El bola* breaks from realist convention and makes eye contact with the spectator as he is detailing his suffering. We, as spectators, effectively assume the role of listener and observer. The film, through its break with normal cinematic codes, calls the spectator to act. Paul Julian Smith observes that "the confession is as cathartic for El Bola as it is for us" (2003). And as one spectator noted: "it made me want to reach into the screen and affect the course of these characters lives. [...] It's rare that a film actually teaches you something about yourself."[10] Through this interaction with the spectator, which has deep roots in the early cinema of attractions, Mañas seems to suggest that the state and its systems are so ineffectual that the burden of rethinking patriarchy rests on the shoulders of spectators, and by extension society. I have written elsewhere that similar moments in contemporary social issue cinema, specifically when the actor makes eye contact with spectator or other unconventional techniques, e.g., *Mar adentro* (Amenábar 2004), do indeed break down the "hollow," realistic illusion of social issue cinema. Yet these moments of what may otherwise be cinematic excess are not necessarily cheap thrills for the masses, as accounts of early cinema hold.[11] Instead, they can be powerful moments that transgress the boundaries that normally separate the victim and the voyeur, creating an impression and perhaps leaving the spectator with a sense of responsibility (Begin 273). *El bola*, in this way, breaks with realist convention in its direct engagement with the spectator while it maintains an effort to present a true account of reality, one that ultimately calls upon the spectator to act, to reconsider what constitutes positive and negative forms of familial structure, and specifically, what constitutes a healthy, socially redeeming form of patriarchy.

Adrienne Rich defines patriarchy as "a familial-social, ideological, political system in which men — by force, direct pressure, or through ritual, traditions, law and language, customs, etiquette, education, and the division of labor, determine what part women shall or shall not play, and in which the female is everywhere subsumed under the male" (57). This form of patriarchy certainly rears its head in contemporary Spanish cinema but is often mocked, as is the case with Almodóvar's films and León de Aranoa's *Familia*. In contrast, each of the three films examined here share a common technique for illustrating a desired and/or "real" shift in patriarchy. In each case study one patriarch derives power from the body — its ability to maintain power through physical intimidation and coercion, as well as institutions and cultural inheritance. These men are then contrasted with figures who, to borrow from Rich, express different customs, rituals, etiquette, education, and ideas on the division of labor that are permeated with mutual agreement and respect as opposed to fear and intimidation. Therefore, in the same way that "traditional" patriarchy was either promoted in film by the state apparatus or used as allegorical critique throughout the Franco years and to some degree the Transition, in contemporary Spanish cinema patriarchy itself, much like the opening scene of *La buena estrella*, is being systematically dissected and reformulated to match more progressive views of masculinity and family, more humanistic views in which what matters is not origin, virility, and power, but rather companionship and egalitarianism. That said, I am in agreement with the sociologist Ralph LaRossa who reminds us that there is a difference between culture and conduct (11). While there may be an abundance of films that do recast patriarchy in alternative ways, this does not mean that the practice or even the collective imagination of patriarchy is as progressive as we see on screen. If Giles Tremlett's account is an accurate indicator, the traditional roles for men, unlike those of women, have not changed much in recent years (202–33). This makes films such as *La buena estrella* a sort of wishful thinking. This may be naïve idealism, but as Manohla Dargis reminds us, "idealism is a form of resistance."

## Notes

1. One example of the shift in male-female relationships as a result of workplace shifts comes from a recent study that found that in heterosexual relationships in which the female partner makes more than the male partner, men are more likely to be unfaithful. See Randy Dotinga. "Infidelity Rises When She Makes More Than He Does." *Bloomberg Businessweek* August 16, 2010, accessed August 16, 2010.

2. It should be noted, however, that because cinema must always be acknowledged as a construct and not as faithful mirror to reality, the dichotomy, realism versus formalism, will always break down: on some level the spectacular can always reveal truth while a documentary can be just as ideological as any Hollywood blockbuster.

3. For more on social issue cinema, see Begin.

4. The contributions to Peter Evans' *The Auteurist Tradition*, for example, deal almost exclusively with sexuality, and particularly female sexuality. Recent editions of *Studies in Hispanic Cinemas* follow similar trends. Almost 20 percent of the articles published in *SHC* are dedicated to issues of gender and sexuality in Spanish cinema.

5. All page numbers for subsequent quotations from this source are given parenthetically. All translations are mine.

6. See, for example, viewer comments at popular sites such as imdb.com, filmaffinity.com, or todocine.com. Viewer comments often revolve around the interpretation of roles by the known actors/actresses as well as the romantic storyline.

7. Quintana writes: "Timid realism is characterized above all, as a laboratory of emotion, sometimes contradictary, such as with the tension between love and indifference in Iciar Bollaín's *Te doy mis ojos*" (19). Enough has been written by academic and popular critics to confirm that *Te doy mis ojos* offers more than a melodramatic tug-of-war. Its raw violence, psychological insights, artistry, and finale all offer a more nuanced view of domestic abuse and patriarchy than your standard "feel good" film. See Begin, Gould Levine, Cruz, Broton.

8. Recently passed legislation requires that men and women who obtain civil marriages share domestic chores. See Dale Fuchs, "Mucho Chores for Macho Men with Spain's New Law." Guardian Unlimited online, June 26, 2005. Accessed June 26, 2005.

9. For a more clinical account of the psychological component of domestic abuse and patriarchy, see Jacqueline Cruz. "Amores que matan: Dulce Chacón, Icíar Bollaín y la violencia de género." *Letras hispanas* 12.1 (Spring 2005): 67–81.

10. See user comments on the Internet Movie Database: <http://www.imdb.com/title/tt0243794/usercomments>, accessed 4 April 4, 2007.

11. Siegfried Kracauer, "The Cult of Distraction: On Berlin's Picture Palaces," *New German Critique* 40 (Winter 1987): 91–96.

## Works Cited

Ballesteros, Isolina. *Cine (ins)urgente: textos fílmicos y contextos culturales de la España posfranquista*. Madrid: Fundamentos, 2001.

Bazin, André. "An Aesthetic of Reality: Neorealism. (Cinematic Realism and the Italian School of the Liberation)." In *What Is Cinema?* Ed. and Trans. Hugh Gray. Berkeley and Los Angeles: University of California Press, 1971. pp. 16–40.

_____. *What Is Cinema?* Ed. and Trans. Hugh Gray. Berkeley and Los Angeles: University of California Press, 2005.

Begin, Paul. "When Victim Meets Voyeur: An Aesthetic of Confrontation in Hispanic Social Issue Cinema." *Hispanic Research Journal* 9.3 (2008): 261–75.

Bollaín, Icíar. "Historia de amor y maltrato." *Te doy mis ojos*. Madrid: Ocho y media, 2003.

_____, dir. *Te doy mis ojos*. Alta Productions, 2003.

Brooksbank Jones, Anny. "Work, Women, and the Family: A Critical Perspective." In *Spanish Cultural Studies: An Introduction*, eds. Helen Graham and Jo Labanyi. Oxford: Oxford University Press, 1995, pp. 386–93.

Dargis, Manohla. "Using the Light of a Star to Illuminate Ugly Truths." NewYorkTimes.com, June 22, 2007. Accessed June 22, 2007.

Feenstra, Pietsie. "Fernando León de Aranoa, autor de género: cámaras intimistas sobre la marginalidad en el cine español." In *Miradas glocales: cine español en el cambio de milenio*, ed. Pohl Burkhard, Jörg Türschmann. Madrid: Iberoamericano/Vervuert, 2007, pp. 201–17.

Franco, Ricardo, dir. *La buena estrella*. Enrique Cerezo Producciones Cinematográficas, S.A., 1997.

Gould Levine, Linda. "Saved by Art: Entrapment and Freedom in Icíar Bollaín's *Te doy mis ojos*." In *Generation X Rocks: Music, Television, and the Revision of Reality in Contemporary Peninsular Literature*, eds. Christine Henseler and Randolph Pope. Nashville, TN: Vanderbilt University Press, 2007, pp. 216–34.

Griswold, Robert. "Introduction to the Special Issue on Fatherhood." *Journal of Family History* 24.3 (1999): 251–4.
Holden, Stephen. "A Father's Brutality, a Son's Defiance." NewYorkTimes.com, April 5, 2002. Accessed April 5, 2002.
LaRossa, Ralph. *The Modernization of Fatherhood*. Chicago and London: University of Chicago Press, 1997.
Mañas, Achero, dir. *El bola*. Canal + España, 2000.
Quintana, Ángel. "El cine como realidad y el mundo como representación: Algunos síntomas de los noventa." *Archivos de la Filmoteca: revista de estudios históricos sobre la imágen* 39 (October 2001): 8–25.
Rich, Adrienne. *Of Woman Born: Motherhood and Experience and Institution*. New York: Norton, 1976.
Smith, Paul Julian. "El Bola." *Sight and Sound* 13.6 (2003): 38.
Tremlett, Giles. *The Ghosts of Spain*. New York: Walker, 2006.
Triana-Toribio, Nuria. *Spanish National Cinema*. London: Routledge, 2003.
Williams, Christopher, ed. *Realism and the Cinema*. London: Routledge and Kegan Paul, 1980.
Williams, Raymond. *Keywords*. Oxford: Oxford University Press, 1985.

# 9

## Meet the Nihilists
### *The Disintegration of the Contemporary Spanish Family in Pedro Aguilera's* La influencia

AMY L. TIBBITTS

The final shot of Pedro Aguilera's film *La influencia* (2007) is that of a young adolescent girl, Jimena, sitting behind the wheel of her dead mother's crashed car, laughing hysterically through blood stained teeth. This violent display of emotion positions the contemporary Spanish family among aspects of emotional hollowness, unanchored familial relationships, ideological instability, and a nihilistic viewpoint of the future. If one considers *La influencia* a contemporary portrait of the Spanish family dynamic or of Spanishness, then questions revolve around how the viewer shall interpret this new bleak landscape of human interaction. Treating the contemporary Spanish family as a post-modern wasteland, the film depicts a vast metaphorical social desert through the use of uncomfortably long extensions of silence and emotional disconnectedness.[1] This essay explores the implications of the bleak state of affairs through an analysis of how spaces (public and private) reflect a consumer-oriented culture, how the representation of the woman (both in motherhood and selfhood) is affected by said culture, and how ultimately the family structure crumbles under the subsequent pressures. One of the main concerns of this study is to question if Aguilera's film portrays the current reality of Spain or, rather, does it attempt to foreshadow the Spain that will materialize if certain globalization forces continue to homogenize society and refocus its attention on commodity over intimacy.

What seems clear, given Jimena's response of gut-bending laughter at the sadness and absurdity that has become her life, is that her implied future, along with the future of the formerly conceived notion of the Spanish family, once considered by the Franco regime as the underpinnings of all that is Spanish, is fragile at best. In fact, the film's rapt attention to hopelessness redraws the notion of social cohesion and pushes the spectator to question (and ultimately acknowledge) that such cohesion ever existed. The conclusions of this study draw in part from a personal interview with director Pedro Aguilera (November 2008) and incorporate work done by cultural theorists working with spatial analysis as well as additional work on the concept of nihilism in contemporary culture. A close reading of the film's use of space, maternal and corporal imagery, tied together with a critique of consumer culture, helps glean an understanding of how this film orients towards a future wrought with apprehension about what is occurring presently and what is coming next for the Spanish contemporary subject.

In most ways, *La influencia* is a departure from the Spanish cinematic landscape of the 1980s and '90s because it does not address questions of nationhood in transition nor does it directly tackle memories of dictatorship. However, it does borrow (or repeat) certain motifs from film and literature that directors and writers from previous generations found useful for these expressions such as incomplete or broken families, and the mad or absent mother. By way of example, one can point to the pre–Transition film *Cría cuervos* by Carlos Saura or Víctor Erice's *El espíritu de la colmena* and *El sur*—all of which deal with damaged childhoods and parents whose impact on their children's development is less than nurturing and wholesome. While those artistic precedents proved effective in expressing the growing pains of a burgeoning democracy or working through the guilt and pain of Francoism, Aguilera develops them for another reason entirely. His repetition of these established codes (dead and/or crazy maternal figures, odd-behaving children, emotional stiltedness, etc.) are not meant to stand as an expression of a new-founded national identity, or as a precarious way of navigating a new political milieu, but rather stand as a latter consequence of those searches still being conducted today. As a director born post–Transition, Aguilera hedges away from having the Dictatorship and the subsequent need to investigate its traumatic legacy dominate his work. Rather, in *La influencia* the viewer is confronted with a disintegration of the individual once he/she is incorporated into the very systems that were put in place to set the subject free. Free markets and the global consumption of all forms of imagery have left the individual adrift, unable to find a cultural or emotional refuge. The result for this particular protagonist is a slow, steady drowning. In this film, the spectator is not invited to witness the entire destruction of self from start to finish, but only invited to the final death throes. Nihilism, the will to nothingness, becomes the new mantra, but one that, by the end of the film, leaves just enough open-endedness to be questioned.

## Consuming Spaces

Read on a visual and spatial level, the film provides a grim cultural commentary regarding both the individual as a solitary being and the individual as part of a communal or family structure. Set in a nondescript Spanish provincial city, the protagonists of the film move within familiar spaces (the house, the pharmacy, supermarkets, the train), none of which provide comfort or a sense of place. From a spatial point of view, *La influencia* mirrors the ideas put forth by Marc Agué concerning supermodernity's production of "non-spaces."[2] Agué argues that such spaces, stripped of their anthropological mores, are "thus surrendered to the solitary individuality, to the fleeting, the temporary and the ephemeral" (78). *La influencia* also uses spaces as means to highlight the individual's aloneness, mostly through the representation of the film's main protagonist, Señora Rivero.

Rivero, a middle-aged mother of two, does not so much inhabit spaces as much as she haunts them. She is what contemporary Spanish novelist Enrique Vila-Matas would call a "fantasma ambulante" [ambulatory ghost]. This manner of "non-being" subtracts from a certain type of agency that cultural theorist Certeau would grant the city dweller as being resistant to absorption.[3] Rivero is already absorbed when the viewer meets her; therefore, she cannot muster up any tension or chaffing against the world of commerce that goes on around her. Rivero's inability to engage in the "everyday practices" that Certeau has embedded as part of an established urban spatial understanding means that she fails, on a certain level, to act the part of resistor.

Removed of nearly all dialogue, *La influencia* depends heavily on imagery and the use of space to communicate its messages. The opening scene is a close up of the back of a woman's head. The camera's eye focuses up close on her barrette, which consists of series of several round and small images that appear to be old paintings but they are for the most part unidentifiable. Here is a moment when the spectator is granted a quick look into how imagery functions in this film because the images are rich in texture, but add nothing to the emotional investment felt for the scene or its participants. However, the viewer does understand the space and actions being presented — Rivero is in a pharmacy buying a bottle of pills of an unknown substance. This is the first of the various "everyday" spaces that occupy the majority of the film. Space in *La influencia* has a heightened communicative importance due to the film's unwavering embracing of silence. In fact, it is in these first moments of the film that one hears the only words uttered of the first 8½ minutes — the price of the bottle. This lack of verbal and emotional interaction frames the trajectory of the rest of the film.

While little information regarding Rivero is communicated in this open-

**The first scene of the film shows the back of Señora Rivero (Paloma Morales).**

ing shot, the viewer does learn that she rents a small space to run a cosmetic and beauty supply shop. The small store, devoid of clientele could be Anywhere Spain, making the geographic specificity impossible to discern and stripping the place from any deeper attachment of meaning. Rivero's days are spent gazing out the window, taking inventory, looking through fashion magazines, and cutting and pasting certain images of feminine beauty (made-up lips, eyes, faces) into a notebook. While there is no dialogue in these opening minutes, there are noises such as the sounds of the street, the jarring finger nails-on-a-chalkboard sound of the protective metal curtain opening, a siren in the distance, etc. All the exterior sounds highlight Rivero's verbal silence and lack of human interaction. In fact, there is only one person who enters the shop during the course of the film. One rainy afternoon an unsuspecting man wanders into the store to buy an elaborate box of make-up, but there is no warm exchange of salutations or an attempt made on the part of Rivero to push the product. After the briefest of exchanges, the man leaves with the box and Rivero quickly locks the door behind him. The shop occupies a miniscule space, and the fact she has no customers, minus the former example, only emphasizes her extreme isolation. As the title of the film, several minutes in, appears on the screen, the camera's shot is from outside the shop and the spectator's view is focused on the other persons on the street, mostly in pairs, walking past the shop in slow motion, never once entering or looking in its direction.

The title of the film takes on several meanings. On the one hand "La influencia" can be read as the effects of various extraneous influences, such as using pharmaceuticals to induce a numbness or disconnectedness. Aguilera, on the other hand, finds the title to reflect more the relationship dynamic between Rivero and her children, recognizing that the kids are in a delicate moment of development in which their mother's behaviors will have an everlasting impact.[4] Focusing in on the vulnerability of childhood, the scars that they will inherit from this episode of their life will determine their identities in the future. And while the children wait for their mother to die, because it is a death that is not only anticipated but desired, there is an inescapable burden of "influence" that the children will continue to live with after she is gone.

It is in the moment of the presentation of the film's title when the audience experiences one of the few lush moments of the film as *Spem in alium* by Thomas Tallis (circa 1570) provides the soundtrack to this depressive stage. This Renaissance motet, with its sacred themes and complex choral setting, layered upon the unimpressive and nondescript backdrop of the street and the comings and goings of anonymous people, not only works to provide an audio heaviness congruent with the already established theme of separation and alienation, but also provides an awareness of the lack of such depth and beauty in the life of the protagonist. In an ironic gesture, it is upon hearing the music that the audience experiences for the first time, her complete emptiness. It is also at this moment that the spectator is treated to one of the concrete themes of the film — its nihilistic view of both the present and the future. Heidegger describes nihilism as "the increasingly dominant truth that all prior aims of being have become superfluous" (5). Put another way, Rivero is what Nietzsche would call a "reactive" subject and she is, when the audience meets her, in the final chapter of completing her "will to nothingness."[5] At this point the viewer is taken along for the advanced stage of decay and annihilation. In some ways, *La influencia* reflects those cultural values so exalted in the Francoist era, such as capitalism and material wealth. What the film shows the viewer, however, is that these commodities do nothing to ease the internal struggle and emptiness of self that are experienced by Rivero. Aguilera points out that culture has shifted to merely reflecting endemic commoditization and consumption and, therefore, has lost its soul. The idea of soullessness in contemporary culture due to overconsumption and the creation of a purely market-driven environment is not a new one nor is it all that noteworthy. What makes this film different and daring is that it never backs away from the destructive forces of its materialistic cannibalism. Rivero's destruction is as much auto-imposed as it is a symbol for the pressures of living in a world driven by elusive ideas of perfection.

Zygmunt Bauman in *Liquid Times: Living in the Age of Uncertainty* explores the general feeling of malaise that infects the contemporary subject faced with consequences of "negative globalization":

> "Progress," once the most extreme manifestation of radical optimism and a promise of universally shared and lasting happiness, has moved all the way to the opposite, dystopian and fatalistic pole of anticipation: it now stands for the threat of a relentless and inescapable change that instead of auguring peace and respite portends nothing but continuous crisis and strain and forbids a moment of rest [10].

While Bauman traces feelings of uncertainty to fears having mostly to do with security, political stability, and personal safety, one can also apply his observations to the behaviors exhibited by Rivero. Her inability to adopt what Bauman recognizes as a counter action to uncertainty — a call to be infinitely flexible and adaptable to the relentless pressures of a modern life — have bled her of any capability of connectedness and intimacy. In addition, we see that her general security is also in jeopardy. She is in danger of her children losing their access to an education; she is losing her business, and is increasingly unable to provide the basic necessities. Rivero's loneliness and solitude reflect how Bauman sees the contemporary individual:

> The messages addressed from the sites of political power to the resourceful and the hapless alike present "more flexibility" as the sole cure for an already unbearable insecurity — and so paint the prospect of yet more uncertainty, yet more privatization of troubles, yet more loneliness and impotence, and indeed more uncertainty still [14].

Bauman emphasizes that on a "negatively globalized planet" that the individual subject faces an insurmountable task of confronting the rapid changes inherent in this process utterly alone: "In such a world there are not many rocks left on which struggling individuals can build their hopes of rescue and on which they can rely in case of personal failure" (24). While Bauman argues solutions to this state of uncertainty and the "fading of human bonds," Rivero is unequivocally not up for such an endeavor. The spatial aspects are significant in this film precisely because they act as non-spaces. The spaces parallel Rivero's life and personal characteristics because, just like Rivero, they lack history and narrative. Rivero consumes endless images of female beauty while the children consume the identifiable images (cartoons, superheroes) of childhood. Unfortunately for the film's characters, the imagery is entirely empty of meaning. Instead, the toys and magazine photos represent a vacuum of emotional stability and availability, which have the protagonists teetering on the edge of annihilation. Hence, the film's framework points towards a negative re-visioning of the mother/child relationship and the institution of the family in general. Agué sees this new form of solitude part of supermodernity and also emphasizes that these "non-places" put a particular burden on the individual: "When individuals come together, they engender the social and organize places. But the space of supermodernity is inhabited by this contradiction: it deals only with individuals (customers, passengers, users, listeners), but they are identified (name, occupation, place of birth, address) only on entering or leaving" (111).

Rivero, in part because she rarely speaks, is not linked to a particular place. In other words, she seems not to identify with the identifying qualities that places infuse onto the individual and this lack of place adds to her emptiness. Feminist geographer, Doreen Massey, while acknowledging that a sense of place comes hand in hand with feelings of belonging, helps to convince that such feelings are constructed around projects of buttressing up national identities.[6] Rivero's lack of cultural mores is cast in a more negative light than the one that Massey might see as a positive outcome of freeing oneself from the culturally and/or politically charged identification of place. The spectator experiences Rivero in public and private space. Even though the private spaces in *La influencia* are some of the most intimate of the domestic realm, the bathroom (the shower), the bedroom (during and after sex), and the kitchen, etc., Rivero is never comfortable and is never completely in control. On the contrary, Rivero is unable to latch herself onto meaningful activities, or persons, or duties. Rather, she is placeless; failing to expresses a local, a national, or a supranational sense of belonging. Perhaps this lack of "sense of place" accounts for Rivero's unwavering zombie-like effect throughout the length of the film. As a result of her sense of uncertainty and lack of direction, she merely succumbs.

In his assessment of American society in the recent decades, *Bowling Alone*, Robert Putnam lists a variety of factors that have led Americans to be less civically engaged and as relying less and less on "social capital," or other factors that help form a sense of community such as time and money stressors, consumption of mass media, transportation, etc.[7] According to Putnam, as Americans have become more affluent, they have also become more solitary, disconnected, and private. A similar assessment could be applied to Spain's Transition to a capitalistic democratic society. As Spain became more and more a part of the larger European and international economic milieu, the individual was more and more left to fend for his or herself. Former social structures were altered or eliminated, leaving behind a void that can be read through a nihilistic optic. As the apertures of free-market Spain widened during the '80s and '90s, the ironic result, according to this film, is the contemporary subject falling into a nihilistic trap — not being able to translate the newly found "freedoms" of consumption and material acquisition into happiness and contentment. As an example, one can see that beyond her children, Rivero has no friends, social circles, hobbies or interests that move her outside of her apartment or claustrophobic (and solitary) job. Likewise, her brief excursions in the city (bar, supermarket, school) are not social outlets. Towards the end of the film, her total isolation is complete as she takes to her bed to die. Rivero's death represents a complete entropy of the will to live, and is, as Aguilera explains it, "an existential death," resulting from a life not worth living.

The intensity of silence is reiterated in a multitude of spaces and in numerous scenes. When what can only be assumed is a lawyer (or dept collector) confronts Rivero outside the shop because she is 6 months behind on payment and will be evicted within the week, she does not say one word to the man, nor does she look at him. Her blankness and lack of reaction is what is most telling. Upon receiving this news, Rivero goes to a café and, as before in the pharmacy, the camera's eye focuses only on her back as she sits on a stool at the bar. Sharing the same space is a seemingly mentally disturbed man, singing a traditional song, attempting to get her attention, or the attention of anyone willing to listen. Once the bartender orders the man to stop, he quietly says to her "déjame algo" [leave me something].[8] These words are meant to refer to money, yet one cannot help but make the association that they also refer to lack of self. The camera moves out to frame both the subjects — the crazy man standing alone in the room and Rivero. A white column divides them visually, driving home the point that sharing space is not the same thing as sharing a connection. Yet, the viewer suspects that they have a commonality or a point of reference based on their mental instability and mutual emptiness. The scene ends abruptly, with no further development. It is worth noting that Rivero's brief interaction with this man is endemic to the very few other scenes involving men. While there exists a conscientious absence of paternal and spousal figures, all of the masculine subjects, with the exception of Romeo, are shot from the front and have a decidedly aggressive, and not quite entirely overt sexual and unsettling presence. This stylistic technique suggests not only an inability to connect across gender lines, but also points to a wider problem of the extreme solitude of the subjects. In fact, Rivero appears even more fragile and isolated when juxtaposed against the male characters.

Paul Julian Smith, in *The Moderns: Time, Space, and Subjectivity in Contemporary Spanish Culture,* addresses the portrayal of the Spanish city in art, film, literature, and architecture. In a chapter on the city space, Smith finds the "death of urbanism" as central to many of the works he looks at, and couples with trends in Spanish urban studies: "Indeed, professional Spanish urbanists writing on their own country have spoken [...] of the 'empty metropolis' and the 'destruction of the city'" (109). The impact that this perceived destruction of space has on the contemporary subject is paramount to *La influencia*'s overall construction. Drawing from the work of Henri Lefebvre's

*The Production of Space*, Smith acknowledges that contemporary Spanish culture confronts issues around "the loss of sociality and monumentality; the irruption of violence and the body; the uncanny persistence of reference to nature and history" and recognizes "the progressive disappearance or dematerialization of both subject and object, citizen and city" (111). Frederic Jameson in *The Geopolitical Aesthetic: Cinema and Space in the World System*, whilst speaking to a specific genre of film, captures the ideological scope of many contemporary cinematic projects that blur the lines of their foundational purpose, of which *La influencia* can be included:

> While the expansion of the former cultural sphere to encompass and include within itself everything else in social life (something that could also be thought of as an immense commoditization and commercialization, the virtual completion of the process of the colonization by the commodity form begun in classical capitalism), it becomes impossible to say whether we are [...] dealing any longer with the specifically political, or with the cultural, or with the social, or with the economic — not to forget the sexual, the historical, the moral, and so on [25–6].[9]

Echoing Jameson's emphasis on contemporary culture's confusion, Rivero cannot find anything or anyone to hold onto, including her role as a mother, and drifts further away from being able to go on living.

## *Maternal Emptiness*

When Rivero leaves her shop, the viewer is introduced to her two children, Jimena (perhaps 13) and Romeo (perhaps 6). One catches glimpses of their daily lives — the preparation of dinner, the comings and goings of taking the children to school, and so forth. Rivero's relationship with motherhood is complicated. While she is a mother and the children occupy a good deal of the cinematic time, the spectator is not treated to emotion-filled interactions. She drudgingly completes her basic duties, in most cases preparing some food and purchasing the occasional toy or game. However, even these moments of (material) affection seem scripted. Not scripted because she is disingenuous, but rather she has no access to an emotional core. As before, now there is no dialogue, and the viewer must make due with only the bare traces of communication. The house is hardly a model of cozy Spanish domesticity, with meals being eaten quickly and in silence, and it further detaches the film from any direct association with models of maternal femininity. In fact, the narrative development reveals no other details that might assist the audience to "know" the protagonist on a deeper level, such as the reason for the father's absence or what is driving her to take pills. Her numbness seems less a consequence of some past trauma, and more a permanent state — Perhaps a choice? In either case, it is clear that what has remained is only a shell, her life substance having been consumed long before the audience sees her for the first time.

The children, meanwhile, engage in normal childhood activities. They watch the cartoon network, Romeo is artistic and draws and paints pictures, Jimena invites a friend over and they put make up on each other and hang out in front of the TV. These seemingly innocent activities are mediated and altered when Rivero is in the scene. When this same friend joins the family during supper, with her and Jimena's faces overly made up, there is no friendly banter or familial chitchat. Everything related to the mother happens in silence, as the last remaining remnants of her personality dissolve away.

In another telling scene, Jimena (the daughter) and Lila (her school friend) decide to go to the park to drink stolen mini bottles of liquor. Lying in the grass, Jimena, in an almost a flood of verbal expression for this film, offers up a frank soliloquy of her mother's emotional difficulties: "My mother is a disaster. She is crazy. She only does stupid things. I don't understand. She doesn't think I realize it. I don't think she works anymore" (*La influencia*). Even though Jimena says these words with her friend lying directly beside her, there is no response and no interaction between the two young women. Lila seems not to hear or care what her friend has just finished saying and the information dissolves into the ether. Jimena ends the scene by throwing back the last swig of the bottle and collapsing beside Lila. Jimena's emptiness mirrors her mother's and the collective fear is that Jimena will have no other choice but to follow her mother's example of engaging in mind numbing activities.

Rivero has a final swan song with her children in the only scene that occurs outside of the city. Feigning an excursion in an attempt to act the happy family, Señora Rivero takes the children to a series of sand dunes and they climb up and down them and eat prepared sandwiches. Romeo, exposing his childish naiveté, is the only one who seems to be enjoying himself and, as always, none of them engage in conversation. Even though the space has been opened up and is visually striking, the fact that the space is a sand desert points decidedly to the lack of vitality in their lives. As with the majority of the other scenes, one cannot pinpoint where geographically speaking the action is taking place. An abstract space stripped of cultural mores; the large sand dunes foreshadow how the family is losing its grip on the last strands of togetherness.

Indeed, following this excursion, Rivero takes to her bed and, within what is a hard timeline to discern (perhaps days or weeks), dies. In these scenes Rivero is vaguely reminiscent of the doomed and consumptive nineteenth century woman, whose last breath is drawn in a tragic demise. What occurs in *La influencia*, however, is that the scenes are stripped of all pretense of Romanticism. Her death is not a poetic gesture, but a pathetic display of meaninglessness. During her final days, the children, in a decided switch of focus, become the film's protagonists. Within the vaguely defined time of Rivero's final days, the children descend into a state of chaos — painting on walls, dirty dishes accumulating, eating whatever they can scrounge together, etc. In fact, the only way for the viewer to understand the chronology of Señora Rivero's death is to witness a decaying bowl of fruit. Upon her death, the children have what can only be described as a tempered response. Romeo slightly whimpers and Jimena looks down on her mother's body, but does not cry and is utterly devoid of emotion. The siblings are numbed and Rivero's death is treated as another symptom of the emptiness that has dictated their lives for many years already.

The shot following the death is of the cityscape and it is during the early hours of the morning with the sunlight barely starting to be visible. Of course, the parallels between a new day (dawn) and a new beginning are well beyond cliché at this point. Nevertheless, Aguilera twists the shot away from a facile interpretation and depicts a dawn of cold light and austerity, showing a stark landscape that looks as uninviting as it is hostile. The image reminds the spectator that theirs will not be an easy path, despite having the mother, "la influencia," erased from their present reality. The viewer understands that Rivero's legacy is that she managed to emboss her "will to nothingness" onto her children and that they will inherit an inability to get out from under the emptiness that was her life.

In an abrupt shift of focus, Jimena now takes control of the action of the film. She arranges her mother's body neatly in the bed, cleans up the spilled paint on the floor, washes the dishes, and scrubs the rest of the house. After the house is neatly arranged, with the evidence of chaotic former weeks tidied up, Jimena takes her mother's car keys and she and Romeo set out in the car. Jimena, perhaps unnecessary to mention, is not of age to drive, and promptly crashes into the wall of a rounded exit ramp. This final scene merits close attention, because it can be read on various, and perhaps opposite, levels. As mentioned at the beginning of this study, having bashed her face into the steering wheel upon impact, Jimena emerges with her teeth bloodied and, slowly, begins to laugh uncontrollably. It is this wild and frenzied laugh, through bloodied and smashed teeth, that ends the film. The viewer is now charged with the task of deciding the future of Jimena and her brother. Does the laughing point to future madness, emptiness, and the hollowness of her mother? Or, opposite of that, does the laugh point to a rupture of her life up to this point, indicating a possible escape?

## Consuming the Body

An earlier crucial shower scene underscores the idea of the self, as represented through the body, slowly disintegrating. Showing Rivero in the shower, the camera angle holds its position from the chest up. The scene occurs in slow motion, with the water slowly running over her head and drowning out the sounds of life coming from other parts of the apartment building. This scene is meant to imitate a kind of pharmaceutically enhanced stupor and should also be read on a more symbolic level as an association with the decay of selfhood. The scene in the shower, relates Aguilera, simulates a baptism in which Rivero attempts to "clean" herself from the decay that is consuming her. The symbolic act fails and she emerges from the shower to brush her hair in front of the mirror, her complete emptiness palpable.

In fact, the "emptying" of the self and body is an important motif for Aguilera. As a case in point, Aguilera acknowledges basing some of the thematic and symbolic pulses of the film on the work done by contemporary Spanish photographer, Davíd Nebrera. Nebrera, a schizophrenic who refuses medication, uses his body, kept in an extreme state of deprivation, as the basis for his work concerning the ravages of mental illness. Aguilera parallels Nebrera's imagery of his emaciated physique with the emotional disintegration of Rivero. Nebrera's photographs, both horrific and oddly intriguing, some say beautiful, mimic the tone and structure that Aguilera is interested in portray-

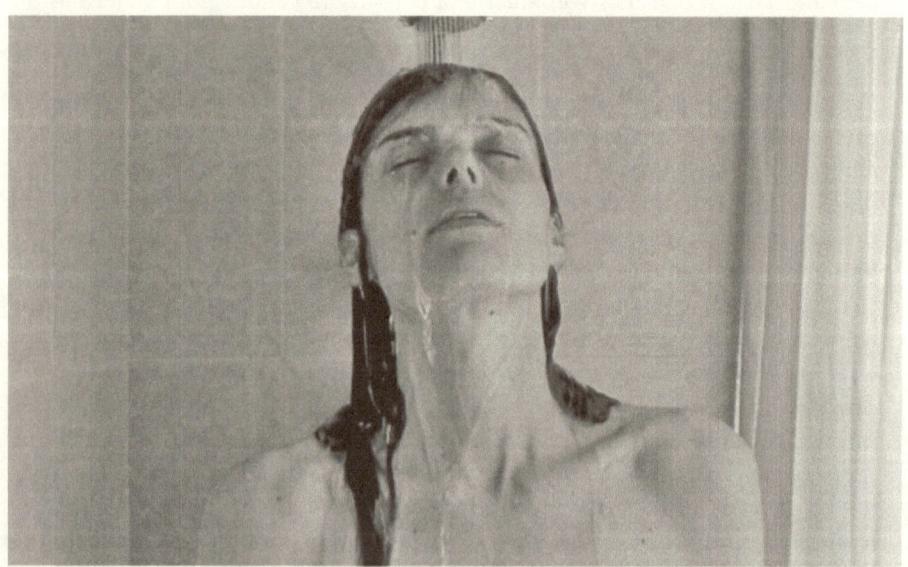

**Señora Rivero (Paloma Morales) in the shower.**

ing. The camera's attention captures, just as Nebrera's photography, a precise moment of decay, suffering, pain, and death. Connected to Nebrera's iconography of self-imposed suffering, Aguilera acknowledges a fascination with the figure of Christ on the cross, especially in works by Renaissance painters Alberto Durero and Fra Angelico, and tries in *La influencia* to emulate the unsteady mixture of violence and beauty found in artists' renderings of the Annunciation on the screen.

A note on Rivero's physical presence on film is worth mentioning. What does come across to the viewer is that by many standards Rivero was once a very beautiful woman. She is tall, pale, slender, dark hair and eyes, and despite her vacant stares and flat affect, one can glimpse a former, more full, person. What this recognition does, however, is emphasize her present blankness and purposelessness and it seems as though whatever used to buttress her up in a previous life has now been shattered. The film offers no real hint as to what or why or even when this fracturing occurred. There are only the meaningless images cut from magazines, coupled with the full collapse of relevance in respect to the other aspects of her life. In a traditional interpretation of Spanish motherhood, this life meaning could be found in the raising of children and in the sanctuary of the home and hearth. *La influencia* does not allow for dependence on such crutches of former roles of femininity.

Echoing this shift, in one of the more difficult scenes, Rivero, revisiting the pharmacy, encounters a man and they seem to be attracted to each other only by way of a common interest in the pills they are buying and an unspoken (at least to the viewer) understanding that they share no emotional connection. As with previous interactions, there is no dialogue between the two. In what is most likely one of the least sexy coital scenes on film, the two are next seen leaving the pharmacy, followed by an immediate shot of them engaged in sex. And, while the scene is not sordid, it is nonetheless unsettling and highly uncomfortable, precisely because its lack of intimacy. A slight ticking of a clock in the background highlights the absence of verbal interaction. In essence, the two could not be further apart, even as their physical (i.e., literal) connection takes place. As the unnamed man slips out of bed and out of her life, Rivero remains semi-unconscious and sleeping, vaguely aware but uncaring that he has left. Barry Jordan and Rikki Morgan-Tamosunas write in *Contemporary Spanish Cinema* that several recent Spanish films engage the body as a locus of feminine subjectivity:

> A number of other contemporary films centre on the female body as the physical, psychological and symbolic focus of their protagonists' sense of self to establish female subjectivity. The spectator is thus confronted, through identification with these characters, with the problematic area of gender difference as a determining factor in existential experience [135].

While one would agree that Rivero is focused on her outward appearance, an aspect that is quickly fading, it becomes more difficult to locate her sense of self as being directly related to her physicality. This is in part due to the face that Rivero is, as the spectator meets her, already selfless and, one would argue, too far gone to find even an incomplete sense of self in her body. In fact, the sex scene does nothing to heighten her sense of self, but rather highlights her emptiness and aloneness. Jordan and Morgan-Tamosunas find that in some contemporary Spanish films, "Explicit sex scenes also negotiate the ambiguous borderland between the progressive representation of sexual identities and subjectivities, and the danger of objectification and exploitation" (138). However, what Rivero experiences during her sex scene is not so much an objectification and exploitation as it is an abandoning of her will. She relinquishes herself without so much as a tinge of regret or meaning. One can only assume that she and the anonymous man are looking for a fleeting moment of pleasure. What is apparent from how the scene is shot, however, is that pleasure does not form part of this equation. The mechanical nature of the interaction and the ever-present silence between them are the most salient features of the event. They "use" each other, but the act is akin to devouring spoonfuls of air, lacking completely in substance.

One of the complications of Rivero's expression, to use a generous word, of her sexuality is that it does not stand in contrast to any identifiable traditional markers. In other words, the binaries concerning sexuality and Spanish womanhood (sexual promiscuity = amoral women; sexual purity = moral women) do not apply in Rivero's case. The problem being that it is impossible for the spectator to put Rivero into context as previously conceived. From a traditional standpoint, when Spanish women were associated with the sustenance of a Catholic hearth and home, as has been well documented and need not be repeated here, Rivero transgresses the domestic space once held sacred as a place of rearing children and fostering family by bringing a strange man home to her bed. On the other hand, those previously held cultural underpinnings do not hold sway in this film. The viewer becomes more concerned with the fact that Rivero is unable to muster up any feelings about the matter one way or another, other than exhaustion and dazedness, and is left with only her apathy. Such behavior, while sexual, is not sexy or erotic and therefore it is not accurate to describe Rivero as objectified or sexualized either by the camera or the others around her. The fact that she fails (also) to be an object of desire points not to some personal defect of Rivero's, but rather stands as a symptom of a larger societal problem of alienation, disjointedness, and an ongoing disinterest in forging lasting connections.

## Final Consumption

Before her death, Rivero's financial situation becomes more desperate as she is confronted with not having the means to pay for the children's school tuition. She begins to steal — a video game and later food. While attempting to shoplift food, Rivero is deterred by a security guard who happens to see her slip some meat into her coat. When she realizes she is being watched, she gingerly places the meat back into the cooler and walks away. It is difficult to tell which situation is causing or perpetuating the other — Is she falling deeper into a foggy melancholy because of her money problems, or are her money problems caused by the self-destruction? Is this a self-imposed ruination or is it meant to be social commentary of the larger alienation of the post-modern subject? The film offers up no definitive answers to these questions. The easiest answer, but yet perhaps the correct one, is that it is a mixture of both. The film suggests a correlation of blame. It is the system of free-market choice that is too big and menacing for the individual to handle and, connected to this, it is the individual who acquiesces to the pressures of the consumer-based structures. Cristina Moreiras Menor in her poignant work *Cultura herida: Literatura y cine en la España democrática* points to Spain's uncertainty upon entering the wider European milieu as a burgeoning democracy as an explanation for certain films and literary expression emerging post 1975 to the present day. Moreiras Menor explains that:

> la mirada confiada al futuro dejan paso a una profunda incertidumbre capaz de transformar lo que antes se había constituido orgullosamente como una comunidad nacional cohesiva y exportable, la "nueva España democrática," en una zona de conflicto que trae a la superficie el agotamiento de la comunidad nacional y, por extensión, de la cultura nacional.
>
> [the confident look towards the future leaves open a profound uncertainty capable of transforming that which before had been proudly constituted as a cohesive and exportable national community, the New Democratic Spain, into a zone of conflict that brings to the surface the end of the national community, and by extension, the national culture] [Moreiras 25].[10]

As connected to the messages conveyed in *La influencia*, Moreiras' explanation fits with nihilism's position on exposing the Western mythos regarding the absolute emptiness of values and beliefs.

As a counter measure against this emptiness, it is possible to read Jimena's display of laughter at the end of the film, at the minimum, as a welcome display of emotion of any kind. Also, there is, at long last, freedom from the closed space of the house as well as the chaos that ensued during their mother's last days of life. Read from a slightly less negative standpoint, her death allows Jimena and Romeo to leave a sullied and dark place. However, this implied

**Jimena (Jimena Jiménez) in final scene, after the accident.**

freedom does not translate easily to the viewer, as a barely adolescent girl laughs through blood stained teeth, sitting in her dead mother's crashed car. If one is forced to read beyond the ending, the future appears tenuous.

Aguilera sees the final scene as a rupture, a point of departure from the oppression that consumed Rivero and interprets Jimena's laughter as a rupture from the past. Perhaps, because the car crashes into the side of a circular structure, there is room to envision a repositioning of the next generation and a hope that the cycle has been disrupted. When speaking about this final scene, Aguilera indicates that he was trying to depict Rivero's death as "sin sentido" [without meaning] by having an ending scene that allows the children to have a moment of catharsis and a chance to "reírse al destino" [laugh at destiny]. He states plainly that "Yo sí creo en ellos" [I believe in them] when referring to the future of Romeo and Jimena. He also points out that the act of laughing is something that their mother was never able to do and that the seriousness of life engulfed her. While there is credibility to Aguilera's explanation, he also acknowledges that the scene can be read from another angle; that the bloody teeth, the lingering sense of sadness and death, the inexplicableness of it all, could indicate a hopeless continuity of the present state. While Aguilera may hope that the two children break with the past, the wounds inflicted by Rivero dying, represented literally by blood and a smashed face, are open and ready to fester, possibly leading the two of them to the same conclusion.

During *La influencia* the viewer is left to fill in the gaps, and there are many. Not only does Rivero lack a sense of place, but she lacks narrative as well. Her personal story and any background information about why she acts the way she does are noticeably absent from the film's trajectory. Instead of overdeveloping the traditional forms of story telling such as exposition, climax, and resolution the film favors silence and questioning. This is why Rivero is not allowed a mythology or even a basic personal history. The viewer simply does not have the privilege of knowing how, why or what has led her to this dark moment, and rather must endure and witness an approximation of a real time demise of an individual.

Aguilera as a director has yet to be classified within or outside of Spain's authorial tradition. Rosanna Maule defines "author" in *Beyond Auteurism* writing, "the author is [...] coterminous with an idea of film-making as an artistic and intellectual practice, whose methods and goals are juxtaposed to those of mainstream cinema, Hollywood in particular" (14). *La influencia* certainly fits this definition and eschews easy conclusions in favor of portraying the gloominess of contemporary life by putting its protagonist on a willing path of annihilation. The images that surround her fail to translate the ideas for which they were invented — beauty, contentment, and life. While the film has an aesthetic attraction, its message is not merely an existential rumination on the meaningless-of-it-all, but rather moves further towards a hopelessness that becomes a search for self-obliteration. In addition, the viewer is left with the question: And what of the contemporary Spanish family? Does Aguilera's viewpoint convey a yearning for a deeper, more connected, familial structure? Is the film attempting to make the contemporary Spanish family seem so desperate and pathetically unappealing as to be a harkening back to a more identifiable and comfortable times of a Francoist past? Aguilera's interest, it seems, lies more in the "telling of the story" of the present, rather than making judgments about the past as more idyllic. The film points more to the feelings of the overwhelming nature of contemporary life and how that life, in its most monstrous capacity, can swallow the individual whole.

For the contemporary subject, *La influencia* forces the question of social cohesion, and begs the question if such cohesion ever existed in the first place. As a "passive" or "weary" nihilist, Rivero's response in confronting this emotional vacuum is to lie down and die.[11] For hers is not quite a suicide and Aguilera insists that she does not die from substance abuse, but rather is "used up." Used up by what, exactly? The answer lies not in the character development of the film's subjects, but in the surrounding imagery and the way it infuses space with empty meaning. *La influencia* shows how nothingness can prevail, how one can move from *fantasma ambulante* to merely *fantasma*. Perhaps Jimena provides the one avenue of escape, but one fears that she is also standing precariously close to the edge of mirroring her mother's fate. Rivero and her family stand out as a model of the futility of living — leaving a gloomy and hopeless prognosis for the contemporary subject.

## Notes

1. *La influencia* stands out as a stark counterbalance to former cinematic portraits of familial bliss, such as Fernando Palacios' *La gran familia* (1962). For more on Fernando Palacio's film see Sally Faulkner's "Chapter 1: Franco's Great Family: La gran familia" [The Great Family], Palacios 1962 in *A Cinema of Contradiction: Spanish Film in the 1960s* (2006).
2. "Meaning spaces which are not themselves anthropological places and which, unlike Baudelairean modernity, do not integrate the earlier places: instead are listed, classified, promoted to the status of 'places of memory', and assigned to a circumscribed and specific position" (Agué 78).
3. See Michel de Certeau. *The Practice of Everyday Life* (Berkeley: University of California Press, 2002).
4. All references to Pedro Aguilera's opinions and insights derive from an interview conducted in Madrid, Spain, in November 2007.
5. For more on Nietzsche's ideas concerning nihilism see Gilles Deleuze, *Nietzsche and Philosophy* (New York: Columbia University Press, 2006).
6. See Doreen Massey, *Space, Place, and Gender* (Minneapolis: University of Minnesota Press, 1994).
7. See Robert Putnam, *Bowling Alone: The Collapse and Revival of American Community* (New York: Simon and Schuster, 2000).
8. The translation is mine.
9. Here Jameson refers to conspiracy theory films that draw in systems so large as to not be easily definable. *La influencia*, while not a conspirator film, eludes definitive classification and crosses and blurs lines of definition.
10. The translation is mine.
11. For more on the concept of "active" nihilism versus "passive" nihilism see David Ohana, *The Dawn of Political Nihilsm: Vol. 1 of the Nihilist Order* (Brighton and Portland: Sussex Academic Press, 2009).

## Works Cited

Agué, Marc. *Non-Places: Introduction to an Anthropology of Supermodernity*. Trans. John Howe. London and New York: Verso, 1995.
Aguilera, Pedro. Personal interview. November 8, 2007.
Bauman, Zygmunt. *Liquid Times: Living in an Age of Uncertainty*. Cambridge, England: Polity, 2007.
Heidegger, Martin. *Nietzsche, Volume IV: Nihilism*. Trans. Frank A. Capuzzi. San Francisco: Harper and Row, 1982.
Jameson, Fredric. *The Geopolitical Aesthetic: Cinema and Space in the World System*. Bloomington and Indianapolis: Indiana University Press, 1992.
Jordan, Berry, and Rikki Morgan-Tamosunas. *Contemporary Spanish Cinema*. Manchester and New York: Manchester University Press, 1998.
*La influencia*. Dir. Pedro Aguilera. Mantarraya Producciones, 2007
Maule, Rosanna. *Beyond Auteurism: New Directions in Authorial Film Practices in France, Italy and Spain Since the 1980s*. Bristol and Chicago: Intellect/University of Chicago Press, 2008.
Moreiras Menor, Cristina. *Cultura herida: Literatura y cine en la España democrática*. Madrid: Ediciones Libertarias, 2002.
*Time, Space, and Subjectivity in Contemporary Spanish Culture*. Oxford: Oxford University Press, 2000.

# 10
# Parents on Stage in Contemporary Spanish Theater

CANDYCE LEONARD

Definitions of the Spanish family and gender roles have been consistently challenged in the late twentieth and early twenty-first centuries as the nation's cultural pluralism and international identity, especially evident as the country sought integration within the European and global communities, have modernized, perhaps even erased, elements of Spain's national traditions and icons. Manifestations of these changes in family life portrayed in Spanish theater were already apparent during the late nineteenth and early twentieth centuries when women's rights movements sprang up throughout Europe and Great Britain. A few examples of the new focus on family roles are *A Doll's House* (1884) by Henrik Ibsen, *Miss Julie* (1888) by August Strindberg, *Mrs. Warren's Profession* (1898) by George Bernard Shaw, *Sacred Blood* (1901) by Zanaida Gippius, *Ashes* (1899) and *Barren Souls* (1908) by Ramón del Valle-Inclán, and *Votes for Women* (1907) by Elizabeth Robbins. Social and economic changes of the historical moment galvanized writers to articulate shifting gender prescriptions, constructions and conflicts.

Ricardo Senabre comments that the "ángel del hogar," for example, is an object of ridicule by Valle-Inclán (1866–1936) in his play *Esperpento de los cuernos de don Friolera* [*The Grotesque Farce of Mr. Punch the Cuckold*] (1921):

> A woman as an *ángel del hogar*[1] [Happy Homemaker] is a fixture appearing with particular frequency in literature of the tear-jerker variety in the second half of the nineteenth century (the *ángel del hogar* is, in fact, the title of a magazine debuted in 1886). Expressions like this one denote the subtly parodic tone expressed in the language of Valle-Inclán's character Mr. Punch [126, n. 9].

Valle-Inclán further addresses progressive social changes in *Luces de bohemia* [*Bohemian Lights*] (1924) when Don Gay discusses his recent stay in England, and a friend asks about the suffragette movement there:

ZARATHUSTRA: Don Gay, what can you tell us about those dykes they call suffragettes?
DON GAY: I wouldn't say they're all dykes [899].[2]

Don Gay offsets Zarathustra's sarcastic assessment of the suffragettes with a suggestive rejoinder that many were attractive women with whom he would like to have connected; we can also assume that some of the New Women[3] were also mothers, such as Emmeline Pankhurst (1858–1928) and as such represented a modernization of the traditional family. Given the historical moment, it is no surprise to find old models laid aside.

Several decades later, historical transitions in twentieth-century Spain continued to influence playwrights in the post–Civil War era, as Gwynne Edwards notes: "any history of twentieth-century Spanish theater reveals that the most significant dramatists of the fifties, sixties and seventies were those whose work was not merely shaped by the circumstances of the dictatorship but was written in opposition to it" (32). Twice awarded the prestigious Lope de Vega Prize, José Martín Recuerda (1922–2007) wrote his powerful Spanish Civil War drama, *La llanura* [*The Prairie*] (1947) to examine the anguish of a war widow seeking justice against the military for her husband's murder by the Nationalists and their furtive disposal of his corpse somewhere on the vast Andalusian prairie. The emphasis on the injustices of the Nationalist brutality that destroy the family does not eclipse the role of the dynamic woman who refuses defeat at the hands of the male establishment. While she finds a certain justice, she also loses her son to the military draft and her daughter is brutally slain as a street prostitute during the desperate times the Civil War produced.

*Los ojos tristes de Guillermo Tell* [*William Tell Has Sad Eyes*] (1955) by Alfonso Sastre (b. 1928) is also a conventional dramatic piece that focuses on the whim of an abusive Nationalist who forces William Tell to shoot an apple from his son's head and prove his reputation as an archer. The son is accidentally killed by his father for the Fascist's sport. *Los ojos* [*Eyes*] (1968) by José Ruibal (b. 1925) is a darker and less conventionally structured play that Bárbara Mujica says is "at its literal level a visceral criticism of the Spanish family.... The mother functions totally in terms of the father's demands, and she is terrified at not fulfilling them. The perfect wife, she worries constantly about the wellbeing of her husband; but she is exhausted and frustrated" (541). Metaphorically, the play refers to the dictatorship, yet the traditional family is at the heart of the drama and the fact that it serves as a criticism of the dictatorship is an implicit critique of the customary family structure with the father at the lead and the mother collapsing under the stress of the inequality.

Each of these dramas, essential to the study of post–Civil War Spanish theater, relies on the traditional family of heterogeneous couples who share parenting responsibilities in the same household. Notably, however, most of these plays use a conventional dramatic formula, except for *Los ojos,* which displays both anti-establishment content and unconventional style.

The 1980s was a pivotal decade since in those years the Second Constitutional Democracy was fully launched and the period of the dictatorship finally edged into history. *Bicicletas son para el verano* [*Bicycles Are for Summertime*] (1984) by Fernando Fernán Gómez highlighted the 1980s, returning to the theme of the Civil War in a touching, anti–Fascist drama where a working-class family — mother, father, daughter, and son — experience the irrationalities of the war amidst the conflict and suffering of their neighbors and friends. *Bicicletas* garnered significant public and critical acclaim, was made into a movie, and reprised in February of 2003 in the Teatro La Latina, again to large and appreciate audiences. It serves as an important dramatic work for its political attention to the Civil War in the aftermath of Franco's death. Without condemning alternative sexual preferences, *Bicicletas son para el verano* affirms the conventional composition of family during that historical period.

The decade of the 1980s established a foundation for plays that more frequently and openly addressed gender roles and sexuality. Such theater pieces were not widely staged in Spain in the 1990s and were viewed by small audiences in marginal theaters; they were, however, published, a vital process for dissemination and research by Hispanists. Even into the first decade of the twenty-first century, alternative representations of the couple are seldom the emphasis of contemporary Spanish drama perhaps, as Catalan playwright Guillem Clua (b. 1973) asserts regarding theater in Barcelona:

> Families are still traditional on stage. Maybe because using another kind of family would divert the audience's attention somewhere else. In other words, playwrights will only use gay parents or single mothers to tell us something about the character or to make it useful for the plot, but never to focus the main concept of the play on their condition as gays or single parents [Personal correspondence with the author].

Many political events have transpired over the past few decades, often with significant impact on Spanish society. They include the constitutional democracy, Spain's participation in the European Union with its common coin, the corruption of the socialist government under the leadership of Felipe González, the arrival of thousands of immigrants, the terrorism of March 2004, the 2005 legislation for same-sex marriage and adoption by same-sex parents, and the recent fixation with memory and the Spanish Civil War. While new marginal sectors have emerged during this time period, they do not represent the majority of theater staged in Spain today.

Dramatic works that suggest a modernization of the role of the parent, the focus of this brief study, include a wide variety of plays such as *Picospardo's* (1995) by Javier Garcia-Mauriño (Madrid 1944), *Bernadita's Place* (1998) by Lourdes Ortiz (Madrid 1943); *The Day I Named You* (2005) by Teresa Calo Fontán (Donostia 1955), *A Mommy and a Daddy* (2005) by Ignacio del Moral (San Sebastian 1957), *Beloved Mother* (2006) by Rafael Mendizabal (Donostia 1940–2009), *Skin in Flames* (2008) by Guillem Clua (Barcelona 1973), *The Free Market* (2008) and *The Path of the Bullet* (2010) by Luis Araújo (Madrid 1956), *Wounds of the Wind* (2004) by Juan Carlos Rubio (Córdoba 1967), and *The Beach of the Doomed Mongrels* (2010) and *Foreskin* (2004) by Nacho de Diego (Alicante 1963).

These and other dramas whose authors demonstrate geographical and chronological diversity vary in their attention to and identity of the parent. Some plays have been staged while others only published thus skewing perhaps our interpretation of present-day Spain and the way we perceive culture. In his study of memory and culture, Alan Confino stresses that "[T]he concept of 'culture' has become for historians a compass of a sort that governs questions of interpretation, explanation and method" (1386). Just as he suggests that memory marks "the ways in which people construct a sense of the past" (1386), our study of theater history in terms of the production of culture often depends on published texts because they are available or we self-select them rather than examine actual theater productions that gain broad Spanish audiences and enjoy the imprimatur of the majority culture.[4] Spanish playwright Ignacio del Moral, author of *Papis* [*A Mommy and a Daddy*] (2005), confirms the absence of new representations of parents on Spain's mainstage: "I believe dramas staged in fringe theater deal a lot with the topic, or at least that's the impression I have, although the plays are unpublished. Probably television series are farther along and have been for quite some time, with large TV viewing audiences. I'm not only talking about comedies, but about serious shows with single parent families or same-sex couples with children" (Personal correspondence with author). Within the larger majority culture, then, there are multiple smaller cultures that connote a praxis that is shaping contemporary Spanish theater history. There are sufficient theater pieces now to make the argument that by 2010 a movement toward normalization of the non-traditional parent is self-evident and growing.

*Papis* is a one-act play that was staged in Madrid's Sala Olimpia in 1992. "Mom" and "Dad" are the two characters, but they are married to others and meet only in the park while taking their babies for a stroll. Eric Ruffin considers their emotional needs:

> Beneath their polite conversation, "the alibi" of children's health, parental obligations, seagulls and an unfinished thesis, the two flirt with each other. They flirt with their ideal spouse. However, because they are both governed by their "married

to another" status, their conversation remains shallow. The ideal, sensitive communicative spouse remains a fantasy, forever existing as an idea [xvii].

Ruffin, rightly so, points to the fantasy — and disappointment — of each character in terms of the reality they cannot escape. The surprise, however, is the standardization of the respective role of each parent: the father is an equal partner in rearing his child, and the mother is completing her doctoral thesis rather than identifying herself as a homemaker within a male-dominated marriage. Each has a "modern" marriage with parental roles that illustrate a new generation of parents, born in the 1950s and 1960s and married in the post–Franco democratic era. More surprising is the unhappiness that both "Mom" and "Dad" suffer. Rather than the ideal marriage as it appeared to be when projected from a 1970s point of view, even a contemporary marriage fails to measure up to its own ideal and leaves couples yearning for something else or something more.

A melodrama starring a married couple in their sixties, Marta and Elías, *Madre amantísima* [*Beloved Mother*] (2003) by Rafael Mendizabal (1940–2009) debuted in September of 2003 at the Centro Cultural de la Villa in Madrid and was published in 2003 and again in 2006. Traditionally structured, *Madre amantísima* opens on a note consistent with the era of Marta and Elías whose marriage is modeled on the governing husband and obedient homemaker wife. The couple bickers and squabbles over petty issues, yet the long-time partnership between them is obvious and strong. The action becomes robustly contemporary when twenty-nine-year-old Juan, the only surviving offspring of Marta and Elías, returns home from Madrid. A successful medical researcher, Juan is gay and dying of AIDS. Marta is jolted from her illusion — that Juan is home to announce an engagement with the promise of long-awaited grandchildren — into the reality of twenty-first century Spanish culture; but disillusionment turns into the abiding love of a parent for her child when she accepts Juan and his partner Carlos into her home and with Carlos' and, ultimately, Elías' help, cares for Juan until his death. Predictably, Elías embodies traditional family values of the Franco era by harshly rejecting both young men, only to incur his wife's unyielding wrath which causes Elías to reconsider his position and his love for his family. Juan remains at home and upon his death, Marta and Elías invite Carlos, also infected with AIDS, to stay and allow them to care for him in their home until his death.

The inclusion of *Madre amantísima* in this study is because Marta and Elías embrace a new family life and indeed signify a new role of parenting, a role that the couple never dreamed they would assume given their own background and environment grounded in conservative attitudes. We see the aging couple lay aside their expectations born of these attitudes and we observe their conversion into contemporary social realities. In his lengthy study included in the 2003 publication of the play, Spanish playwright Pedro Víllora (b. 1968) emphasizes the importance of the traditional format of the play since the drama is directed at a conventional, middle-class audience:

> *Beloved Mother* is neither a revolutionary nor a vanguard text, and perhaps all the more important from a social perspective.... This is a work about everyday people, written for everyday people, for individuals who have not questioned certain convictions and customs about what it means to be different; it is a play that affirms that one can be different but equal, that we can and should change, that there are essential values that should be permanent while others that are thought to be basic human values really are not ["Mendizabal" 14].

Mendizabal is the author of more than fifty full-length plays and over one hundred one-acts, almost all associated with comedy and commercial theater so that his writing on an arguably volatile topic was not perceived as an overt political statement by an activist as much as a drama about family life in the twenty-first century. Víllora stresses that there are no hysterical moments or flashy, sensational scenes; rather, some scenes are quite painful, "not because they stir the audience with shrieking but because they stab the heart with a silent knife" ("Mendizabal" 16). Marta and Elías are readily familiar to Spanish audiences: a hard-working, salt-of-the-earth couple who years earlier suffered the loss of their elder son and now must grieve again, this time within a traditional culture that might condemn their son as well as them, a risk they are willing to accept.

Rafael, the same age as Marta and Elias, is the pivotal character that drives *Las heridas del viento* [*Wounds of the Wind*] (2004) by Juan Carlos Rubio (b. 1967), although he is deceased and never appears on stage. His son, David, a thirty-one-year-old architect, is the offspring designated to go through his father's belongings, discovering among them a bundle of passionate love letters from Juan, a man in his sixties. David knows nothing about Juan or about this secret part of his father's life. The homosexuality of a man born in the 1940s, an accomplished attorney, dutiful husband, and father of three who spent his life as a heterosexual is connected to Rubio's investigation of identity. Rather than making homosexuality the crisis of the play, the author explores an adult son's inquiry into his parent's life after his death, a provocative theme in itself.

Life as a gay man was so forbidden to Rafael that he was unable even to write secret love letters to his "partner," Juan. Some twenty years earlier when he received Juan's declarations of love, Rafael was too constrained by traditional prescriptions of masculinity to respond in kind, yet he wanted to be a part of Juan's life. As a solution, Juan proposed that he write letters to Rafael, and that Rafael respond with blank paper which Juan would then answer with his words of burning desire and devotion for Rafael, words that Rafael not dare articulate. Juan relates this story to David over the course of several meetings as David slowly comes to understand his father's unfulfilled longings as well as his kind yet slightly cool attitude toward his spouse, David's mother. The conclusion of Juan's narration to David about the "true" identity of Rafael is also the end of the play: David sobs over the loss of his father, his father's silent aching, and his own culture-based inhibitions that caused him to be blind to differences and, thus, to deny his father's identity and the loving father-son relationship that he could have had.

Víllora writes that *Las heridas del viento* definitively surpasses all of the Rubio's other plays with its focus on perception: "If there is one play in which Juan Carlos Rubio talks about the differences between who a person is, who the person believes he is, and who everyone else believes him to be, without a doubt this is it" ("El otro Juan Carlos Rubio" 8). The conflict between reality and perception undergirds Rubio's discussion of homosexuality within a culture that proscribes differences and rewards conformity. Written in 1999 and awarded the Antonio Machado theater prize in 2000, *Las heridas del viento* was published in Spain in 2004 and again in 2006 and has been performed for audiences in Mexico, the United States (New York), and Spain in multiple productions since 2005. At its writing in 1999, the play was on the cusp of social and political changes that would result in the 2005 legislation approving same-sex marriages and adoption by same-sex couples. Such legislation belongs to David's generation, but remained far out of his father's reach.

*Las heridas del viento* does not follow conventional format as do other of the plays discussed above, yet neither is it of a vanguard style that would restrict it to small or elite audiences. Like *Madre amantísima*, Rubio's play avoids gay stereotyping, over-the-top scenes, or harsh censure of conventions established decades earlier. The play does, however, unequivocally argue for the acceptance of sexual preference, for the open expression of love, and for the possibility of a fulfilling affective life. Perhaps the most poignant and iconic element of the play are the blank pieces of paper that Juan shows to David, a vacuum corresponding to the absence of the intimacy Rafael could never express, and evidence of his condemnation to an "invisible" subculture within a heterosexually dominated and intolerant society.

The most pronounced indicator of the normalization or standardization of alternative couples following the 2005 legislation approving same-sex marriages and adoption by same-sex couples is the newly formed Certamen de Textos Teatrales Leopoldo Alas Mínguez [Competition of Dramatic Works Leopoldo Alas Mínguez], an international competition specifically for theater texts in Spanish whose themes or protagonists are gay, lesbian, bisexual, or transsexual. Formed in 2007 in honor of the writer and activist Leopoldo Alas (1962–2008), great-grandson of Spain's celebrated nineteenth-century novelist Leopaldo Alas, *Clarín* (1852–1901), this international competition is sponsored by the Fundación Autor [The Author Foundation] of the Sociedad General de Autores y Editores [SGAE: The General Society of Authors and Editors], and the Asociación Cultural Visible [The Association for Visible Culture] with the purpose of "stimulating and normalizing the presence of the LGTB community for writing contemporary theater in the Spanish language, and supporting via this award the social visibility of the community with the full rights and privileges of all citizens" (Certamen de Textos). The annual competition, which has received entries from Spain, the United States, and various countries of Spanish America, confers 2,000 euros to the winning playwright, a dramatic reading of the play, its production in the annual Festival Visible Madrid, and publication in the theater series published by SGAE (Alan). Collaboration with the influential and long-time institution SGAE is a powerful sanction that favorably promotes LGTB[5] theater that has long been marginalized or totally eclipsed by the majority culture. The production of the play at the annual festival of the Asociación de Cultural Visible as well as publication in SGAE's theater series assures the accessibility of these theater pieces and provides a foundation for broader expansion and exploration of the topic.

The third recipient of the International Competition of Theater Texts Leopoldo Alas Mínguez, 2009, is Nacho de Diego (b. 1963) for his play *La playa de los perros destrozados* [*The Beach of the Doomed Mongrels*] (2010). Diego's drama shuns conventional format and style yet remains very accessible. As Ariel Alan describes the play:

> The story is sustained within a structure that increases in tension, and the conversations are actions in and of themselves. The play is written in language that is radically contemporary but fully poetic at the same time, alternating between scenes that seem pulled from an Internet Chat Room — dry and rapid dialogue — and other scenes in which the characters set up complex situations or present themselves to us via meditative monologues that reveal who they are more completely.

Rather than acts and scenes, Diego uses "passages," sixteen of them, each assigned a musical rhythm: "Passage 1: *Sostenuto*," "Passage 2: *Adagio*," and "Passage 3: *Andante*." The scene titles give the reader a convincing sense of changing rhythms and intensities (although we do not know how these textual clues work in a production of the play), while also emphasizing the cultural allusions to art, music, and theater that appear throughout the dramatic work. Second, the structure gives us a sense of the reality of the moment. Whereas "history can be (or appear to be) chaotic and meaningless," Eric Bentley argues, "drama cannot" (11). In terms of *La playa* ... the montage vs. linear structure, the emphasis on rhythm changes via the music notations, and the abandonment of chronologically arranged scenes all correspond to the psychic and personal fragmentation the characters feel after the discovery of Roberto's betrayal of his wife and his subsequent suicide. The drama retains the coherence that Bentley rightly contends undergirds the dramatic work, but the fragmentation of both linear time and rhythm connects us to the chaos that Roberto's infidelity has brought his wife, Diana, as well as the sense of bewilderment Roberto's friends and even his mother-in-law feel about the devastating breakup of their marriage, and his suicide wrought by guilt for hurting Diana and behaving so recklessly.

Roberto is also attracted to men with whom he has had multiple relationships and, unknowingly, is HIV positive. The concept that Diego works with and the relationship to the title is the abandon of self-indulgence that destroy individuals, people "destroyed by a lack of respect, destroying that which they don't know how to respect" (Víllora, "Nacho de Diego a solas" 17). In *La playa de los perros destrozados*, the factor of the character's HIV status is like an STD: concrete proof of duplicity and the harm it imposes on a relationship; it is pain rendered physical that disloyalty imparts to the partner. In his introduction to the 2010 edition of the play, Pedro Víllora lends perspective to the emphasis of the drama:

> I don't believe that *The Beach of the Doomed Mongrels* is a play about AIDS, nor am I convinced that we could say it is a play about homosexuality.... The issue is that Roberto has betrayed Diana, destroying the trust she had placed in him and breaking their marriage vows. AIDS, therefore, does nothing more than expose his betrayal.... *The Beach of the Doomed Mongrels* is the story of lonely people that live among the tumult, about individuals that cause harm by their own inertia, about resentment that produces trauma and impulsive behavior, and about disagreements that turn into animosity ["Nacho de Diego a solas" 15–17].

*La playa de los perros destrozados* received a dramatic reading in the Manuel de Falla Auditorium at the SGAE in July of 2010 as part of the Festival Visible Madrid 2010, with a focus less on Roberto's bisexuality than the crisis created by Roberto's infidelity to Diana.

Roberto's infidelity, in fact, is the core of the dialogue when close friends and Berta, Diana's mother, voice their confidence regarding Roberto's steadfast love for his wife. Berta, expresses no shock that her son-in-law is bi-sexual and asserts her knowledge and unqualified acceptance of Roberto's not having wanted children, noting that children were not a priority for her daughter either. Diagnosed with HIV and recovering from pneumonia, Diana talks with deep anger to her mother about her father, drawing a parallel between Roberto's infidelity and that of her father who abandoned his family for the "sluttiest chorus girl in the company," as Berta describes his seductress. A parent in her mid– to late fifties, Berta is familiar with a husband's betrayal, an age-old paradigm, and she directs herself toward calming her daughter and caring for her rather than censuring Roberto's bisexuality. Berta's inclusion in the play is essential since she is a bridge between generations and because she brings with her the experience and knowledge of survival that Diana must depend on as she finds her own pathway to a new life.

In Nacho de Diego's *Prepucio* [*Foreskin*] (2004) staged in 2006 at the Sala Triángulo in Madrid, the mother, Consol, of the protagonist, Marc, is "an attractive woman" (70) probably in her early sixties. She has minimal stage time, yet talks on the phone with her handsome son throughout the day on his thirty-ninth birthday in preparation to visit him for a small celebration. Her attention to what seems to be an excessive grooming regimen prompts the phone calls from the hair salon and the gym as her schedule deteriorates and she chatters about her ordeal at one place or another. Marc's conversations with his sister and friends are quite different and reveal his homosexuality even as they reference the discussion Marc will have with his mother once she arrives:

Sergi (José Navar, left) and Marc (Nacho de Diego) in *Prepucio* (Foreskin) by de Diego in a 2006 production at the Sala Triángulo in Madrid (courtesy Nacho de Diego).

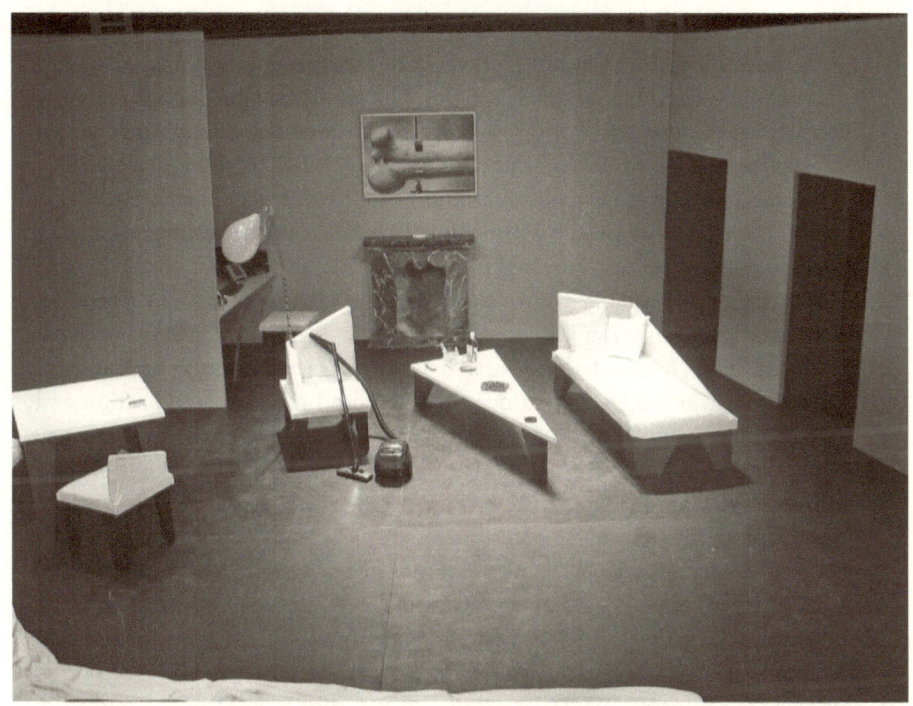

**Set design for *Prepucio* [Foreskin] at the Sala Triángulo (courtesy Nacho de Diego).**

MARC: I will likely mention the issue to her today.
SERGI: "Mention the issue"? Marc, don't beat around the bush or the same thing will happen that always happens.
MARC: Okay, I won't casually "mention" anything; I'll be straight upfront about it [82].

An initial assumption is that Marc will inform his mother that he is gay, so no plans for a traditional wedding are in order. Yet at thirty-nine, his hesitance seems unwarranted and his phone calls to the International Center of Urology leaves the audience uncertain about what stirs Marc's anxiety.

In the full unpublished manuscript,[6] Marc's apprehension is fueled by deep-seated anger: "I've been bitter these thirty-nine years for something you know about only too well and today, specifically today, I've decided to talk about it with Mother" (n.p.). Ignacio Amestoy Egiguren writes that it is a topic "extraordinarily personal on the surface, but that has unsettling social, religious and political dimensions" (17), and those very dimensions connect Diego's play to long-held tradition. Marc is furious that his mother allowed his circumcision — in his view, mutilation — when he was an infant and as a result is less able to function sexually as fully as he would like. The conclusion of the 2004 published version closes with Marc's anger and his problem unresolved. In the lengthier unpublished version, the closing scene includes a conversation between Marc and his sister Nuria, then Marc again calls the International Center of Urology, but this time schedules an appointment for possible restoration of his foreskin.

Nacho de Diego has chosen a bold topic for his play and intentionally directs attention away from his protagonist's homosexuality, thus normalizing sexual preference rather than making it the point of dramatic conflict. As it turns out, Consol has long known that her son is a homosexual. The hypocrisy of the traditional marriage is illustrated in the example of Marc's parents. Before his death, Marc's father visited his mistress every Saturday and, in fact, was with her when the accident occurred that lead to his hospitalization and death. Consol knew about her husband's long-time love affair from the day it started and although she had bouts of jealous rage when she fought bitterly with her husband, ultimately there was nothing she could do within a social system that permitted males such liberties.

At the anecdotal level the play examines Marc's anger about his circumcision thirty-nine years ago; at the figurative level, the story reveals Nacho de Diego's attack against traditions that no longer apply — such as uniform sexual preference. Marc's resentment against his mother and a parental/religious decision that has affected his entire adult life is a direct rejection of tradition. Diego argues "The doctrine of circumcision, that in the historical moment when it became law had in its genesis basically sanitary and hygienic purposes, has long since stopped having meaning in a society of wealth and wellbeing" (Amestoy 17). Marc's parents, born in the 1940s during the Franco era, inhabit gender roles and prescriptions that no longer apply in today's Spanish culture. Parents are central to Diego's drama. Marc's circumcision at the insistence of his Jewish father almost forty year earlier signifies the old way of life that contradicts Marc's life today. Similarly, the heterosexual couple who defined the era of Marc's birth is no longer the singular model. The character of Marc's mother, Consol suggests the transition to a new culture due to her full knowledge and acceptance of her grown son's sexual preference rather than embarrassment or shame at his lack of conformity.

Dramatic roles for actresses playing single mothers that include widows or wives abandoned by their husbands are relatively easy to find since women have played those roles in reality for millennia. In his two theater pieces *Mercado libre* [*Free Market*] (2008) and *Trayectoria de la bala* [*The Path of the Bullet*] (2010), Luis Araújo (b. 1956) demonstrates the transfer from the traditional Spanish *madre* to a contemporary model that incorporates the influx of immigrants into the European Union in general and into Spain in particular. The immigration that began in the late 1980s has altered the demographics of

Spain as well as raised the issue of illegal status that appears in numerous late twentieth and early twenty-first century Spanish dramas. *Mercado libre* earned the Premio Esperpento 2008 de Textos Teatrales [The 2008 Esperpento Prize for Dramatic Texts] and premiered in March of 2009 in Madrid's Teatro Español, the same year that the Teatro Español re-published the text in an impressive color edition with production photos and several essays about the play and its thesis: the power that money buys and the abuse of that power.

The two characters are named *A* and *B* so that even in their names the male, *A*, has dominance over the female, *B*, who comes in second and is inferior to the powerful male attorney infatuated with her. *B* is a prostitute and *A* is the insatiable client who wants to possess her in this formula of buying and selling that so perfectly elucidates the social inequality that Araújo indicts:

> It is a free market for citizens of Class A, of course. Because if the citizen of Class B tries to get into the game, s(he) is immediately reminded of the insufficiency of merits to belong to Class A. (S)he does not have the right legal status, the lack of scruples, the right pedigree, the right skin color, the right nationality, the assistance of a clan or social group, (s)he does not have.... How can (s)he even try to own the right to freely compete, equal to equal? [Araújo "Introduction" 11]

The author is less concerned about prostitution per se than about a human being made vulnerable by a democratic society that promises freedom while repressing it within a capitalist economy that emphasizes buying and selling within a power-structured hierarchy. Jorge Urrutia writes: "For me, for however tragic the theme of prostitution is, it is nothing more than a symbol ... the entire dramatic circumstance is a symbol of the always cruel social structure" (55). Any eroticism, then, that exists in the story is merely a metaphor of the profound avarice and the physical abuse that *A* imposes on *B*, clear evidence of society's prostitution of the vulnerable.

That *B* is a single mother is essential to the storyline because she is desperately trying to provide a better life for her three children. We know nothing of their father(s), but we learn that her first sexual encounter occurred in her native country where she was raped at the age of twelve, victimized by the abuse of an older man who exercised his power over her. Luis Araújo agrees that her condition as a parent is critical to *Mercado libre*:

> That she is a mother is fundamental in developing the plot because without her three children, the woman would never have allowed these levels of humiliation.... Nevertheless, within the social metaphor that the play establishes, I believe that it is vital to note that people accept their exploitation in manual labor, and social scorn (segregation, discrimination, etc.) because they are trying to give their children a life they themselves could not have [Personal correspondence with author].

When *B*'s two sons, aged fourteen and fifteen, are arrested for raping a schoolmate (yet another frightening commentary about generational gender

Daniele Freire in the role of A in *Mercado libre* [Free Market] by Luis Araújo in the 2009 production at the Teatro Español in Madrid (© Sergio Parra).

Yoima Valdés portrays B in *Mercado libre* [Free Market] at the Teatro Español (©Sergio Parra).

power and cyclic behavior), the mother anxiously turns to the formidable attorney for help, promising him payment or whatever is necessary to save her children and return them to her. He is successful, but the price seems far too dear.

José Monleón fittingly addresses the excesses of the power and greed that money buys, the thesis that is repeated throughout the dialogue: "It is all a question of how much.... Except that — and here is where the drama stops being an anecdote — the moment arrives when possession is not enough, when it is no longer the goal. It simply no longer satisfies" (11). *B* is the voice of humanity and reason, both in dialogue and action, while *A* is the devouring and insatiable demon. In the penultimate scene, *A* is tying and gagging *B*, as she screams that he must swear that he will protect her children. The action of the final scene takes place one year later as *A* waxes eloquent to the news media, explaining that the mother has disappeared, that "she is a poor woman who had no other solution than to prostitute herself in order to give her children a good life" (2008, 71) and that out of his sense of humanity, he will graciously assume guardianship of the pathetic woman's three children. His double-edged explanation implicitly signals his continuing demand that she belong only to him. In these final bone-chilling moments the audience can only assume that she either remains imprisoned somewhere for his private use, or that his excessive craving has indeed killed her. The closing of the play is poignant: "A flash illuminates his smile that hangs floating in the darkness" (2008, 72). *A* is vile.

Luis Araújo's most recent play, *Trayectoria de la bala*, merited the *Premio International de Dramaturgia Cultura Frontal* [International Prize for Theater on Advanced Culture]. The thesis ostensibly is racism as the father (unnamed) and elder son, Chema, are involved in illegal activities (legal on paper, thanks to their family attorney) and cannot tolerate the presence of immigrants in Spain, legal or not, or anyone else that seems unfit for whatever reason. The younger son, Pablo, aged twenty-three, is in love with thirty-eight-year-old Janirah, an Iranian living in Spain illegally. Her skin color, her Mid-Eastern origin, her imperfect Spanish all disqualify her to be the wife of Pablo and mother of his children — she is pregnant with their first child. Even her status as a human being is called into question. Arújo's theater is uncompromisingly political, ever challenging the relativity of culturally dictated norms that define the human condition. It is Chema that personifies moral vacuity in *Trayectoria de la bala*. He and his cohorts have burned Janirah's shabby dwelling to the ground and while she is hospitalized briefly to treat her burns, Pablo's father intends to coerce an abortion of her unborn child with the assistance of an accommodating doctor. Extending the pressure, he threatens to reveal her illegal status and have her deported unless she consents to abort her child.

Pablo senses the urgency of the situation when his father suddenly leaves, so he races to her side thereby saving his child.

Whereas the actions of the three male characters motivate the dramatic conflict, the greatest force of the piece rests on the two women: Pablo's mother, Clara, a traditional Spaniard in her late fifties, and Pablo's soon-to-be-wife, Janirah. Conversations between Clara and her husband as well as between Clara and Chema suggest she is a somewhat passive wife and mother. Yet she is clearly a woman who recognizes and condemns the wrongdoings of her husband and son. She is also an individual who chooses to investigate what is new rather than outright reject what she does not know.

The first act concludes with Chema on his way to the hospital after accidentally shooting himself when he tried to kill Pablo, and the second act opens a few days later with the burial of the father. The father's death from a heart attack is barely mentioned or grieved, and Chema's survival as a paraplegic after the shooting is not detailed. These are crucial events in the life of the family that serve metaphorical rather than melodramatic functions: the father must die since he personifies an old way of life that has no place in contemporary Spain and global, twenty-first century identity and culture. Chema is paralyzed from the shooting and, like his father, demonstrates a hatred so comprehensive and irrational that it must be paralyzed if Spanish society, like the family itself, is to move forward in harmony. Further, the playwright proposes that just as the bullet brought destruction upon the one who fired the shot, unbridled and vitriolic discrimination ultimately backfires on the individual (Araújo "El camino hacia el *otro*" 139).

These two events ultimately enable Clara and Janirah to talk openly with each other and experience communication and understanding in their own relationship as women. Their dialogue is characterized by very brief sentences in contrast to the longer passages in the rest of the play, and with every word the gap between two very different cultures and countries closes:

MOTHER: And you are from Morocco.
WOMAN: No. Iran. You know Iran?
MOTHER: Iran, me? No. Well, Ceuta...
WOMAN: Tehran is very big. Much bigger than Madrid.
MOTHER: Ah! Very big...
WOMAN: Seven million are living.
MOTHER: Inhabitants.
WOMAN: Yes, seven million.
MOTHER: Seven million?
WOMAN: Yes, much people.
MOTHER: Muslims.
WOMAN: No all. Also Christians and Zarathustran. Do you say Zarathustran in Spanish?
MOTHER: There are Christians in Iran?

WOMAN: Yes, a few. Before, also Jews. Today almost not.
MOTHER: Today there are no Jews?
WOMAN: No, much hate, fanatic. Jews go in Israel...
MOTHER: You are Arab.
WOMAN: Not Arab; I Persian.
MOTHER: Well, Muslim, right?
WOMAN: No.
MOTHER: No?
WOMAN: No.
MOTHER: Why not?
WOMAN: No. I agnostic.
MOTHER: Agnostic?
WOMAN: Yes.
MOTHER: Oh, no!

*Silence.*

MOTHER: Do you mean that ... you don't believe in anything?
WOMAN: I don't know ... perhaps ... Jesus? Mohammed? I don't know, good men. They love goodness. I love goodness, too.
MOTHER: You love goodness?
WOMAN: Yes. You no?
MOTHER: Yes, of course. I'm Catholic. How could I not love goodness.
WOMAN: Yes. We love goodness. Men love power, dominating, they crazy. Men hate, they make war. We no.
MOTHER: We?
WOMAN: Women.
MOTHER: What? Ah, I see.

*Silence.*

MOTHER: Women.
WOMAN: Yes. [183–184]

With few words, Janirah transcends the cultural clutter of the historical moment, the alleged impenetrable differences, and the fear of change to articulate their similarities and the common humanity that they share. But Araújo takes it a step further when Janirah, the "other" from a faraway land, summarizes the blight on Spain's heritage epitomized by Chema:

WOMAN: You think much problems. Because you not know problems, not know about problems. Problems is other thing. Hunger, disease, no water, war, no medicine, no school, no rights, no freedom ... that is problems. Spain is very good. Money, party, laughter is very good. Everyone eat, everyone have home, everyone have medicine [n.p.].
...
Women in Iran not free. But here ... no is my country. Here is democracy, women free.
MADRE: Free? [186–187].

Brief or one-word sentences usually give audience members a heightened sense of rhythm and increased intensity in a stage production, but the conversation between Clara and Janirah is paced, almost deliberate as guided by the stage directions: "*Silencio.*" and "*Pausa.*" These stage directions specify a rhythm of process as Clara considers what she is learning about Janirah, and as Janirah serenely anticipates a future in which her son will enjoy a new world of freedom, peace and love.

The dramatic works contained in this discussion record the trajectory of contemporary Spanish theater history and the theatrical landscape of the twenty-first century. Aimed specifically at theater pieces that include characters in the role of a parent, this essay demonstrates a political discourse that at present remains at the margins of the majority culture rather than at the center where "endorsed texts"[7] thrive. Spanish playwright Jerónimo López Mozo (b. 1942) proposes that non-traditional roles is not a typical theme in contemporary Spanish theater and suggests that one reason we do not see a broader range of representations is that "Up until 1975, censorship did not tolerate even questioning the traditional concept of the family. After 1975, few authors have approached the topic, perhaps because such plays would likely be poorly received by audiences" (Personal correspondence with author). Political or ideological censorship is more fully understood when contextualized within Joseph R. Roach's analysis of theater history and inscription/erasure where he argues that "Inscription is the ideological production of bodily images and behavior.... Inscription foregrounds and reiterates favored representations; erasure occludes the undesirable ones" (159). It is arguable that theater works that dominate commercial Spanish stages are less politically challenging and more crowd pleasing so that the "production of bodily images and behavior" *vis-à-vis* the single parent or same-sex parents remains outside of the traditional sphere of Spanish culture.

A second factor for consideration is that of the published playtext vs. its production on stage. Maria M. Delgado points out in her study of erasure and inscription in contemporary Spanish theater: "the interest invested in Spanish playwrights by foreign academics is not matched by the presence of their plays on European stages" (3). She further argues that "theater needs to be performed. Theater is a collective work, and it doesn't happen on its own" (1). There is no question that playwrights compose their dramatic works for the stage and spectators and not solely for reading. In his prologue to *Las heridas del viento*, Juan Carlos Rubio insists: "I believe that my work as an author does not become real theater until an actor breathes life into the role" (7). French theorist Patrice Pavis argues that "more than any other art, theater demands, through the connecting link of the actor, an active mediation on the part of the spectator confronted by the performance; this happens only during the *event* of aesthetic experience" (70), while Michael Issacharoff responds to the troublesome polemic of the ephemerality of the production and, I would add, to the inability of everyone to attend a performance in Spain: we turn to "the script — the only constant element" (57). I concur with Delgado regarding the possible skewed outcome of evaluating thematic representations in Spain when we examine and emphasize only the published dramatic text or unpublished manuscript without proper attention to stage productions and audience experience and reception since these factors are indelible components of culture.

The increased publication and production of contemporary Spanish plays with new characterizations of parents is a signpost of a more open environment where the concept of family is broadly defined. The dynamics and composition of the Spanish family have been modifying for decades so that what has been the practice in social reality is revealed on stage by playwrights. Their characters are educated, articulate individuals with self-agency, thus re-inscribing the stage with a new "ideological production of bodily images and behavior."

## NOTES

1. See, for example, Bridget Aldaraca's study, "El ángel del hogar: The Cult of Domesticity in Nineteenth-Century Spain."
2. All translations of citations, excluding some of the titles, are mine unless otherwise noted in Works Cited.
3. See Elaine Showalter 38–58 for her discussion of New Women.
4. See Maria M. Delgado 1–5 for her discussion of text vs. production, marginalized texts and Hispanists' choices regarding texts for research and classroom teaching.
5. I am using the acronym LGTB (Lesbian, Gay, Transvestite, Bisexual) since this is the one used by the Festival Visible Madrid (see <http://www.festivalgayvisible.com/index2.html>), by the Asociación Cultural Visible (see <http://www.festivalgayvisible.com/coleccionVisible.html>), and in the call for papers for the Certamen de Textos Teatrales Leopoldo Alas Mínguez (see <http://www.festivales.com/ver/festival/leopoldo-alas-minguez> and <http://www.festivalgayvisible.com/Certamen.html>).
6. Eight of the original thirteen scenes in the manuscript appear in the published version.
7. See Maria M. Delgado 1–5 for her discussion of text vs. production, marginalized texts and Hispanists' choices regarding texts for research and classroom teaching.

## WORKS CITED

Alan, Ariel. "Nacho de Diego, ganador del 'Certamen Internacional de Textos Teatrales Leopoldo Alas Mínguez.'" June 3, 2009. <http://teatro.universogay.com/nacho-de-diego-ganador-del-certamen-internacional-de-textos-teatrales-leopoldo-alas-minguez_03112009.html>.
Aldaraca, Bridget. "El ángel del hogar: The Cult of Domesticity in Nineteenth-Century Spain." In *Theory and Practice of Feminist Literary Criticism*, eds. Gabriela Mora and Karen S. Van Hooft. Ypsilanti, MI: Bilingual Review, 1982, pp. 62–87.
Amestoy Egiguren, Ignacio. "Introducción: Libertad de creación." *Teatro: piezas breves*. Madrid: Fundamentos, 2004, pp. 7–24.
Araújo, Luis. "El camino hacia el *otro*." *Trayectoria de la bala*. Madrid: El Teatro de Papel, No. 12. Ediciones Primer Acto, 2010, pp. 135–143.

———. "Introducción." *Mercado libre*. Ed. Ángel Facio. Madrid: Teatro Español, 2009, pp. 9–12.
———. *Mercado libre*. Madrid: Asociación de Autores de Teatro, 2008.
———. Personal correspondence with author. December 2, 2010.
Bentley, Eric. "The Science Fiction of Bertolt Brecht." *Galileo* by Bertolt Brecht. Trans. Charles Laughton. Ed. Eric Bentley. New York: Grove, 1966, p. 9–42.
Certamen de Textos Teatrales Leopoldo Alas Mínguez. "Bases legales 2010."
Clua, Guillem. Personal correspondence with author. September 8, 2010.
Confino, Alan. "Collective Memory and Cultural History: Problems of Method." *The American Historical Review* 102.5 (1997): 1386–1403.
De Diego, Nacho. *La playa de los perros destrozados*. Madrid: Ediciones y Publicaciones Autor, 2010.
———. *Prepucio. Teatro: Piezas breves*. Madrid: Fundamentos, 2004, pp. 69–93.
———. *Prepucio*. Unpublished manuscript.
Delgado, Maria M. *"Other" Spanish Theaters. Erasure and Inscription on the Twentieth-Century Spanish Stage*. Manchester: Manchester University Press, 2003.
Del Moral, Ignacio. Personal correspondence with author. September 21, 2010.
Edwards, Gwynne. "Post-Franco Spanish Theater, Jaime Salom and *Casi una diosa (Almost a Goddess)*." *Contemporary Theater Review* 7.4 (1998): 31–44.
Issacharoff, Michael. *Discourse as Performance*. Stanford, CA: Stanford University Press, 1989.
López Mozo, Jerónimo. Personal correspondence with author. September 10, 2010.
Mendizabal, Rafael. *Madre amantísima*. Madrid: Editorial Fundamentos, 2006.
Monleón, José. "Prólogo." *Mercado libre*. Madrid: Asociación de Autores de Teatro, 2008, pp. 9–11.
Mujica, Bárbara. "Sobre *Los ojos*" *Texto y vida*. Fort Worth, TX: Holt, Rinehart and Winston, 1990, pp. 541–42.
Pavis, Patrice. *Languages of the Stage: Essays in the Semiology of the Theater*. New York: Performing Arts Journal, 1982.
Roach, Joseph R. "Theater History and the Ideology of the Aesthetic." *Theater Journal* 41.2 (1989): 155–168.
Rubio, Juan Carlos. "Prólogo." *Las heridas del viento*: *Humo. Arizona*. Madrid: Fundamentos, 2009, p. 7.
Ruffin, Eric. "A Note on the Plays." Ignacio del Moral. *Dark Man's Gaze; A Mommy and a Daddy*, and *Little Bears*. Trans. Jartu Gallashaw Toles. Ed. Phylliz Zatlin. New Brunswick, NJ: Estreno Plays, 2005, pp. xv–xvii.
Senabre, Ricardo. Note to *Los cuernos de don Friolera: Martes de carnaval* by Ramón del Valle-Inclán. Madrid: Espasa-Calpe, 1990, p. 126, n. 9.
Showalter, Elaine. *Sexual Anarchy: Gender and Culture at the Fin de Siècle*. New York: Penguin, 1991.
Urrutia, Jorge. "Del mal como conocimiento: el teatro de Luis Araújo." *Mercado libre*. Ed. Ángel Facio. Madrid: Teatro Español, 2009, pp. 31–58.
Víllora, Pedro M. "Mendizabal: escrito para gustar." Madrid: Centro Cultural de la Villa de Madrid, 2003, pp. 9–76.
———. "Nacho de Diego a solas." *La playa de los perros destrozados* by Nacho de Diego. Madrid: Ediciones y Publicaciones Autor, 2010, pp. 15–18.
———. "El otro Juan Carlos Rubio." *Las heridas del viento* by Juan Carlos Rubio. Madrid: La Avispa, 2004, pp. 5–10.

# 11

# Basque Identity on Stage
## *History, Family Constructs, and the Troubled Mother in Maite Agirre's* Bilbao: Lauaxeta, tiros y besos *and Teresa Calo Fontán's* El día en que inventé tu nombre

TRACIE AMEND

Like many postmodern authors, Spanish dramatists of the twenty-first century engage in a re-examination of recent history in order to address shifting identities. In the case of Maite Agirre's *Bilbao: Lauaxeta, tiros y besos* [Bilbao: Lauaxeta, Shots and Kisses] (2002) and Teresa Calo Fontán's *El día en que inventé tu nombre* [The Day I Invented Your Name] (2004), the female protagonists struggle with two roles: unconventional motherhood, and their place within Basque (and Spanish) history. In both plays, the female characters' positions as mothers and Basque citizens become two intertwining and often conflicting forces in their lives, particularly when the women are forced to confront the past. In this way, Agirre and Calo Fontán use the stage to explore the relationship among history, family, and "national" identity in a twenty-first century context.[1]

As a revisitation of the Spanish Civil War from the Basque perspective, *Bilbao* offers not only a new historical version of the conflict, but also examines alternative maternity and family constructs as a central component for Basque identity then and now. Although the characters ultimately fail in their attempts to form successful Basque family units, the potential for such constructs finds relevance for twenty-first century Basque society. Specifically, Agirre implies that the realization of an alternative family in the thirties might have forged a productive path for Spain and for Basque citizens had history turned out differently.

After a brief exposition set in the early twenty-first century (to be discussed in detail later), the spectator is plunged into the recreated history of the Civil War. Specifically, an old woman, later revealed to the spectator as Mertxe Adulta, enters and remembers her youth as one of four ardent Republican activists in the thirties. The setting is a bar in Bilbao, where Republican youths discuss their ideals, conflicts, and hopes for the future. The four principal characters are Mertxe Joven and Leire, two girls who discuss their future as potential wives and mothers, and Luís and Ángel, the boys in love with Leire. Although Luís supports the political and social ideals of his peers, Ángel is an ardent Republican on the front who places his ideals before everything— even his own life.

Whereas the first half of the play presents a series of political and personal discussion, the second half delves into concrete problems of the individual. While the men argue and drink, Leire reveals to Mertxe that she is pregnant with Ángel's child. As the war progresses, she must decide whether to marry the dependable Luís, risk an alternate familial identity with Republican activist and soldier Ángel, or choose both men, thereby subverting the traditional family construct. Once she reveals her secret to the men, Luís and Ángel fight to determine who will act as husband and father. Despite Leire's suggestion that they form a family unit together, both men reject that option. The result is that Ángel returns to the battlefield while Leire, Mertxe, and Luís shield themselves during a night of bombing. Although all three survive the bombing, the play's conclusion is not a happy one. When Ángel returns from battle several weeks later, he learns that Luís and Leire stayed inside the bar without proper medical care. Luís explains that both Leire and her baby died during his absence, and the flashback ends with the two men fighting physically and emotionally over their lost love/potential family. As the action returns to the twenty-first century and the bar ruins, the only character that survives into old age is Mertxe Adulta—the sole conduit into the past.

Within the central plot narrative of Basque youths during the Civil War, Agirre creates a layered and complex analysis of the conflicting political and social ideals of the time period. In her analysis of the play, Candyce Leonard focuses on the celebration and discussion of a distinctly Basque culture ("Fantasmas" 72). The emphasis on Basque icons and visual symbols informs the characters' passion for national identity. Even within the setting of the bar, the youths listen to Basque musicians playing the *trikitixa* (a Basque accordion), hang up regional flags, and recite verses in *euskara*. As the title suggests, the characters are dedicated to a celebration of Basque expression through the most famous Basque poet of the thirties, Lauaxeta. Lauaxeta and his verses foster political and artistic inspiration throughout the play. In Leonard's words, the recitation of the national poet "es un acto de homenajear al poeta, y también es el espejo del rol de la poesía de Lauaxeta en la cultura popular vasca" [it's an act of homage for the poet, and it also mirrors the role of Lauaxeta's poetry in popular Basque culture] (72).²

While this recognition of a national poet serves to contextualize the Civil War from a distinctly Basque perspective, the characters also allude to and discuss ideas within the greater Republican movement, including the support of unions and communist organizations from other regions. Ángel often conflates Basque regional culture and Republican ideals, proclaiming at one point, "Bizkaiko miatze gorri, zauri zarae mendi ezian en la calle se escuchan rumores de huelga, brazos duros, trajes azules" [red mines of Bizkaia, deep wound on the green mountain on the streets one hears rumors of strikes, strong arms, blue suits] (84). In this recitation, Ángel combines some of Lauaxeta's verses describing the "red mines" of Bizkaia with the red fervor of the proletariat and the fight of the people. Ángel's code-switching from Basque to *castellano* throughout the play suggests his dedication to a dual culture, an ideal that the other characters allude to as well. The combination of Basque patriotism and the support of Republican efforts seems to suggest the hope for a national identity within the context of Spain; that is, that Basque youths may embrace both their regional identity as well as their place in a future Spanish nation. However, this reconciled notion of Basque identity only reaches as far as the characters' naiveté. When Nationalist bombs land on Bilbao, the characters realize that all of their ideals — whether personal, political or social, will be buried with the rubble of the bar.

While the exploration of Basque culture and identity is the overarching focus of the play, a crucial component of that exploration is the family structure. Within this hybrid nation of Basque culture and Republican ideals, does the family remain the basic building block of post-war society? It is this question that quickly becomes the crux of the characters' choices and their futures as Basque citizens. Because of Leire's pregnancy, the characters must examine their true beliefs regarding sexuality, gender roles, and parenthood. In this way, the characters' political debates lead them into the discussion of family and its place in the future of the nation.

Initially, the dialogue in the play concerns different political opinions, particularly the small disagreements between Luís and Ángel. Although Luís supports his friend's efforts during the war, he is enough removed from battle that he becomes a philosophical counterpart to Ángel's ardent soldier. Their differences crystallize as they fight over Leire:

> VOZ DE ÁNGEL: ¡Eres un cobarde! Mientras tú te entretienes en robarme a Leire y en resolver tus problemas existenciales sobre el amor libre y no la patria, otros lucharemos en primera línea y trataremos de resolver los problemas del país, los problemas de todos.

Voz de Luís: ¡Déjame en paz!
Voz de Ángel: No. Todavía no. Luís, ¡Estamos en guerra!
Voz de Luís: Yo odio vuestra mentalidad militar, vuestros amores patrios.... Os regalo vuestra guerra sin fin, perennemente justificada. ¡Viva la revolución! ¡Fuera la patria! ¡Ni Dios, ni amo, ni Rey!
Voz de Ángel: ¡Siempre igual! Nos robáis mientras os damos la vida!
Voz de Luís: ¡Yo no te he pedido tu vida. Mátate por tus ideales, pero no por mí! ¡Adiós!

[Ángel's Voice: You're a coward. While you're busy trying to steal Leire from me and resolve your existential problems about free love and not our homeland, others are fighting on the front line and trying to resolve the country's problems, the problems of everyone.
Luís's Voice: Leave me in peace!
Ángel's Voice: No, not now. Luís, we're at war!
Luís's Voice: I hate your military mentality, your love of homeland.... I'll give you your unending, always justified war. Long live the Revolution! Out with the homeland! Out with God, owner and king!
Ángel's Voice: It's always the same with you. You rob us while we give you our lives.
Luís's Voice: I haven't asked you for your life. Kill yourself for your ideals, but not for me! Goodbye!] [110].

The two men's differing views parallel their romantic rivalry — specifically, the men form a traditional erotic triangle with Leire as the object of desire. According to Eve Kosofsky Sedgwick's discussion of the erotic triangle, the rivalry between men creates a homosocial relationship in which the men express different types of desire towards one another.[3] In the case of Luís and Ángel, the desire within the erotic triangle is not so much homoerotic as it is the yearning to form a productive union with Leire. In other words, both men are fighting to establish themselves as the best husband and father of the "new" nation, whether it be as part of Republican Spain or within a Basque state (or both). Of course, neither vision of this post-war nation materializes, and the hope for a productive family dies with the Republicans' defeat. Ultimately, neither man is able to forge a productive unit — their rivalry fails to produce a solution, and both Leire and her child are lost to the trials of the war as a whole.

Although the early scenes in the play seem to focus primarily on Republican efforts and Basque regional pride, the rhetoric concerning sex and marriage enters into the discussion from the first moments of the play. Even before Leire reveals her secret to her friends, the issue of individual freedom, and especially, free love for both men and women, is a common topic for the youths. Luís in particular supports secular free love, even toasting "Viva el amor libre" [Long live free love] in the early moments of the play (80). All four characters show disdain for traditional Catholic notions of marriage at different moments. Ángel and Mertxe Joven are quick to point out that a traditional marriage (and the Catholic system that supports it) no longer serve the public's (or Republican activists') interest. Ángel proclaims "En lugar de bodas y leches más nos vale a todos alejarnos de las Iglesias, por si acaso..." [Instead of weddings and mother's milk we should work on getting get away from churches, just in case] (85), and Mertxe chimes in, saying, "Tienes que admitir, Leire, que las Iglesias ya no son muy seguras" [You have to admit, Leire, that churches aren't very safe these days] (86). Along with criticizing the traditional aspects of a "church" marriage, the youths express admiration for artists and activists who defy the dominant rhetoric concerning love, sexuality and marriage. Specifically, the young Basques discuss a recent production of *Bodas de sangre* and the plight of the lovers who defy convention. It is in this metatheatrical moment that the spectator first witnesses the passionate and eventually naive interaction between Ángel and Leire. Ángel applies their free will to his relationship with Leire, who in turn plays along in the tragic drama of scandalous love and sex:

> ÁNGEL: (Off) y fuera de la Iglesia le espera su gran amor que ... podría ser yo.
> LEIRE JOVEN: Y que yo te matara... (*Coge a Ángel y atrayéndole hacia ella le besa en la boca. Vemos a la pareja en el marco de la puerta*).
> ÁNGEL: (*Se pone a recitar*)
> "Hmmm ... la boca sirve para comer" (*Hace unos pasos de danza cogiendo a Leire por la cintura*)
> "Las piernas sirven para la danza"
> "Y hay una cosa de la mujer...." (*Dice algo al oído de Leire. Ésta se santigua como escandalizada*).
> LEIRE JOVEN: ¡Jesús!
> MERTXE JOVEN: (*Signándose y haciendo que se escandaliza*). "Son indecencias de los pueblos." (*Todos se echan a reír*).
> [ÁNGEL: (Off) And outside of the church awaited her beloved, who could be I.
> YOUNG LEIRE: And I could kill you... (*She grabs Ángel and pulls him over to kiss him. We see the couple in the outline of the door*).
> ÁNGEL: (*He begins to recite*). "Hmmm ... the mouth is for eating" (*He dances a few steps slipping his arm around Leire's waist*)
> "Legs are for dancing, and there is one thing of woman...." (*He says something in Leire's ear. She crosses herself as if scandalized*).
> YOUNG LEIRE: Jesus!
> YOUNG MERTXE: (*Crossing herself and pretending to be scandalized*). "Those are common indecencies." (*Everyone breaks into laughter*)] [81–2].

This early performance among the four main characters serves several different purposes. On an artistic level, the youth's knowledge and appreciation of Lorca's works (including references to *Dona Rosita*), indicate their sense of camaraderie with other marginalized persons/regions in Civil War Spain — in this case, the gay poet of Andalucía.[4] In this moment, the youths identify with Spanish culture as a whole rather than isolating themselves as solely Basque citizens. Along with expressing their national identity, the performance also indicates the characters' longing to break away from conventional notions of love and marriage — to avoid the tragedy that unconventional, star-crossed love brought to Lorca's characters.

In theory, all four youths support a sense of free love unbound by matrimony or conventional, Catholic notions of the family. When pushed to put their ideals into practice, however, the characters' instinct is to embrace traditional notions of love, sexuality and marriage. Even before Leire reveals her pregnancy, Luís and Ángel begin to form a rivalry within the traditional erotic triangle. When Luís dances with Leire and they accidentally kiss, Ángel immediately assumes the stance of a territorial boyfriend:

> ÁNGEL: Aclaremos algunas cositas, amigo Luís. Primera, nada de robarme a mis novias. (*Las mujeres se ríen haciendo comentarios burlones*). Segundo, creía que no leías ciertos periódicos y por último el bar está cerrado así que se acabó la fiesta por hoy, amigo.
> LUÍS: Tengo suficientes argumentos para rebatir tus miserables argumentos contra mí. Primero, la mujer no es una propiedad y además la propiedad privada se ha abolido. Segundo, la poesía de vuestro Lauaxeta es puro cancionero popular y también esto es colectivo y no una propiedad privada. Tercero y último, el bar no está cerrado porque lo abro yo, como primer cliente, antes de una dura jornada en la fábrica, y como hoy estoy de muy buen humor pues venga, ¡todos a bailar!
> [ÁNGEL: Let's get a few things straight, Luís. First none of this stealing my girlfriends. (*The women laugh and make teasing comments*). Second, I didn't think you read those types of newspapers, and finally, the bar's closed so the party's over for today.
> LUÍS: I have plenty of rebuttal arguments for your miserable little complaints against me. First, women aren't property and furthermore, private property has been abolished. Second, the poetry of our Lauaxeta is popular verse, which is also collective and not private property. Third and finally, the bar isn't closed because I open it as the first customer after a long, hard day at the factory, and since today I'm in an excellent mood, everybody dance! ] [87].

Although this early exchange maintains a light-hearted tone, the scene acts as a precursor to the play's key conflicts; that is, the desire for love and family juxtaposed with the Republican cause and Basque patriotism. Both Ángel and Luís support the idea of a political collective, but they are reluctant to extend these ideals to their romantic/sexual relationships. This conflict between the youth's social ideology and traditional practice quickly becomes the central argument of the play, as Leire's pregnancy forces each character to consider his/her role as potential parent. Despite Luís's recognition of the men's hypocrisy throughout the play, neither Ángel nor Luís is able to break out of the traditional family construct.

For much of the play, Leire herself vacillates between trying to secure a stable family (potentially represented by Luís), or sacrifice her own wellbeing and security to the Republican cause (as espoused by Ángel). Unfortunately, neither path satisfies the requirements for a protected, productive family during and after the war. Once she reveals her secret to Mertxe, Leire is able to explain her conflicted feelings towards the movement and her role as mother:

> Ángel y yo, aunque no quiero hablar de Ángel, solo decirte que íbamos, bueno, eso creía yo, muy en serio ... lo malo es esta guerra asquerosa que me lo está complicando todo, pues, cuando más ilusionada estaba, va y me dice que quiere dejarlo, que la situación no está por romanticismos, que somos libres, que cada uno tenemos que contar nuestro sitio en esta "coyuntura" como ésta ... seis meses son largos, se mire como se mire y ahora me da una patada, como se hace a los perros y me dice, hala, busca tu sitio ... luego ha empezado con lo de que no tenemos por qué ser una pareja convencional, y yo ¿convencional? ... y todo me sonaba muy bien dicho, pero yo todo el tiempo con una sensación de que me estaba echando a patadas de su lado, pero disfrazando las patadas con palabritas, total que me coyunturé por mi cuenta buscándome a mí misma y ... qué fácil es todo para ellos, que fácil.
>
> [Ángel and I, well, I don't want to talk about him, I'll only say that we were getting, well, at least I thought we were getting, serious ... the hard thing is this horrible war that is complicating everything in my life ... well, when I was more hopeful, he comes to tell me he wants to leave our relationship, that this situation isn't one for romantics, that we are free, that every person has to find his place in this "situation" ... six long months, no matter how you look at it, and now he kicks me like you kick a dog and he tells me, go look for your place ... then he starts with this we don't need to be a conventional couple business, and me, conventional? ... and everything sounded well said, but I was thinking the whole time that he was just kicking me out of his life, but disguising the kicks with pretty little words with the result that I get tied up in a mess looking for myself ... how easy everything is for them, how easy!] [89].

Leire's monologue acts as a turning point in the play's trajectory — whereas the early scenes were a series of hypothetical discussions and declarations of beliefs, the second half of the play asks whether it is possible, practical and just to apply these ideals to the "real" world — in this case, the responsibility of parenthood. In this moment, Leire realizes that as good as Ángel's rhetoric sounds, it is as restrictive and oppressive to women as the traditional gender roles that the characters criticized in the early scenes of the play. Initially Leire hopes to provide a "padre normal" [normal father] for her child, but she realizes that a traditional union with Ángel is not an option (97). If all three characters are trapped in a traditional erotic triangle, and the alternative "coyuntura" is just as oppressive, then it is necessary to create a new family construct that allows for a just distribution of labor between mother and father.

After Leire articulates the challenges she faces as a Basque/Republican mother, both women discuss the benefits of an improvised family that steps outside of the ineffective, (and eventually, tragic) participation in the erotic triangle. Whereas Luís and Ángel only see a rivalry in which one man must triumph, Leire and Mertxe view their opposition as an opportunity to create familial (and consequentially, national) unity and productivity. From Leire's perspective, her optimal position as wife and mother is one in which she enjoys the men as a complementary set. When Ángel insists that she choose one of the them as the "only father," Leire replies, "Os amo a los dos y no puedo vivir sin ninguno de los dos.... Ángel, estoy enamoradísima de ti, y tú ya lo sabes, pero quiero también a Luís porque me siento muy protegida a su lado ... junto a él me parece que soy una mujer fuerte" [I love you both, and I can't live without either one of you.... Ángel, you know I'm crazy in love with you, but I also love Luís because I feel protected with him ... with him I find myself to be a strong woman] (105). She, as well as her child, is served by combining the paternal qualities of both men. Not only does she benefit from Luís's stability and Ángel's passion; she also ensures protection and stability for her child.

Unfortunately, the women's alternative ideas of familial structure are too progressive and not practical in the midst of civil war violence. Once Ángel leaves for battle, Luís and Leire attempt to survive by themselves, with the result that both mother and child perish. In this sense, Leire's assertion that she can't live without both men becomes a prophecy of her approaching death. The ideal of a better family dies with Leire and the Republican cause, and as a result, Leire's dream becomes buried with the other forgotten ghosts of the Civil War. It is only when Mertxe Adulta excavates them in the twenty-first century that both the political and social ideals of her youth may find new life.

Although the majority of *Bilbao* takes place during the Civil War, the play's trajectory is set in motion through memory—specifically, the memory of an old woman who conjures the ghosts of the past. In fact, the plot of the erotic triangle is framed by an exposition and conclusion in the twenty-first century. It is only through Mertxe Adulta's memory that the vision of the Basque youths appears; therefore, the twenty-first century bookends are crucial to the overall interpretation of the play as a whole. The first scene begins with Mertxe Adulta entering the vestiges of an old bar in Bilbao. As the spectator hears construction noises, it becomes obvious that the bar will soon be demolished. Although the spectator first sees the ruins of the old life, it is only a matter of minutes before Mertxe's memory brings forth the scene in which both the bar and its inhabitants are young and vibrant. Since Mertxe exists in the twenty-first century (and also conjures the memory of herself as a young woman), she becomes the spectator's conduit between past and present, between historical ghosts and the physical vestiges of those ghosts in the present. This opening scene allows Agirre to resuscitate a personal historical narrative from the perspective of the present. Rather than merely presenting the story of the bar in its "own" period from the beginning, Agirre ensures that the present sustains the memory of the past — in other words, that the present invents the past, and that in turn, the past reformulates the present. As Candyce Leonard notes in her introduction to the play, the memory of the past "sirve para crear — o recrear — la historia de un país y su gente hasta el punto de constituir una identidad actual" [works to create — or recreate — a country's and its people's history in order to make up a current identity] (69). By the end of the play, it becomes increasingly clear that the role of the mother is a crucial component of this "current identity." In other words, Leire's potential as a good, albeit unconventional, mother becomes a bastion of hope for a productive family unit of the future. Just as Mertxe Adulta resuscitates the ghosts of the past through her memory, she is also able to resuscitate and reflect upon the ideology that was lost during that unique period of Spanish history.

The concepts of re(created) history, national trauma, the appearance of ghosts through memory, and the assemblage of ruins are reminiscent of Jo Labanyi's depiction of haunting in her article "History and Hauntology; or, What Does One Do with the Ghosts of the Past? Reflections on Spanish Film and Fiction of the Post-Franco Period." In her analysis, Labanyi explains how the ghosts of the past reemerge to seek "reparations" due to the fact that those in power have repressed or ignored their memory (66). In her words, the ignored ghosts have existed in "historical hells" in which they are "denied a narrative" (72). The lack of vestiges, or Derridean traces, prompts the ghosts to reappear and restore the lost memory — specifically, they create a postmodern *bricolage* formed from the ruins of the past (69–70).

This assessment of haunting applies effectively to the use of ghosts on stage in *Bilbao* in that Mertxe Adulta is able to reconfigure the past through her memory and the physical ruins of the bar. In other words, she provides the missing traces from which the ghosts of the past will find their "narrative" — in this case, the visual representation of their lives and struggles during the Spanish Civil War. The visual nature of the theater also gives a powerful embodiment to the ghosts. Not only does Mertxe Adulta look them at; they also receive the gaze of the audience, thereby legitimizing their presence and the validity of their lost history. Thus, the spectator sees recreated history though Mertxe's eyes, and the story of Basque Republican youths is resurrected and legitimized. At times, the ghosts themselves look back at their conjurer, thereby also enjoying the position of the gazer.[5] In this sense, the relationship between ghosts, Mertxe Adulta, and the spectator provides a powerful exposition for the historical trajectory of the theatrical action.

Because the hope for a loving, unified family dies with Leire, it seems that the play's ultimate message is one of sadness and regret. However, this interpretation is not entirely accurate- although the potential for the productive family and just nation dies out with the characters, the dream of such a nation lives on through the memory of Mertxe Adulta. Her ability to recreate past hopes within the ruins of the bar suggests that the ideals of the thirties could be resurrected. Mertxe secures their memory in the hopes that that narrative might serve a purpose for the twenty-first century; that is, that a new perspective on the past will reframe Basque identity in the present.

While Agirre presents a hypothetical model of an alternative family, Teresa Calo Fontán examines the problematic family construct that is created when one grows up without the continual presence of both parents. In her play *El día en que inventé tu nombre* [*The Day I Invented Your Name*], Calo Fontán examines the nature of the mother-daughter dynamic in relation to the debate over Basque nationality in the twenty-first century. Unlike the young Basques in *Bilbao*, the characters in *Día* are flesh and blood beings that exist in an exclusively twenty-first-century setting. Despite these significant differences in structure and setting, both plays include similar thematic threads. Specifically, both dramatists play with the concept of dual culture/nationality through the prism of the family construct. In other words, Agirre and Calo Fontán explore the ability of the Basque people to develop their identity as both Basques and as Spaniards. Moreover, both dramatists recognize the importance of the family construct in the process of nation-building (although the type of nation built remains the central point of debate), and both present the obstacles inherent in the creation of a productive, happy, family. Finally, both dramatists explore the role of the mother as the central building-block of individual/national identity.

Esperanza, the mother in *Día*, is charged first with meeting the teenage daughter whom she abandoned, then convincing her to leave the ETA-inspired street-gang *kale-borroka*. Throughout this process, both mother and daughter attempt to define themselves through the prism of national history and their forsaken familial roles. Like in *Bilbao*, the majority of the action involves political and social debates between characters. Esperanza attempts to explain the reasons she was not present in Bego's life, and Bego attempts to explain the reasons she has participated in *kale-borroka*. Although the characters form a bond as they pour out their souls, Esperanza eventually fails in her attempts to "set her daughter straight." Eventually, Bego slips out of her mother's house in order to rejoin *kale-borroka*. In the last scene of the play, Espe reads a newspaper article that explains that Bego has been arrested for her participation in a violent demonstration. Without Bego's physical presence, Esperanza is left wondering whether she could have altered Bego's path. Ultimately, she can only mourn the loss of her daughter from afar.

As in *Bilbao*, the drama's trajectory depends upon two thematic threads — the debate over Basque nationality and identity, and the construction/deconstruction of the family. The political debates pertain to the definition of Basque nationality — that is, how Basque citizens define themselves. Having lived through the oppression and violence of the dictatorship, Esperanza rejects *kale-borroka* as senseless, ineffective violence. Moreover, she suggests that Basques can play an important role in the Spanish democracy while also retaining a sense of regional patriotism. Bego, on the other hand, eschews all authority as an extension of Spanish oppression. Throughout the play, she defends violence as a necessary means to fulfill the denied Basque identity — that is, an autonomous *Euskadi*.

In both cases, the view of individual and national identity is wrapped up in a sense of trauma. In his article "'¡Malditos pueblos!': Apuntes sobre los vascos a finales del siglo XX" [Damn Villages!: Notes on Basques near the End of the Twentieth Century] Philip Silver characterizes this trauma as a lingering psycho-social condition that plagues Basque citizens for years after the Transition. Specifically, Silver mentions the decimation of northern Basque territories during the war as one origin of trauma (47). This physical destruction was compounded by the continual denial of *Euskadi* as a nation-state, leading to a widespread Basque melancholy (48). As an ultra-marginalized group, Basques suffer and relive the trauma of their continual "otherness." This trauma manifests itself in the extreme polarization of Basque politics, fostered by two main groups — the *españolizantes* (those who support Basque cultural and political integration into Spain) and the *nacionalistas* (those who desire a completely autonomous Euskadi without Spanish influence or occupation) (51). Both groups deny and negate the other, which perpetuates the sense of otherness and the history of trauma among the Basque people (51). Those who support a middle ground are usually forced to take one side or the other: "si los nacionalistas estatales y los españolizantes quieren negar la existencia de la patria o nación-estado de los nacionalistas vascos (los abertzales), estos últimos pretenden obligar a tragar por la fuerza a los no-nacionalistas su concepción minoritaria de lo "vasco" y su diseño de Euskadi ... un modelo de vasquidad elegido por ultra-abertzales" [if regional/state nationalists and españolizantes want to deny the existence of the country or nation-state that Basque nationalists, or abertzales, fashion, the latter group attempts to force the others to swallow their minority concept of Basqueness and their concept of Euskadi ... a model "Basqueness" chosen by uber-abertzales] (51–2).

This sense of trauma and the resultant political polarity of the Basque people becomes the canvas onto which Calo Fontán paints the troubled mother-daughter relationship. Although both Espe and Bego have identified themselves as rebellious or Other (Espe as a relatively leftist hippie, and Bego as a punk *etarra*), their political ideologies become an increasing point of contention between them. After Bego confirms her participation in *kale-borroka*, Espe remains dubious towards Bego's ideology and shows disdain for ETA-like violence:

> ESPE: No lo entiendo. Puedo entender tu rebeldía ante una situación que te parece injusta, pero...
> BEGO: ¿Me parece?
> ESPE: Es posible que lo sea.
> BEGO: ¿Es posible?
> ESPE: Vale, lo es. Al menos, para una parte de la población. Pero lo que no entiendo es la forma de lucha. Es cruel, injusta, y estéril.
> BEGO: ¿Me vas a dar la charla sobre los procedimientos democráticos?
> ESPE: No. Primero porque la democracia me ha decepcionado bastante. Es un lavado de cara de muchas injusticias, no tienes que convencerme. Pero yo he vivido una dictadura, ¿sabes?, y te aseguro que la mierda de la democracia no parece tan mierda si se compara con lo otro. Pero ya no quiero hablar de política contigo.
>
> [ESPE: I don't understand it. I can understand your rebellion in a situation that seems unfair to you, but...
> BEGO: It seems to me?
> ESPE: It's possible that it is.
> BEGO: It's possible?
> ESPE: Ok, it is. At least, for a part of the population. But what I don't understand is the way in which you fight. It's cruel, unjust, sterile.
> BEGO: Are you going to lecture me about democratic procedures?
> ESPE: No, because democracy has disappointed me considerably. It's a way of washing away many injustices; you don't have to convince me. But I've lived through a dictatorship, you know? And I assure you that democratic shit is nothing compared with that. But I don't want to talk politics with you] [182].

Despite Esperanza's proclamation, the debate quickly returns to the question of violence and destruction. Specifically, Espe confronts Bego about her alleged participation in a recent demonstration in which members of *kale-borroka* burned a bus:

> ESPE: ¿Contra quién vais?
> BEGO: Contra el sistema.
> ESPE: ¿Qué sistema? ¿El de transportes? ¿Cuál es el objetivo? ¿Que quiten los autobuses y os pongan tranvías?
> BEGO: ¿Ves porque no quiero hablar contigo? No tengo por qué aguantar tu ironía.... Esa acción sale en la prensa y evidencia que hay un conflicto armado, o sea, que Euskadi ya no se ha rendido y sigue luchando contra el invasor.
>
> [ESPE: Against whom are you fighting?
> BEGO: Against the system.
> ESPE: What system? The transportation system? What is the objective? You want them to take away buses and give you streetcars?
> BEGO: Do you see why I don't want to talk with you? I don't have to bear your sar-

casm.... That demonstration was covered by the press and it is evidence that there is an armed conflict, or in other words, that Euskadi has not given up and will continue fighting the invader] [183].

In this moment of dialogue, Calo Fontán puts forth the heart of the argument of Basque nationalism. The nationalists (in this case represented by Bego) adopt a position of independence through rebellion and violence, both of which are justified in order to overthrow an oppressive occupation. As Bego explains simply earlier in the play, "en el momento en que se vayan, acabará la violencia, ya está" [the moment they leave, the violence will stop, and that's that] (174). Esperanza not only represents an older generation, but also the more mainstream position of the Basque people — that is, that while the Basque Country may have been occupied unjustly, the road forward is one of consolidation. In other words, Espe indicates that Basques should continue to fight for regional respect while also contributing to the overall nation-state — a possibility that seems possible to some Basques who had already survived oppression, alienation and violence under Franco.

Due to the sophistication of Esperanza's argument and Bego's petulant tone, the spectator tends to "side" with Esperanza's more tempered and intellectual vision of Basque nationality. As Candyce Leonard asserts, the theater-going public would most likely identify itself with Esperanza ("Construyéndose" 147). Nonetheless, the spectator may not discount Bego's (and by extension *kale-borroka* and ETA's), ideology. Calo Fontán seems to suggest that the extreme Basque nationalists are entitled to their resentment, and that their actions and presence as citizens may not be extricated from Basque history or identity. Just as a crucial piece of Esperanza's identity is wrapped up in Bego (and vice-versa), so too is the mainstream Basque citizen required to recognize the struggle for national autonomy.

This political debate is firmly entrenched in a twenty-first century context, including the discussion of the effects of the Transition, the development of Spanish democracy, ETA, post 9/11 terrorism, and the train-bombing in Madrid. However, the underlying political conflict remains one that has existed throughout the twentieth century; in many ways, Espe and Bego's disagreements parallel the ideological debates of Luís and Ángel in *Bilbao*. Like Ángel, Bego is an extreme activist who will fight for her ideals to the point of self-sacrifice; like Luís, Esperanza fears the consequences of unending violence and supports a more peaceful/intellectual activism. Once again, the two debating characters represent two crucial sides of the Basque attitude towards its nationality and identity.

Although Calo Fontán does not use ghosts as explicitly in *Día* as Agirre does in *Bilbao*, the plot and themes in *Día* still rely upon the notion of retracing personal and national history. Specifically, the play taps into the legacy of

Basque-Spanish interaction from the beginning of the dictatorship to 2004. For Esperanza, the ghosts of the dictatorship still loom in her memory; for Bego, she wishes to resurrect not only the ghosts of Basque resistance, but also her own memories of her lost childhood.

During a later scene in the play, Esperanza describes victims of the dictatorships as ghosts who continue to haunt those Basques of her generation. Upon telling the story of a baker who lost their son and their bakery, Espe describes the couple as "fantasmas" and "sombras de sí mismos" [ghosts] and [shadows of themselves] (203). In a particularly emotional political debate regarding execution and torture, Espe further explains the legacy of the dictatorship from both sides: "En más de una ocasión tu madre, después de llorar por la víctima, cercana, ha llorado de nuevo al conocer la identidad del verdugo" [On more than one occasion your mother, after mourning the victim, nearby, cried again upon finding out the executioner's identity] (202). In this sense, Espe recognizes how the more general (i.e., Spanish) trauma of the dictatorship is connected and related to the post-war, regional trauma that impedes Basque unity.

Although Bego has not yet developed much trauma through a series of political memories, she too is haunted by the memories of familial trauma. Specifically, Bego uses the visual tool of Espe's portrait to create a sense of memory and identity: "Me sé tus fotos de memoria, las he mirado y remirado cada noche durante horas" [I know your pictures by heart, I have looked and looked again at them for hours every night] (185). She also recounts how she longed to look like her mother's photos to the extent that she cried when her father cut her hair: "Creo que sentí de alguna forma que me estaban cortando la cuerda que nos unía. Y así fue, porque no volviste a aparecer" [I think I felt in some way that they were cutting the cord that united us. And that's just how it was, because you didn't come back] (186). As a near-adult, those "happy" memories have become reminders of absence — both of her mother and of self. The traces of abandonment, as exemplified by objects (hair, photos, books) become visual signs of Bego's personal trauma. Ultimately, Bego's angst manifests itself as political rebellion — a connection which is continually explored throughout the mother-daughter encounter.

Although Esperanza is not necessarily an *españolizante*, her attempts to assuage Bego's trauma and argue against her radicalism puts mother and daughter on opposing ends of the spectrum. Of course, the political trauma is mirrored by familial trauma. Bego's feelings of abandonment as a child, and the absence of a mother are conflated with her assertions that she (and the Basque collective) have been denied a crucial piece of identity. Although Esperanza attempts to explain her past to Bego, the daughter cannot see past her own trauma and the bad memories of her childhood. Concurrently, Esperanza is haunted by her choice to relinquish her place as Bego's mother.

In this sense, both characters grapple with their past but fail to find a clear-cut solution to their lingering trauma. Like Bego, the spectator wonders why Esperanza chose to leave her child; and like Esperanza, the spectator wonders if the model of a traditional, or at least, present, mother would have prevented Bego's political radicalism. Through the emotional confrontations and discussions between mother and daughter, Calo Fontán seeks to explore those questions.

The familial trauma expressed in the play circles around two pressing issues — initially, Bego seeks to understand why Espe left her. While this discussion is important, the true question becomes how much of Bego's identity is dependant upon her relationship with her mother. How has her mother's presence and absence influenced her development as a young adult, and is she ever separated from her past or her parent's actions? According to Candyce Leonard, Bego is forever linked not only genetically to Espe, but her life's trajectory is forever influenced by the relationship with her mother. In Leonard's words, Bego's identity has been formed by "el mundo aftectivo de su madre," [the world her mother's affection created] and despite her rebellious actions, Espe remains "su centro" [her center] (146). If the link between mother and daughter may never be broken, then this fundamental relationship becomes the key to healthy individual identity, and by extension, healthy national identity. For Bego, however, her sense of self remains wrapped up in the dual traumas of personal abandonment and the legacy of Spanish occupation.

When prompted to explain her abandonment, Espe's primary explanation is that she loved Bego too much, but knew too little. Later, Espe explains that she wished to give Bego a more stable, financially secure life that only her father could provide. With this explanation, the spectator begins to see the schism of the two parents as one that goes beyond a physical separation. Bego's father represents the relatively rich bourgeoisie (and probable *españolizante*), and Espe offers his foil — an anti-traditional hippie who in her own words, is "la única persona de tu familia incluida tú misma que no es burguesa" [the only member of your family, including you, who isn't bourgeois] (172). This characterization is fleshed out with Espe's ideology concerning love, marriage and parenthood. Even before deciding to leave Bego with her father, Espe describes how she rejected traditional marriage with Bego's father, calling their marriage "un follón" [a big commotion] (165) and later proclaiming that even the wedding bucked tradition — "Ahí me puse inflexible, nada de iglesia" [In that case I was inflexible, no church] (188). Despite her explanations, Bego remains unconvinced and continues to conflate her parents as part of the same political and social ideology.

Although Espe is unable to convince Bego to leave *kale-borroka*, the troubled teen does receive a sense of closure during certain moments of self-discovery. After several rounds of political debate, Bego remembers the time she did spend with her mother, and also learns of the origin of her name. During a particularly poignant moment, Espe explains that Bego's first name was Beitu, which in *euskara* means "to look" or "to observe." In a tender monologue, Espe explains:

> Intuía que no tenía en realidad nada que ofrecerte y el nombre ... era como una especie de herencia. Debía ser hermoso, sonar bien, y acompañarte en la vida. Transmitirte lo que quizás no podría decirte ... porque aunque en este momento ni siquiera pensaba en ello, no pensaba en irme, ni nada parecido, tenía una especie de presentimiento, un nudo en la garganta, un presagio de que yo no iba a estar allí, contigo, mucho tiempo.... Yo quería depositar mi mensaje de vida en tu nombre. Así que por fin, di con "Beitu."
>
> [I knew that I really didn't have anything to offer you and the name ... was a sort of heritage. It had to be beautiful, sound well, and accompany you in life. Transmit to you what I might not be able to tell you ... because although in that moment I didn't even think about it, I wasn't thinking about leaving or anything like it, I had a sort of premonition, a lump in my throat, a sense that I wouldn't be there, with you, for much longer.... I wanted to deposit a life message with your name. And that's how I came up with "Beitu"] [196].

It is in this moment that the two are able to connect not only through memory, but also through a sense of shared identity. Despite her absence, Espe maintains a figurative presence in Bego's life by inventing her identity—that is, giving her a meaningful name. This mark of identity ensures that Espe is always a part of Bego's development, even though her absence has caused trauma in her daughter's life. The fact that Bego's name denotes both Catholic tradition and Basque intellectualism implies that she has the potential to be the child of the future—that is, she could embody the consolidation that has been lacking among Basque citizens.

In this sense, Calo Fontán ties together deftly the debate over political identity with the universal yearning for a family and a sense of individual identity. Not only are mother and daughter separated (and then brought together) by political ideology; they are also separated and brought together through the broken and restored family construct. In this way, the debate over the Basque "nation" is inextricably linked to the re(construction) of the family unit.

Unfortunately, this promise of a hopeful future is dashed by the dysfunctional trajectory of the family and the political polarization among Basque citizens. While Bego may have represented the new future of Basque identity, the promise remains unfulfilled. As in *Bilbao*, the productive family is more of an idea in its embryonic stages that ultimately fails to develop due to personal problems, wars, and regional crisis. Once again, ideology and hope fall victim to personal and political upheaval. Yet, both dramatists suggest that there may be hope for the Basque Country in the twenty-first century. The alternative, productive family unit remains a powerful image that can reappear and potentially materialize. In a sense, the dream is performed through the visual medium of the theater; that is, both dramatists show the *potential* for Basque greatness. Concurrently, both dramatists also present the obstacles that subvert the dream, and both realize that history must be unearthed, retraced, and recreated. Moreover, national trauma must be resolved before the crucial building-block of national identity — the family — may be reconstructed in a healthy, productive way.

## Notes

1. I have placed "national" in quotation marks due to the ever-changing definition and political complexities that the concept of a nation-state evokes. Within the context of this chapter, nation may connote democratic Spain as a whole, the Basque Country as an autonomous nation (Euskadi), or any number of other configurations. Spain as national label is in itself inadequate, as Randolph Pope suggests in his semiotic analysis of the language of nation-state: "This word 'Spain' needs to be handled with all the caution that Wittgenstein recommends when one is faced with ... an imprecise construction subject to multiple and debatable delimitations" (360). In the plays studied, national identity is viewed from a variety of perspectives and historical moments, and Basque nationality itself remains a constantly shifting construct. Thus, the concept of nation depends upon the dramatic and historical context of that particular moment of the play and is not meant to be an all-inclusive term.

2. All translations from *castellano* to English are mine; however, Candyce Leonard has provided translations of Basque words for both plays. I have taken her translations into *castellano* as a guide for my own translations where Basque words are used.

3. For a thorough discussion of the spectrum of desire shared between men in an erotic triangle, see Eve Kosofsky Sedgwick's *Between Men*.

4. Leonard notes that Lorca is tied to Basque culture in that the organization of Basque poets, *la Asociación Libre de Ensayos Artísticos,* produced and performed *Bodas de sangre* in Bilbao (72). Furthermore, Lorca and Lauaxeta were colleagues who were both executed by Nationalist troops in 1936 (72). In a sense, Lorca becomes an Andalusian version of Lauaxeta, and therefore represents the same ideals expressed in the verses or songs of Basque patriotism.

5. Labanyi also pinpoints the subjective position of the ghost as related to the gaze. In her analysis of the film *Soy Ana,* Labanyi notes that ghosts vacillate between positions — acting as the gazer one moment and becoming the object of the gaze in the next (78).

## Works Cited

Agirre, Maite. "BILBAO: Lauaxeta, tiros y besos" in *Teatro español del siglo XXI: actos de memoria,* eds.
Candyce Leonard and John P. Gabriele. Winston-Salem, NC: Editorial teatro, 2008, pp. 77–122.
Calo Fontán, Teresa. "El día en que inventé tu nombre" in *Teatro español del siglo XXI: actos de identidad,* eds. Candyce Leonard and John P. Gabriele. Winston-Salem, NC: Editorial teatro, 2009, pp. 153–211.
Labanyi, Jo. "History and Hauntology; or, What Does One Do with the Ghosts of the Past? Reflections on Spanish Film and Fiction of the Post-Franco Period." In *Disremembering the Dictatorship,* ed. Joan Ramón Resina. Amsterdam: Editions Rodopi, 2000, pp. 65–82.

Leonard, Candyce. "BILBAO: Lauaxeta, tiros y besos: fantasmas del pasado" in *Teatro español del siglo XXI: actos de memoria*, eds. Candyce Leonard and John P. Gabriele. Winston-Salem, NC: Editorial teatro, 2008, pp. 69–76.

———. "Construyéndose la identidad en El día en que inventé tu nombre" in *Teatro español del siglo XXI: actos de Identidad*, eds. Candyce Leonard and John P. Gabriele. Winston-Salem, NC: Editorial teatro, 2009, pp. 145–51.

Lewis, Tom. "España fuera de sí: Representing San Sebastián in Antonio Muñoz Molina's *El invierno en Lisboa* and *Ardor guerrero*." In *Spain Beyond Spain*, eds. Brad Epps and Luis Fernández Cifuentes. Lewisburg, PA: Bucknell University Press, 2005, pp. 331–59.

Pope, Randolph. "Spain Imagined from Outside Spain: The Space of Autobiographical Memory." In *Spain Beyond Spain*, eds. Brad Epps and Luis Fernández Cifuentes. Lewisburg, PA: Bucknell University Press, 2005, pp. 360–72.

Sedgwick, Eve Kosofsky. *Between Men*. New York: Colombia University Press, 1985.

Silver, Philip. "'¡Malditos pueblos!': Apuntes sobre los vascos al final del siglo XX." In *Disremembering the Dictatorship*, ed. Joan Ramón Resina. Amsterdam: Editions Rodopi, 2000, pp. 43–64.

# 12

# Mother–Daughter Relationships in Contemporary Spanish Theater

## Cristina Casado Presa

Few works have been more influential in contemporary Spanish theater than Federico García Lorca's *La casa de Bernarda Alba* (1939).[1] This drama, "about women in rural Spain" portrays the struggle between Bernarda, the absolute and sinister mother, and her daughters, who are subjugated and dominated while they suffer in fear of openly rebelling against her. While Lorca wrote his work in the 1930s, the theme of the mother-daughter relationship reemerges as a recurrent one in literature written by women from the 1950s onwards. Toward the end of Franco's dictatorship a new group of female playwrights became part of the theater scene and undertook the task of creating theatrical productions that showed what a woman truly is, how she spoke and how she felt. These plays show different perspectives on the mother-daughter relationship that reflect, both on the authors and on Spanish women. Conflict and the struggle are the common denominator within these plays. Bernarda Alba is the starting point from which to analyze later theatrical texts that reconsider the mother-daughter relationship. Through the analysis of plays by Concha Romero, Lidia Falcón and Pilar Pombo, I will discuss the problem of matriarchy and solidarity, or a lack of it, in contemporary Spanish theater.

Federico García Lorca's study of the feminine personality has been widely written about and analyzed by the critics as shown by the extensive number of interpretations of his plays, particularly *La casa de Bernarda Alba*.[2] Michael D. Thomas emphasizes how opposition and conflict are at the core of the dramatic movement in *La casa*. He writes: "the discord between Bernarda and her daughters; between Bernarda and Adela; between tradition, custom, austerity and rebellion, change, vivacity; between old age and youth; between blackness and color, between false appearance and evident truth" (Thomas

390). This friction and tension stem from the clash of two worlds with opposing value systems, ideals and conventions.

Bernarda embodies a bigoted obsession with an archaic principle of honor, forcing her daughters to an unconditional and extreme submission to her own fanatical concept of decency. As Summer M. Greenfield points out "neither deeply rooted personal dignity nor religious piety is the basis of her fanaticism" (Greenfield 457). Bernarda perpetuates patriarchal values in her household, symbolized by her ever-present cane, which makes her the protector and enforcer of a confining but socially accepted and acknowledged code of conduct and propriety. As John P. Gabriele notes "mothering, for Bernarda, involves enforcing certain traditional beliefs or conventions with regard to gender roles, namely submissiveness or obedience for the female and permissiveness for the male" ("Of Mothers and Freedom" 190). As in other Lorca plays, women's activities take place inside the house while the masculine world happens outside of the house.[3] Bernarda says "hilo y aguja para las hembras, látigo y mula para el varón" [needle and thread for women, whip and mule for men] (11).[4] However, in spite of being a woman, Bernarda has armed herself as a man and manifests a possessive and controlling nature that finds its expression in a variety of ways.

After the gathering following her husband's funeral for example Bernarda announces: "En ocho años que dure el luto no ha de entrar en esta casa el viento de la calle. Hacemos cuenta que hemos tapado con ladrillos puertas y ventanas. Así pasó en casa de mi padre y en casa de mi abuelo" [In eight years of mourning the wind from the street should not enter this house. We'll pretend we have covered doors and windows with bricks as it was done at my father and my grandfather's house] (128). As a result, any form of socialization beyond the house is made literally impossible, the only exception being Angustias, the eldest daughter, who is going to marry Pepe el Romano. Any visit is carefully screened and viewed in a negative way. Even contact with La Poncia, the maid, or the distant singing of the peasants is considered as dangerous and an intrusion. Ironically as a woman, Bernarda is the most strict and unsympathetic when passing judgment upon other women, including her own daughters.

Only two characters show some type of rebellion, neither of which meets with success. María Josefa, Bernarda's demented mother, echoes in her songs the truth of the unspoken feelings that float in the house, but she is locked up. Adela, young and rebellious, shows open opposition to Bernarda's power. She rebels through escalating bold, individual actions, from giving her mother a fan decorated with flowers and wearing a green dress to having an illicit relationship with Pepe el Romano and finally breaking Bernarda's cane. As John P Gabriele points out, Adela's character grows to be the exact opposite of her mother and expresses her desire to break free ("Of Mothers and Freedom" 194). However, Adela's quest for freedom through her prohibited love won't be successful, either. Bernarda cannot accept Adela's desire to break away and will once again have the last word ("Silencio"). Bernarda represents what Nancy Chodorow defines as a "controlling, invading mother who does not allow her daughter to develop a secure sense of her separate body and separate self" (*Reproduction* 50). For Bernarda's daughters there is no escape from this imprisonment.

The older sisters Angustias, Magdalena, Martirio and Amelia all resent their mother but are unable to confront her. This becomes evident in the weak personality of Angustias, but also through the other sisters' interactions with each other. Their confinement has engendered jealousy, loneliness, and isolation as well as produced repressed wishes and desires that have turned into compulsion and aggression. The daughters' suppressed anger and hatred has found an open manifestation in their constant teasing of each other and in little games such as the hiding of Angustias's portrait of Pepe el Romano. Nonetheless, these same feelings will result in Adela's betrayal by Martirio and will provoke the tragic denouement of the piece. The ending leaves the audience without a resolution. Life in the house of Bernarda means adhering to her rules and any attempt to break the circle and attain self hood ends in either death or madness. Thus, *La casa de Bernarda Alba* shows a story of domination and dependence that illustrates both the physical and psychological violence that a mother figure can exert and the submissive-rebellious behavior of the daughter.

The mother-daughter bond has proven to be conflictive by nature. Freudian theories defend how the conflict arises from the penis envy in girls and the competition with the mother for the father's attention. According to Freud "the daughter gives up her wish for a penis and puts in place of it a wish for a child: and with that purpose in view she takes her father as a love object. Her mother becomes the object of her jealousy (253–256). However, new theories have emerged since the mid–1970s from a series of works which have focused on the relationship between mothers and daughters. From Simone de Beauvoir to the above quoted Nancy Chodorow or Adrienne Rich, the popularity of these studies is a direct consequence of the rise of both American and European feminist movements which became more prevalent as many prejudices overtime disappeared when talking about family.

While Adrienne Rich analyzes motherhood as an institution and experience in the context of western patriarchal society (*Of Woman Born: Motherhood as Experience and Institution*), other authors such Nancy Chodorow describe how the mother figure maintains certain political, economical and cultural assumptions and behaviors to her own detriment. This results in the continuation of a series of values such as obedience and good behavior creating a pattern of subordination. As she states in *The Reproduction of Mothering* (1978), the idea is still present in other works that show how these circumstances create difficulties "for daughters to develop self-esteem," as "the mother inevitably represents to her daughter regression, passivity, dependence where the father represents progression, activity, independence, and reality orientation" ("Family Structure and Feminine Personality" 64–65). Much of this literature also had a wide reception in Spain, where a number of sociological and psychological studies have further highlighted the growing interest in the problems within mother-daughter relations. With the increase of feminist consciousness and the breaking of many taboos concerning family life and family relations, many women writers have dared to step back from their own life-givers, their most powerful individual influences in their lives, and they have critically examined the effects of the mother-daughter bond in order to understand their own identities. The uniqueness of that primary relationship was suddenly been recognized as paramount importance for the understanding of women's self-definition and their relation to the other. These new voices and approaches to the relationship between mothers and daughters will result in revisions and retellings in which its tensions and contradictions are fully explored and depicted in all their manifestations.

As Patricia O'Connor points out, women playwrights in Spain have been virtually nonexistent until the late nineteenth century ("Solidarity and Revision" 573) while women novelists have challenged male assumptions for decades. When talking about theater it isn't until after General Franco's death and the establishment of Democracy that a new group of women playwrights becomes more visible.[5] Authors like Paloma Pedrero, Maribel Lázaro, Concha Romero, Lidia Falcón or Pilar Pombo vindicate the existence of a feminine dramatic production with a language of its own. Pedrero believes that there is a female language that seeks to be projected while Maribel Lázaro adds that as playwrights they seek to raise their world to a protagonist role, mainly through their characters and a true commitment to them ("Los horizontes del teatro español" 15). By writing plays from this perspective, introducing the woman on stage, these writers are creating a new form of writing, a new theatrical language. These playwrights create female-centered works that subvert the male canon and show women in a new light.

According to Hélène Cixous a feminine text must be subversive because, when women write themselves there is the invention of a new writing. Individually, when written, the woman returns to the body that has been denied, or at least distorted. She writes, to censor the body is to censor the word. On the contrary, to hear the voice of women describe how it feels and looks to be a woman ensures that the one who is represented will be heard (*Laugh of*

*Medusa* 62). Therefore, many of the issues portrayed in these theatrical productions belong to the feminine, exploring themes such as lesbianism and motherhood. The experience is created and described by a person who has the ability to live them firsthand.

There are obvious differences among these dramas including the temporal and geographical settings and the generations of women portrayed. They also differ in their perception of the historical and social reality of Spain. However, the relationships depicted seem unable to escape the legacy of Bernarda Alba as they share a similar lack of resolution. Once again, "there can be no end to the tension between mother and daughter" (Arcana 118) and such tension is reflected in many different ways.

In *Juego de reinas* [*Queens' Game*] (1989), Concha Romero revisits the figure of Isabel the Catholic.[6] The young princess has become the sovereign of the world's most powerful empire as she herself admits in the proximity of her death. However, on this occasion, the drama is not centered on the figure of the Catholic Queen but rather her daughter, Juana. This shift introduces a new dynamic. While *Juego de reinas* is set in the tradition of the Spanish historical drama, the two-act play that premiered in 1989, shows the clash of views and interests of Queen Isabel of Castille, a woman raised to accept sacrifice, and her daughter Juana, who finds herself unexpectedly the heir to the Spanish throne.[7]

The crucial aspect of Queen Isabel and Juana's relationship is underlined by the simplicity of the scenic elements of the drama that emphasize the confrontation between the two women. Isabel lacks many aspects of the mother figure to which Chodorow alluded, as she doesn't adhere to a female model that is passive and submissive to the will of her husband. The mise en scène is conceived as a space in which the words of Isabel and Juana cannot be lost. In fact, they are the only characters on stage throughout the entire performance. The rest of the characters such as Fernando the Catholic and Felipe el Hermoso, much the same as Lorca's Pepe el Romano, only appear in the play by means of conversations between the two women.

Despite years of separation, the love between mother and daughter remains deep and sincere as evidenced by their conversations. The play begins with Juana interrupting Isabel's work late at night: "no tengo ni pizca de sueño y me apetece mucho hablar contigo [I am not sleepy at all and I really want to talk to you] (2). Juana shows her affection by remembering scenes from her childhood and the care she received from her mother. She concludes the dialogue with a heartfelt outburst in which she says, "no quiero ni pensar que algún día me faltes" [I hate to imagine that one day you won't be here] (4). Isabel responds to these affectionate comments: "¡Mi pequeña Juana! Tan sensible, tan alegre, tan vital" [My little Juana! So sensitive, so happy, so lively]

(5). Inevitably, the two women remember lost loved ones as they share in person for the first time, their feelings of sadness.

However, this initial harmony begins to disappear as the conversation progresses and they have their first disagreement about clothes. Isabel is depicted as an old woman, dressed in black not only for mourning, but also, "porque había que rebajar gastos" [because we had to reduce expenses] (11). Juana, in contrast, wears a red dress that emphasizes her youth, and beauty and a reflection of her life in the court of Burgundy. While Juana describes her new residence as "colorista y exultante" [colorful and exhilarating] (10), Isabel considers these new customs as "algo relajadas" [somewhat relaxed] (10). Furthermore, Juana Isabel questions Juana about the fact that she disregarded her Spanish confessors. While Juana believes that this change does not matter "si pertenecen todos a la misma religión" [if all belong to the same Church], (10), Isabel is upset at what she describes as "bebiendo, alternando y confesando con franceses" [drinking, socializing and confessing with the French] (10), showing her open rejection of Juana's lifestyle in Burgundy.

Isabel's possessiveness of Juana becomes evident even in this first scene. All of her criticisms are directed to the princess' new independence, highlighting the fact that Juana must progress through a continuity, repetition, and affiliation to her own ideas, in short, a reflection of herself. This emerging conflict becomes a full confrontation that turns the mother-daughter bond into a maternal struggle for dominance and an attempt to make the daughter an extension of her own personality. Thus, Isabel tries to instill into Juana the principles she herself has successfully internalized to reign Spain: "lo primero es el deber, después todo lo demás" [first is duty, then everything else] (27). She places particular emphasis on the dangers of mixing politics and love. This is due to the fact that Isabel has assumed an absolute self-sacrifice for the good of Spain, but also because she has a deeply negative view of men. Isabel is convinced of the inevitability of abuse from men that will cause suffering and a strong dependency on the part of women: "Los hombres suelen ser infieles por naturaleza, con sus esposas y hasta con sus amantes y hay que estar preparada para cuando suceda" [Men tend to be unfaithful by nature, with their wives and even their lovers and you have to be prepared for when it happens] (30).

It is not surprising; therefore, that Isabel tries to inculcate into Juana some awareness of her feelings towards her husband, Felipe, in order to avoid suffering and also to make decisions as a capable and competent sovereign. Juana hopes that Felipe will help to rule but Isabel is adamant: "No, Juana. No esperes que nadie te resuelva los problemas. Debes tener criterios propios y saber imponerlos incluso a tu marido si es necesario. Tú serás la reina. El solo rey consorte. No lo olvides nunca" [No, Juana. Do not expect anyone to resolve your problems. You must impose your own criteria even upon your husband if it is necessary. You'll be the Queen. He will be the consort. Never forget that] (23). When France and Spain go to the war, Felipe escapes to Burgundy leaving behind his wife, who intends to follow him. However, Isabel is inflexible and says "No puedes ir mientras dure la guerra ...Juana y España, no lo olvides nunca, ya sois una misma cosa" [You can not go while the war lasts. Do not forget that Juana and Spain are now the same] (27)."

While Isabel is adamant in relation to matters of the Crown we must not assume that she does not love Juana, but rather quite the opposite. Isabel constantly warns her daughter about the dangers of love based on her own experience, as evidenced when she says "he sido mujer antes que reina" [I have been a woman before being the Queen] (44). Isabel admits her suffering because of Fernando's infidelities and that she cried "lágrimas de desamor, de sufrimiento, de celos vulgares y corrientes" [Tears from a heartbreak, from suffering, from vulgar and ordinary jealousy] (29). It is precisely this double identity of tyrant and victim that is one of the more disturbing aspects of the relationship.

Romero's representation of Isabel is a strong contrast to the historical Isabel of Castile. The mighty Queen reveals how she has succeeded in life through a manipulation of characterizations of her sex and gender. Isabel wants to turn Juana into a continuation of herself, creating a form of imprisonment for both women. Isabel's experience has been the lack of recognition as an independent, individual subject. Her personality and feelings have always been hidden under her status as a political figure and we understand that her control over Juana is a liberation for her. According to Jessica Benjamin, violence is an apt medium for the assertion of masculine identity. The use of physical confinement as a means for Juana to come into her senses, i.e., to accept the necessities of the state and the sacrifices they entail, helps Isabel to establish her own autonomy and reveal themselves as "a way of repudiating dependency while attempting to avoid the consequent feeling of aloneness. It makes the other an object but retains possession of her" (151). Isabel's dominating and androgynous appearance is expressed through her constant reminder of her obligations to Juana. She even resorts to violence, locking up her daughter in her room and preventing Juana from any contact with another person: "Si no me obedeces como madre, me obedecerás como reina" [If you don't want to obey me as a mother, obey me as your Queen] (41). In the eyes of Isabel Juana must leave behind her passion for Felipe to save herself from the perils of male seduction.

Juana's attempts of rebellion and resistance are always thwarted by Isabel's warnings and value judgments about her behavior. Isabel is aware of the passion Juana feels for her husband: "¿También tienes espías en mi dormitorio?"

[Do you also have spies in my bedroom?] (37) and is appalled by the behavior of her daughter.

Although showing sadness and compassion, she does not abandon her educational effort "trata de comprender las razones de estado" [try to understand the reasons of state] (39). Despite the lessons Isabel tries to share, Juana has lost all interest in Isabel's teachings and regards the throne of Spain with an open revulsion and also as a threat, fearing that she will become her mother's replica. Juana defines Isabel as "la mujer más dura que he conocido...Un monstruo" [the harshest woman I have ever met... a monster] (40) and accuses her of being neither a woman nor a mother. Despite Juana's words the play ends with an unforgettable passage. The war is over and Felipe has claimed Juana. Isabel attempts one last conversation with her daughter that becomes an unexpected confession in which she looks for acceptance of her actions: "El amor es importante, pero no lo es todo. Ya lo verás con el tiempo. Tienes un destino grandioso. No permitas que lo tuerza nadie. A punto estuve yo de perder el mío con tantas amarguras y tantas lágrimas, pero gracias a Dios el trabajo y el amor por España me salvó (...) cumplí mi destino como un hombre aunque haya sufrido como una mujer" [Love is important but not everything. You'll see over time. You have a great destiny. Do not let anyone thwart it. I almost lost mine with so much bitterness and tears, but thankfully, work and love for Spain saved me. I fulfilled my destiny as a man but suffered as a woman] (46–7). With these words Romero seeks to mitigate the extreme negativity of the relationship between Isabel and Juana, leaving, at the same time, an even greater "bitter taste" in the mouth of the audience. As viewers learn about the terrible resignation of Isabel, her allusion to her love for country exasperates Juana. She leaves the scene without saying goodbye and without hearing the words that could have resolved the conflict with an understanding between mother and daughter. When Isabel discovers Juana's absence, of which the audience is already aware, Isabel pronounces the final words of the drama: "¡Ay Juana, Juana, mi pequeña Juana, mi última esperanza! [Oh Juana, Juana, my little Juana, my last hope!] (47). Thus, the play ends merging with History in that Juana and Isabel never see each other again. It also offers audiences valuable additional information that explains both the distance between the two women and Juana's madness.

*Juego de reinas* represents a disturbing example of a relationship that confirms what many feminist approaches have suggested about the enduring influence of mothers on their daughters. This relationship can result in the transmission of certain established roles and patterns of behavior that prevent the development of the latter. However, the representation of the clash between Isabel and Juana demonstrates that both women live in different realities that are mutually exclusive. Romero's drama follows the idea present in

Lorca's *Bernarda* that the heroines cannot successfully set themselves free from the mother bond. However, Romero shows the dual condition of victim and tyrant that Isabel occupies while portraying the necessity of reformulation of the feminine sphere, as both models seem to be invalid.

While Lorca focuses on the impossibility of escaping the tradition and Romero denounces the necessity of different options for women, Lidia Falcón presents a process of development that delineates causes and effects, origins and outcomes. She defines herself as a feminist and has always used her dramatic production to highlight and raise awareness of the injustices related to women.[8] Falcón believes that the first area in which women are subordinate is the family institution, as it promotes the thought that women leave their single condition under their father's guidance and enter into the husband's guardianship. In *Siempre busqué el amor* (1983)[9] the family is identified as the space in which domestic violence is part of the education of children. Falcón provides the audience with a feminist critique of family and motherhood as the foundation of women's suffering.

In this play we witness the tribulations and humiliations that Fuensanta and her children endure at the hands of her husband. The siblings recount the constant beatings, how the father locks them up at home without enough food and how they are forced to work in his country estate for countless hours without rest. Violence becomes unnaturally normal in the house. As one of the sons, Juan, says: "No ha pasado nada nuevo, tampoco. Más o menos lo de siempre" [Nothing new has happened, more or less, the usual] (*Siempre* 121).[10] Fuensanta has gone to the police several times but her claims have been unanswered and this has led to further beatings. Violence against women seems to be normal in the eyes of society. Amparo, the maid, has been a witness to the family suffering for years but she advices Fuensanta, "Si te callaras y le llevaras la corriente quiza fuera un poco mejor" [If you shut up and play along with him, maybe things will improve] (146). Therefore, the blame is put on Fuensanta even though Amparo knows very well that Fuensanta has suffered the frequent brutality of her husband.

Fuensanta admits she married her husband because he was rich and she wanted a luxurious life: "Encontraré un hombre rico y guapo que me quiera" [I will find a rich and handsome man who loves me] (133). Unfortunately, she has paid a terrible price for the fulfillment of her wish. The beatings started immediately after their marriage and their sons and daughters are the result of constant rapes. As she explains: "los gemelos nacieron de esa violación, y después otras para María, Nina y Noya" [The twins were born from that rape and then it happened again for María, Nina and Noya] (134). She admits she was always scared of getting pregnant over and over as every child has bound her closer to her abusive husband.

Fuensanta's experience of motherhood has proven to be the ultimate oppressive and subordinating mechanism. As Falcón points out: "la mujer no se reproduce voluntariamente por el agrado que ello le produce. La mujer se reproduce forzosamente para proporcionar a la sociedad la fuerza de trabajo humana que precisa, obligada por la coacción económica y extraeconómica que contra ella utilizan los hombres" [women don't reproduce by pleasure. Women are coerced to reproduce by men, economically and extra economically, in order to provide society with the necessary human work force][10] (*Razón feminista* 60). Fuensanta's children have become both cheap laborers for her husband as well as objects for his violence.

While trapped by her unwanted maternities, Fuensanta transmits patterns of inferiority and submission to her children. As she herself admits she is unable to confront her husband: "¡Yo quiero tener valor, solo un poco de esa fuerza que él tiene para luchar contra él! [I just want to be courageous, to have just a little of that strength in order to stand up to him!] (*Siempre* 146). Fuensanta craves opportunities for self-assertion, in order to give herself life. She has always searched for those opportunities through love, but now torture and love have become synonymous. Her husband, as we have seen, imposes himself on his wife and children through violence and he takes advantage of Fuensanta's weakness to exert his supremacy.

This pattern repeats itself in her infatuation with Ramón, who she sees as a way of escaping and finding the love she is desperately looking for: "Ramón...creo que tengo derecho después de tantos años de sufrir, a buscar el amor, a encontrar un buen hombre que me quiera y me proteja" [Ramón...I think I have the right after all these years of suffering, to find a good man that loves me and protects me] (148). Once again, her escape through love will fail as she learns that Ramón has been trying to abuse her daughters, Luisa and María. All her hopes are shattered when Luisa screams at her: "¡Estúpida! ¡Un buen hombre que te quiera...¡Sí! ¡Metiéndome mano a mí también!" [Stupid! A good man that loves you! Yes! He has been sexually harassing me as well!] (149). Fuensanta cannot bear to hear the truth and accuses her daughter of lying to her in order to hurt her. Years of abuse and isolation along with her obsession for love have drawn her to men whose affection and recognition are to be won, she believes, by utter self-humiliation. Thus, complexes, obsessions and frustrations are the legacy that Fuensanta can offer her children, while confined in a closed environment where violence is the training ground.

Confinement engenders the daughters' dependence, loneliness and social isolation as well as producing wishes and desires that turn into compulsion, obsession and aggression. This appears mainly through the characters of Luisa and María. Love and hate, reproach and excuse, condemnation and forgiveness are their mixed response to their attachment to Fuensanta's love, which is both sought and needed as it was never completely given to them. After confronting her mother about Ramón's actions and letting her know that her hope of freedom through love is ineffectual, they decide that they must kill their father. María insists that, "Ya es hora...hay que matarle" [It is time, we must kill him] (155).[11] Thus, as John P. Gabriele points out, Fuensanta's wish for freedom materializes in the effort of the children to escape their father's tyranny through murder (*Lidia Falcón: Teatro Feminista* 110). The truth about Ramón and the realization that she has been looking for freedom in the wrong place is what brings a resolution as Fuensanta agrees that the only solution for them is to eliminate the source of their suffering. As Gabriele remarks, "muerto el padre...se restaura el acuerdo y la tranquilidad" [once the father is dead, agreement and peace will be restored] (110). Violence is the means by which Fuensanta finally bonds with her children and especially with Luisa and María. Fuensanta offers to be the one to shoot the father but María intervenes: "No, mamá, yo lo haré. Soy pequeña y no pueden encarcelarme" [No mom, I will do it. I am a child and they can't put me in jail] (*Siempre* 162). The play ends with María's statement: "los niños del reformatorio me llaman asesina de mi padre" [the kids in the detention center call me a father's murderer] (162), perhaps hinting at the fact she will inherit the legacy of her father's violence.

Falcón's portrayal of the victimization and torture of the mother and children provides the audience with a feminist critique of male hegemony as the foundation of women's suffering. She places her focus in a setting populated by men who are portrayed as sexual abusers or sadists that indulge in humiliating women, and by women who have been taught to suffer without rebellion. The audience is forced to ask him/herself about the social and psychological reasons for Fuensanta's behavior, leading to the dominant patriarchy, its laws and the way they affect women's hopes, actions, thoughts and feelings.

The last play analyzed in this chapter shows a different perspective with an interesting twist in the mother-daughter relationship. *Remedios* (1988)[12] by Pilar Pombo[13] takes its name from its one and only character, a widow in her sixties. Remedios has been persuaded by her daughter to sell her apartment and move in with her in order to help provide childcare for their family. The monodrama begins with a phone call from Remedios daughter, Rosa, who has called in the last minute to tell her that the family will not be home for dinner. The way Remedios answers shows that she is used to this kind of situation as she just mumbles in an uninterested way " sí hija sí... sí, sí, sí" [yes dear yes..., yes, yes, yes] (129).[14] The call gets cut off and Remedios stays alone on her end of the line.

This moment is symbolic of Remedios' living situation. She feels lonely even though she is living with her family due to the treatment she gets from them, especially from Rosa. Her family either treats her like a child or uses her as a maid. She recalls that she is not allowed to touch anything in the house because her daughter fears she will break something. Ironically, she also remembers that her hands are good enough "para limpiar culos" [to clean butts] (135).

The monodrama depicts an imaginary conversation she has with her family. Remedios initially moved in to help her daughter so she could return to work after the birth of her second child. She made many sacrifices, giving up her friends and neighborhood where she lived for many years and now she suspects they want to put her into a retirement home. However, she has met another widower, Esteban, and doesn't want to accept the future her family thinks is best for her.

Remedios expresses herself with a sharp tongue in a humorous and sarcastic way becoming sad and angry at times, especially when addressing the imaginary version of her daughter, Rosa. She pretends to explain her relationship with Esteban to Rosa: "Tú no te puedes imaginar lo que puede suponer para mi, y sobre todo a mi edad...encontrar el calor de un hombre a mi lado" [You cannot imagine what means for me at my age to find the warmth of a man next to me] (139). Also, she emphasizes how important it is to feel "querido, útil, necesario" [loved, useful, necessary] (139). She realizes that her daughter refuses to admit that older women, too, have the need for love and sexual desires. As Mary F. Yudin points out, *Remedios* offers us a rare glimpse into the concerns of "a forgotten member of our image conscious world" (24). Because she is no longer a young and beautiful woman, she seems to have lost her intrinsic value, even to her own daughter.

Rosa is a part of the society that takes advantage of the elderly while alienating them. This applies in particular to mothers, who have become maids and babysitters for their families. These women are being discarded, placed into retirement homes when they are no longer useful to their families. Rosa seems to be more preoccupied about her material goods than the wellness of her own mother. Pombo explains that her house is "una casa moderna en un barrio moderno" [a modern house in a modern neighborhood] where everything is "absolutamente despersonalizado" [absolutely despersonalized] (129). Rosa regards her mother as an instrument of maintaining her status in an ever-consuming society. Remedios has given up her economic independence and also lost her support from other women in her old neighborhood. She recalls, "Allí tenía mis amigas...Me querían y me tenían mucha confianza...todo el mundo estaba pendiente de mi" [I had my friends there...they loved me and trust me...everyone paid attention to me] (134). Now, she feels economically and emotionally trapped by her family and has exchanged sisterhood for exploitation.

Remedios decides to take action and escape her situation. Through a second phone call we learn that she is going to move in with Esteban and marry him. This time the conversation is full of life and "escucha y se ríe" [she listens and laughs] (141). When she hangs up the phone she expresses her happiness, leaves the house slamming the door and looks forward to her new life, where she hopes to reclaim her happiness and dignity, in other words, her "old self."

This drama presents striking differences with the previous one and yet, it still shares fundamental themes. While men have been depicted as oppressive members of the patriarchal system, Remedios finds her freedom through her marriage to Esteban. We must understand that Esteban signifies the opportunity of returning to the life Remedios gave up, where she was considered a human being, part of a community. Nonetheless, the critique of patriarchal society is still implicit in the drama as Rosa has become an accomplice in the moment she considers her mother as a useless tool, following the precepts of a society that will regard her the same way in the future. Rosa's alienation of her mother will likely become her future in a society in which any trace of solidarity, especially among mothers and daughters, will be obliterated.

After considering and analyzing this group of plays we must go back to our initial consideration. Can we talk about the long shadow of Bernarda Alba? Certainly none of the mothers in the plays we have analyzed match the bigotry and tyranny of Lorca's character. Even though all of these plays show different aspects of the mother-daughter bond, they also all point to the oppression of women in the hands of patriarchal hegemony, and the complicity of women in its conservation.

Bernarda goes to extreme measures to keep the reputation of her household intact, that is, to meet the standards of what a respectable woman is for society. She promotes the conflict and betrayal among her daughters through her unreasonable eight-year period of mourning. Bernarda even prioritizes the opinion that the community may have about her and her siblings over the death of the Adela, her youngest daughter.

"Silence" is the final word she declares at the close of the play. Lorca opens and closes his work with the same expression and the story comes full circle in a metaphor of the confinement of women in a society where they have no voice or presence and where they certainly cannot expect solidarity from other women, as they are prisoners themselves. This portrayal of unhealthy mother-daughter relations is compelling because extreme, abnormal examples of family relations are presented in a straightforward, realistic language, thus blurring the boundaries between fact and fiction.

There is a final rationalization of the maternal circumstances and experiences, but there is no reconciliation or understanding of these experiences as we have seen the same pattern in the later plays. Juana makes a radical break with her mother, Remedios abandons the daughter's house, and while Fuensanta stays with her children, she has proven her inability to have a healthy relationship with them.

The texts of the plays studied offer different approaches to the mother-daughter relationship, and this difference is significant when it comes to achieving a deeper understanding of the history of Spanish women. In the three plays analyzed, the female characters perform a review of their lives, in which the connection and separation among mothers and daughters play a role in the development of their identity. The ultimate consequences of the exercise of memory are also important on two levels: all the characters and their respective environments represent different stages of their personal story and the collective history of a country that went through radical but gradual change, from a dictatorship to a democratic system and in which, certain aspects and ideas about women and society, are still in existence. Therefore, the material these playwrights bring through their theatrical representations of mother-daughter relationships, sorority and sisterhood, are extremely enriching within the context of Spanish culture.

It is important to note the existence of female aesthetic strategies of representation in these plays as we are offered characters that through their unique natures, show a clear awareness of themselves, their thoughts and emotions. The protagonists are fighting the precepts learned at the time. The representations of these women push back the boundaries of what it means to be "subversive" or "disobedient." Little by little, what was once unthinkable is now represented or at the very least published.

Gradually, issues that were taboo are emerging in these works. At the same time, these playwrights allow their characters to question certain concepts previously taken for granted, like the silence of women during the Dictatorship, censorship, self-imposed in many cases or self-denial and passivity traditionally inherent to womanhood. That is why the analysis of these works and the representations of women that we find in them, lead us to reconsider the characteristics of women who populated the Spanish theater scene previously. These plays claim the necessity of solidarity among women while representing the lack of it and, most importantly, dare to question the stability of society, sexuality and ultimately, the social, cultural and moral values rooted in the hegemonic ideology of Spain.

## NOTES

1. The play was not staged until 1945.
2. To name a few, Caroline Gallerstein draws a parallel between Bernarda's tyranny and the political situation in Spain in the months previous to the Spanish Civil War. Francisco Ruiz Ramón focuses on the different spaces of the play in terms of closeness. John Ozimek explores the speech in the play to establish a power hierarchy. Sumner M. Greenfield explores the lyricism and stagecraft in the play by studying the symbols and images that interwoven with the dramatic action. For further references see Francesca Colecchia, "A Selected Bibliography of Studies on Federico Garcia Lorca's La casa de Bernarda Alba," *Estreno: Cuadernos del Teatro Español Contemporáneo* 21 (2): 3.
3. See *Yerma* and *Bodas de Sangre*.
4. All translations are mine. Subsequent translations will appear parenthetically.
5. As Patricia O'Connor notes, in 1986 approximately twenty female authors of dramatics texts reunite in Madrid for their first meeting. Their common interests and goals lead them to form the Asociación de Dramaturgas Españolas (Spanish Female Playwrights Association). The authors we analyze here were part of it, but there were other members such as Paloma Pedrero, Carmen Resino or Maribel Lázaro. For further information see Patricia O' Connor, *Dramaturgas españolas de hoy: Una introducción* (Madrid: Fundamentos, 1988).
6. Another play by Romero, *Las bodas de una princesa* [*The marriage of a princess*] (1982) focuses on the figure of Queen Isabel the Catholic. Romero's representation is, however, atypical. Isabel appears in this work as a young woman, different to the contemporary histories of her character. The work stages her tricks to gain the throne and achieve the reaffirmation of their identity.
7. Juana was not destined to be queen and became heir only upon the death of her brothers and sisters. Juan died in 1497, Isabel in 1498, and her son, Prince Miguel, in 1500.
8 Falcón has been a key figure within Spanish feminism. She was an activist during Franco's time and even went to jail. She was one of the founders of the Feminist Party and as a lawyer she has defended women's rights. Her theatrical production includes topics such as domestic violence, as seen in the play analyzed here, abortion, or feminism and the ideal feminine. For further information see John P. Gabriel, *Teatro feminista de Lidia Falcón: Las mujeres caminaron con el fuego del siglo; Siempre busqué el amor; La hora más oscura* (Madrid: Fundamentos, 2002).
9. *Siempre busqué el amor* [*I always looked for love*] is based on a true story. Maria Nieves Soldevila and her siblings plotted the murder of their father, Juan Vila Carbonell, in 1981. Vila Carbonell abused his wife and children for years, until they decided to end his cruelty and violence by killing him.
10. All translations are mine. Subsequent translations will appear parenthetically.
11. All translations are mine. Subsequent translations will appear parenthetically.
12. *Remedios* is published in Patricia O' Connor's *Dramaturgas españolas de hoy: Una introducción* (Madrid: Fundamentos, 1988), pp. 129–141.
13. *Remedios* is not the only monodrama written by Pombo. Other works include *Amalia, Purificación, Isabel, Sonia* and Ginés "El Figurante." For further information see Virtudes Serrano's "El presente doloroso y esperanzado en la obra dramática de Pilar Pombo," *Estreno* 24 1 (Spring 1998): 39–44.
14. All translations are mine. Subsequent translations will appear parenthetically.

## WORKS CITED

Arcana, Judith. *Our Mothers' Daughters*. Berkeley, CA: Shameless Hussy, 1979.
Beauvoir, Simone de, Constance Borde, and Sheila Malovany-Chevallier. *The Second Sex*. New York: Alfred A. Knopf, 2010.

Benjamin, Jessica. "The Bonds of Love: Rational Violence and Erotic Domination." *Feminist Studies* 6.1 (Spring 1980): 144–174.
Cazorla, Hezel. "Conversación con Pilar Pombo." *Estreno* 25.2 (Fall 1999): 9–11.
Chodorow, Nancy. "Family Structure and Feminine Personality." In *Woman, Culture and Society*. Stanford, CA: Stanford University Press, 1974.
\_\_\_\_\_. *The Reproduction of Mothering: Psychoanalysis and the Sociology of Gender*. Berkeley: University of California Press, 1978.
Cixous, Hélène. "Laugh of Medusa." In *Feminisms: An Anthology of Literary Theory and Criticism*, eds. Robyn R. Warhol and Diane Price Herndl. New Brunswick, NJ: Rutgers University Press, 1991.
Colecchia, Francesca. "A Selected Bibliography of Studies on Federico Garcia Lorca's *La casa de Bernarda Alba*." *Estreno: Cuadernos del Teatro Espanol Contemporáneo* 21 (2): 39.
Coloquio: "Los horizontes del teatro español. Nuevas autoras. Un coloquio moderado por Lourdes Ortiz." *Primer Acto* 220 (1987): 10–21.
Falcón, Lidia. *La razón feminista*. Barcelona: Fontanella, 1981.
Freud, Sigmund. "Some Psychical Consequences of the Anatomical Distinction between the Sexes." *The Ego and the Id and other Works*. Vol.19 of *The Complete Psychological Works of Sigmund Freud*. Ed. James Strachey. London: Hogarth, 1961, pp. 173–179.
Gabriele, John P. "Of Mothers and Freedom: Adela's Struggle for Selfhood in *La casa de Bernarda Alba*." *Symposium* 47.3 (Fall 1993): 188–197.
\_\_\_\_\_. *Teatro feminista de Lidia Falcón: Las mujeres caminaron con el fuego del siglo; Siempre busqué el amor; La hora más oscura*. Madrid: Fundamentos, 2002.
García Lorca, Federico. *Bodas De Sangre*. Madrid: Espasa Calpe, 1987.
\_\_\_\_\_. *La casa de Bernarda Alba*. Edición de Allen Josephs y Juan Caballero. Madrid: Cátedra, 1986.
\_\_\_\_\_. *Yerma: Poema Trágico En Tres Actos Y Seis Cuadros*. Madrid: Ediciones Cátedra, 1976.
Greenfield, Sumner M. "Poetry and Stagecraft in *La casa de Bernarda Alba*." *Hispania* 38.4 (1955): 456–461.
Harris, Carolyn J. "Love, Madness and Silencing in Concha Romero's *Juego de Reinas*." In *Entre actos: diálogos sobre teatro español entre siglos*. University Park, PA: Estreno,1999.
Jones, Susan. "*Remedios*, a Play by Pilar Pombo." *Studies in the Humanities* 25.2 (December 1990): 74–90.
Lerner, Gerda. *The Creation of Patriarchy*. New York: Oxford University Press, 1986.
O'Connor, Patricia. *Dramaturgas españolas de hoy: Una introducción*. Madrid: Fundamentos, 1988.
\_\_\_\_\_. "Solidarity and Re-Vision in the Plays of Two Spanish "Dramaturgas": Maribel Lázaro and Pilar Pombo." *Revista Canadiense de Estudios Hispánicos* 14.3 (Spring 1990): 573–578.
Ragué-Arias, Maria José. "Introducción a la obra de Lidia Falcón." *Estreno* 10.2 (Fall 1984): 26–31.
Rich, Adrienne. *Of Woman Born: Motherhood as Experience and Institution*. New York: Norton, 1986.
Romero, Concha. *Las bodas de una princesa*. Madrid: Lucerna, 1988.
\_\_\_\_\_. *Juego de Reinas o Razón de estado*. Madrid: J. García Verdugo, 1997.
Serrano, Virtudes. "El presente doloroso y esperanzado en la obra dramática de Pilar Pombo." *Estreno* 24.1 (Spring 1998): 39–44.
Thomas, Michael D. "Lenguaje poético y caracterización en tres dramas de Federico García Lorca." *Revista de Estudios Hispánicos* 12 (1978): 390.
Thwaites, Lilit. "Limpiaculos, cucarachas and marujas: Pilar Pombo's monólogos and the Older Spanish Women." *The Space of Culture: Critical Readings in Hispanic Studies*. Newark: University of Delaware Press, 2004.
Yudin, Mary F. "Nunca he tenido tiempo para ser yo: A Study of the Protagonists in Two Monodramas by Pilar Pombo." *Estreno* 21.1 (Spring 1995): 24–27.

# About the Contributors

**Samuel Amago** teaches courses in contemporary Spanish literature, cinema and culture at the University of North Carolina at Chapel Hill, where he is an associate professor in the Department of Romance Languages and Literatures. His most recent book is *Unearthing Franco's Legacy: Mass Graves and the Recovery of Historical Memory in Spain*, a co-edited volume dedicated to an analysis of how the country's violent authoritarian past continues to manifest itself in the cultural present.

**Tracie Amend** is an assistant professor of Spanish at Wayne State College in northeast Nebraska. She specializes in the literature (and specifically, theater) of Spain. She has published articles in *Hispanófila*, *Mediterranean Studies*, and *Gestos*. Along with her interest in peninsular studies, she participates in interdisciplinary classes and projects within the performing arts.

**Diana M. Barnes** teaches Spanish language and literature as a visiting assistant professor at Skidmore College in upstate New York. Her studies focus on the mother-daughter relationship during Spain's Transition, as well as Civil War literature. She has worked as a journalist and in addition to her scholarly investigations of contemporary Spanish narrative, she writes and presents on U.S./Mexico border issues.

**Paul Begin** is an assistant professor of Hispanic studies at Pepperdine University, where he teaches course on Spanish literature, cinema, culture, and history. Some of his publications on Spanish cinema may be found in *Screen*, *Bulletin of Spanish Studies*, *Hispanic Research Journal*, and *Studies in Hispanic Cinemas*.

**Catherine Bourland Ross** is an associate professor of Spanish at Southwestern University in Georgetown, Texas. Her interests include the contemporary Spanish novel, Spanish film, and contemporary Spanish culture, with a focus on women's concerns. She has published articles on 20th century Spanish novelists in journals such as *Letras Peninsulares* and *Revista monográfica/Monographic Review* as well as an article on the mother figure in Spanish film in *Letras Femeninas*.

**Cristina Casado Presa** is an assistant professor of Spanish at Washington College in Maryland. She primarily studies Spanish contemporary theater. In particular, she has focused on women playwrights and their depictions of women's roles.

More recently, she has been working on representations of witches in contemporary Spanish theater. Her current research focuses on witchcraft in young adult Spanish fiction.

**Renée Craig-Odders** is a professor of Spanish at the University of Wisconsin, Stevens Point. She is the author of *The Detective Novel in Post–Franco Spain* and *Democracy, Disillusionment and Beyond* and co-editor of *Hispanic and Luso-Brazilian Detective Fiction: Essays on the Género Negro Tradition* (McFarland, 2006) and *Crime Scene Spain: Investigations of Place in Contemporary Spanish Crime Fiction*. She has also published articles and chapters on various contemporary Spanish writers including Alicia Giménez-Bartlett, Francisco González Ledesma, Juan Madrid, Andreu Martín, Carlos Reigosa and Lorenzo Silva.

**Candyce Leonard** is a professor at Wake Forest University and has worked with contemporary Spanish theater since 1980, is the co-editor of seven volumes of contemporary Spanish plays, and is the author of numerous articles and published interviews with Spanish playwrights.

**Marisol Rodríguez Rodríguez,** originally from Galicia, received a master's degree from the University of Santiago de Compostela and a Ph.D. from the University of Auckland. In particular she has written on the importance and impact of the literary careers and works of Galician women writers from two different generations within specific cultural and historical contexts: the final years of the Franco regime and Spain's ensuing democracy. These writers were Xohana Torres, María Xosé Queizán, Carmen Blanco and Teresa Moure.

**Lorraine Ryan** completed her master's and doctoral degrees at the University of Limerick, Ireland. Her research interests center on the family in contemporary Spain, contemporary Spanish literature, Spanish cultural and collective memory, and sociology of memory. Her articles have appeared in *Clues, History of the Family: An International Quarterly, Memory Studies, Hispanic Research Journal, Modern Language Review, International Social Science Journal,* and *Romance Studies,* as well as in various edited collections.

**Amy L. Tibbitts** is an assistant professor in the Department of Modern Languages and Literatures at Beloit College in Beloit, Wisconsin. Her work focuses primarily on contemporary Spanish narrative and, more recently, contemporary Spanish film. Her areas of interest are gender studies, urban and spatial studies, and representations of childhood in Spanish film.

**Tiffany Trotman** is a senior lecturer in Spanish at the University of Otago, Dunedin, New Zealand. She is the author of *Eduardo Mendoza's Crime Novels: The Function of Carnivalesque Discourse in Post-Franco Spain, 1979–2001*. In addition, she has published articles and chapters on various contemporary Spanish writers including Lucía Etxebarria, Carlos Ruiz-Zafón, Antonio Gala and Eduardo Mendoza.

# Index

abortion laws 2
*Los abrazos rotos* 5, 93–107
adoption 3, 5, 66, 68, 126; adoptive parent vs. biological parent 131; same-sex 165
adultery 52
Agirre, Maite: *Bilbao: Lauaxeta, tiros y besos* 6, 180–189, 195
Aguilera, Pedro: *La influencia* 6, 141–158
Alberdi, Inés: *La nueva familia española* 1–2, 25
Almodóvar, Pedro 93–108, 129, 138; *Los abrazos rotos* 5, 93–107; and family deviancy 94–95, 100; and fathers 95–96, 103, 129–130; film noir 96, 98, 101, 103; *Hable con ella* 94; and historical memory 94, 101–106; *Ley de deseo* 130; light as motif 101; *La mala educación* 94, 101–103, 105; *Mujeres al borde de un ataque de nervios* 104; and nuclear family 96–97, 100–102, 106, 130; and paternity 96; *Pepi, Luci, Bom y otras chicas del montón* 102; *¿Qué he hecho yo para merecer esto?!* 94, 97, 102, 130; *Tacones lejanos* 94; *Todo sobre mi madre* 94, 96; *Volver* 94–97; x-ray imagery 98–104
alternative sexuality 4
Amago, Sam 5, 93–108, 215
Amenábar, Alejandro: *Mar adentro* 132, 137
Amend, Tracie 6, 180–197, 215
androgeny 119
*ángel del hogar* 24, 40, 43, 52, 159
anxiety 32
Araújo, Luis 162; *Mercado libre* 170–174; *Trayectoria de la bala* 170, 174–177
*Atlas de la geografía humana* 4, 40–58

*Un barco cargado de arroz* 79, 85, 87
Bardem, Javier 128

Barnes, Diana 5, 109–125, 215
Basque national identity 6, 180–196
Basque theatre 6
de Beauvoir, Simone 61
Begin, Paul 5, 126–140, 215
*Bilbao: Lauaxeta, tiros y besos* 6, 180–189, 195
bisexuality 167
blended families 5
*El Bola* 5, 126, 135, 137
Boullaín, Icíar: *Flores de otro mundo* 134; *Hola, ¿estás sola?* 134; *Te doy mis ojos* 5, 126, 129, 132–134, 136
Bourland Ross, Catherine 3–4, 9–23, 215
Brooksbank Jones, Anny 2–3
*La buena estrella* 5, 127, 130, 132, 134, 138
*La buena hija* 41
Bustos, Goyo 9, 11, 20–22

Calo Fontán, Teresa: *El día en que inventé tu nombre* 6, 162, 180, 189–196
cartographic imagery 5, 94
*La casa de Bernarda Alba* 6, 198–200, 206, 210–211
Casado Presa, Cristina 6–7, 198–213, 215
*Centro de investigaciones sociológicas* 2
Clua, Guillem 162
*El club de las malas madres* 3, 9–22
contraception 2
*El corazón helado* 40
Craig-Odders, Renée 4–5, 75–92, 216
crime fiction 75–76, 89–90
cult of beauty 53–54
custodial fathers 4, 29–30

Davies, Catherine 40
de Diego, Nacho 162; *La playa de los perros destrozados* 166–168; *Prepucio* 168–170
dependency care 19

*El día en que inventé tu nombre* 6, 162, 180, 189–196
*Diario de una madre imperfecta* 9–10
divorce 2–3, 14
domestic violence 5, 129, 132–137, 206–208

*Las edades de Lulú* 40
*The Empire of Fashion: Dressing Modern Democracy* 27
*A escrita da certeza* 4, 65
*Los estados carenciales* 4, 24–39
Etxebarria, Lucía: *El club de las malas madres* 3, 9–22

Falcón, Lidia 6, 198; *Siempre busqué el amor* 206–208
family: alternative 6, 28, 180–189; and Catholicism 34–37, 130; deviancy 94–95; disintegration of 96; extended 2; under Franco 44–45, 52, 93–95, 100, 109, 126, 130, 138, 160; heteronormative 5, 96, 160; hypermodern 28–38; non-heternormative families 3, 122; nuclear 2, 5, 72, 96–97, 126; in the Transition 46–49; *see also* gay and lesbian marriage; same-sex parents
female body 152–154
feminism 60–63, 76–77, 80–82, 89, 201–202
*femme fatale* 75
*Flores de otro mundo* 134
Franco, Ricardo 133; *La buena estrella* 5, 127, 130, 132, 134, 138
Freixas, Laura 41

Galician women writers 4, 59–74
García Lorca, Federico: *La casa de Bernarda Alba* 6, 198–200, 206, 210–211
García-Mauriño, Javier 162
García-Zarza, Isabel: *Diario de una madre imperfecta* 9–10
*Gary Cooper que estás en los cielos* 5, 109–111, 114, 116, 118–123
gay and lesbian marriage 3, 126
gender: autonomy 41, 45; equality 117; inequality 43
*generación activa* 41, 43
generation 41
Giménez Bartlett, Alicia 4–5, 75–92; *Un barco cargado de arroz* 79, 85, 87; *Muertos de papel* 80, 84; *Nido vacío* 79, 83, 85, 89; *Ritos de muerte* 76–79, 82, 84;

*Serpientes en el paraíso* 80, 83–84; *El silencio de los claustros* 79, 87, 89; "La voz de sangre" 82–83
Gómez, Fernando Fernán 161
González de Chávez, María Asunción 13
Grandes, Almudena: *Atlas de la geografía humana* 4, 40–58; *La buena hija* 41; *El corazón helado* 40; *Las edades de Lulú* 40; *Malena es un nombre de tango* 41; *Modelos de mujer* 41

*Hable con ella* 94
happiness 25–26; and parenting 46, 49, 50, 55–56, 163
*Herba moura* 68–71
*Las heridas del viento* 164–165
historical inquiry 5, 6, 142
historical memory 187–189
HIV/AIDS 163, 167
*Hola, ¿estás sola?* 134
Homer: *Odyssey* 33, 38
homosexuality 80, 95, 122–123, 163–165, 168–170
*Hypermodern Times* 27, 30
hypermodernity 24–39

individualism 25
infidelity 167, 170
*La influencia* 6, 141–158
International Competition of Theater Texts Leopoldo Alas Mínguez 166
interracial marriage 5
intertextuality 94

*Juego de reinas* 202–206

legislative bill 13/2005 3
Leonard, Candyce 6, 159–179, 216
*Ley de deseo* 130
Lipovetsky, Gilles 4, 26–28; *The Empire of Fashion: Dressing Modern Democracy* 27; *Hypermodern Times* 27, 30

*Madre Amantísima* 162–164
*La mala educación* 94, 101–103, 105
*Malena es un nombre de tango* 41
Mañas, Achero: *El Bola* 5, 126, 135, 137
*Mar adentro* 132, 137
marriage 84–86; failed 32; same-sex 165; in the Transition 51
*Maternidade biológica* 63
*Maternidade social* 63
matrophobia 62
Maushart, Susan 9, 14

Mendizabal, Rafael: *Madre Amantísima* 162–164
*Mercado libre* 170–174
Miró, Pilar 109–125; *Gary Cooper que estás en los cielos* 5, 109–111, 114, 116, 118–123; *El pájaro de la felicidad* 5, 109–115, 118, 122–123
*Modelos de mujer* 41
Moral, Ignacio del 162; *Papis* 162–163
mother/daughter relationships 6–7, 41, 48–49, 115–117, 189, 194–195, 198–213
motherhood 3, 4, 5, 9–23; and anger 111; ascriptive 44; in the Franco regime 43–47, 109–110, 119; generational differences 5, 112, 115–116, 122; instincts 44–45, 72; intensive model 45; legal 65; literature 9–11; as magical act 70–71; in the media 13–15, 19–20, 47; myths and ideals 10–13, 41, 43, 64, 72, 82; as patriarchal imposition 63; rejection of 31–33, 46–47, 71, 76, 82, 112–113; representations of 62; revindication of 61–62, 68, 71; role of government 20, 111; and sexuality 52, 62–64, 68, 154; social/biological 64, 71; in the Transition 46–48, 51, 110–111, 113; unfulfilled 40, 49, 51–55, 149–150; vilification of 83; *see also* happiness; parenting
Moure, Teresa: *Herba moura* 68–71; *A xeira das arbores* 4, 60, 68–69
*Muertos de papel* 80, 84
*Mujeres al borde de un ataque de nervios* 104

negative globalization 146
*Nido vacío* 79, 83, 85, 89
nihilism 142, 145
non-custodial mothers 32
non-spaces 143

O'Connor, Patricia 201
*Odyssey* 33, 38
Ortiz, Lourdes 162

*El pájaro de la felicidad* 5, 109–115, 118, 122–123
*A palabra das fillas de Eva* 60
*Papis* 162–163
parenting: 14, 24; gender roles 16–17, 24, 41, 44–45, 126, 134, 162; literature 16–17; in the media 15; solo parents 2, 28–29, 45, 48, 68, 171; *see also* custodial fathers
*Parir o pensamento* 63
patriarchy 5–6, 97, 117, 120, 126–127, 129–136, 138, 199; as construct 68–72
pedophilia 4, 65

*Pepi, Luci, Bom y otras chicas del montón* 102
*La playa de los perros destrozados* 166–168
polyandrous unions 4, 33–34
Pombo, Pilar 198; *Remedios* 208–210
pregnancy in the workplace 42
*Prepucio* 168–170
prostitution 171

*¿Qué he hecho yo para merecer esto?!* 94, 97, 102, 130
Queizán, María Xosé 59; *A escrita da certeza* 4, 65; *Maternidade biológica* 63; *Maternidade social* 63; *A palabra das fillas de Eva* 60; *Parir o pensamento* 63; *Ten o seu punto a fresca rosa* 4, 60–61, 65, 71

racism 174
Recuerda, José Martín 160
*Remedios* 208–210
reproductive technologies 64–67, 72
Rich, Adrian 61, 200–201
*Ritos de muerte* 76–79, 82, 84
Rodríguez Rodríguez, Marisol 4, 59–74, 216
Romero, Concha 6, 198; *Juego de reinas* 202–206
Rossetti, Ana 40
Rubio, Juan Carlos 162, 177; *Las heridas del viento* 164–165
Ruibal, José 160
Ryan, Lorraine 4, 40–58, 216

Saez Buenaventura, Carmen 12
same-sex parents 34–36
Santos, Care: *Supermami: mil maneras de ser una mamá feliz* 9
Sastre, Alfonso 160
Schopenhauer, Arthur: *The World as Will and Representation* 25–26, 38
*Sección Feminina de Falange* 44
Second Demographic Transition (SDT) 76
separation 2–3
*Serpientes en el paraíso* 80, 83–84
*Siempre busqué el amor* 206–208
*El silencio de los claustros* 79, 87, 89
space 143, 147–149
Spanish cinema 93–94, 142; and feminine subjectivity 153; and patriarchy 129–131, 138; and realism 3, 127–129, 132–133, 136–137; and social discourse 128–129
Spanish Civil Code 3
Spanish Civil War 180–189
Spanish Constitution 3

Spanish theater 159–179; 198–213; history 162, 177
step-parents 88
*Supermami: mil maneras de ser una mamá feliz* 9

*Tacones lejanos* 94
*Te doy mis ojos* 5, 126, 129, 132–134, 136
*Ten o seu punto a fresca rosa* 4, 60–61, 65, 71
Tibbitts, Amy 6, 141–158, 216
*Todo sobre mi madre* 94, 96
togetherness 37–38
*Trayectoria de la bala* 170, 174–177
Trotman, Tiffany 4, 24–39, 216

del Valle-Inclán, Ramón 159
Vallvey, Ángela: *Los estados carenciales* 4, 24–39
*Volver* 94–97
"La voz de sangre" 82–83

women writers 43
women's literature 42
work/life balance 5, 18
working mothers 18, 21, 31, 41–42; 90; 112–113; *see also* pregnancy
*The World as Will and Representation* 25–26, 38

*A xeira das arbores* 4, 60, 68–69

www.ingramcontent.com/pod-product-compliance
Lightning Source LLC
Chambersburg PA
CBHW032054300426
44116CB00007B/727